I0816175

Praise for *The Jesus Stories*

Jesus Christ is the most interesting Man in the world. In *The Jesus Stories*, Georgia Tanner takes us on a brilliant journey that focuses on the King who came to save us. Like any good mystery, we want the details. This great mystery of the ages unfolded in Jesus, and Georgia unearths information that will thrill the reader in this greatest rescue story ever told. Her excitement is contagious as she points us to the wonder of Christ. Set your heart's table and enjoy this feast for the soul!

Charlotte Travis
Author, Speaker, and President of Abide in Him, Inc.

Georgia has done her homework, and through due diligence, she has painted high-definition snapshots of Jesus Christ, the most amazing person to ever appear on the stage of human history. Her book is a direct route without detours to the destination of clarity of understanding of Jesus, the one person who truly deserves not only your highest respect but your worship.

Dr. James Saxon
Director of Evangelism and Adult Bible Classes
The Church of The Apostles Atlanta, Georgia

Georgia is a uniquely gifted author with the rare ability to paint a picture with her well-chosen, descriptive words that make the stories she tells come alive so that the reader feels they are in the midst of them—like entering into a 3-D painting. As a reader who has heard the stories she shares many times before, I saw Jesus and aspects of the events surrounding Him with fresh eyes as Georgia highlighted many details of the stories that brought new illumination to them. I am especially excited to give this book as a gift to family and friends who are not as familiar with Jesus and the Biblical accounts of Him, as I believe they'll experience a compelling, life-transforming encounter with Jesus and behold Him not only as the Savior of the world but also be drawn to receive Him as their personal Savior and Lord.

Julie Van Gorp
Co-founder and President of True View Ministries

Scripture is an endless well beckoning us to come and drink deeper. Tanner has done this deep dive into the gospels and has revealed her findings in a way that is effortless for us, the reader. *The Jesus Stories* is for anyone desiring to draw a little nearer to the heart of Christ. This book is one I will return to over and over again to deepen my understanding of the gospels and to simply enjoy.

Kaitlyn Fiedler
Author of *What Now? Finding Renewed Life in Christ After Loss*

Georgia's gift for bringing Scripture to life is on full display in *The Jesus Stories*. She invites us to walk alongside Jesus day by day and see firsthand how He reveals Himself to ordinary people in extraordinary ways. You will certainly be blessed by this front-row seat to the Gospel accounts!

Elise Wilkes
Director of Women's Ministry
The Church of The Apostles, Atlanta, Georgia

It seems like everybody likes Jesus. Sort of unpopular to be anti-Jesus. However, it seems that very few people are absolutely in awe of Him. And very few bow the knee and acknowledge that Jesus is Lord. In her wonderful book, "The Jesus Stories: Seeing Jesus Through the Eyes of Those Who Saw Him," Georgia Tanner helps us see Jesus in deeper and more refreshing ways. The book is thoroughly researched and biblically faithful. And your heart will be warmed by reading what she has written. I predict you'll be in awe of Him and joyfully call Him "Lord"!

Rev Bob Cargo
Director of Church Planting
Perimeter Church

The Jesus Stories

The Jesus Stories

SEEING JESUS THROUGH THE EYES OF THOSE WHO SAW HIM

Georgia Tanner

Carpenter's Son Publishing

The Jesus Stories: Seeing Jesus Through the Eyes of Those Who Saw Him

Published by Carpenter's Son Publishing
Carpentersonpublishing.com

Cover Design by Kathi Roberts

Author Photo by Seleesha Mathews and Elizabeth Whaley

Interior Design by Suzanne Lawing

Printed in the United States of America

ISBN: (print) 978-1-956370-76-8

That which was from the beginning,
which we have heard,
which we have seen with our eyes,
which we have looked at and our hands have touched
—this we proclaim concerning the Word of life.
The life appeared;
we have seen it and testify to it,
and we proclaim to you the eternal life,
which was with the Father and has appeared to us.
We proclaim to you what we have seen and heard,
so that you also may have fellowship with us.
And our fellowship is with the Father and with his Son, Jesus Christ.
We write this to make our (your) joy complete.

1 John 1:1-4 NIV

Table of Contents

To
All Who Desire to See Jesus

Introducing the Eyewitnesses

I have heard his name my entire life—Jesus. That name has always been associated with the descriptor of *Son*. I have always accepted the Son of the Father, God with a capital G. I believed it. I never doubted it. Since childhood, I have prayed in his name and heard his stories. It is time for me to read his story line by line and thoroughly explore God's words about Jesus for myself.

My friend Jane used to stumble and immediately start to cry whenever she talked about Jesus. She would lose her words and be unable to continue what she was in the middle of saying. It was always very touching, and I would think, "Oh, I would love to have a faith and a relationship like that; just the thought of Jesus would overwhelm me with deep love and emotion!" It took years on our faith journey together before she confided to me that she had prayed years before to *know Jesus more deeply.* Her tears were not of knowing him, but of her sorrow that she didn't know him as deeply as she longed to! It was profoundly fascinating that God gave her such overwhelmingly deep feelings for not knowing Jesus that her desire was precisely what led her to know him more intimately.

Perhaps I am on this same journey.

It is so easy for me to say, Father God. And the Holy Spirit feels like my constant companion. But Jesus? It is so hard for me to relate to this man-God. His stories are larger than life. And his walk toward death is heroic. His resurrection is so unreal. I am like the desperate father waiting for a miracle, crying out to Jesus, "I believe; help my unbelief!" (Mark 9:24).

I read recently in Glyn Evans's profound devotional *Daily With the King,* "Jesus is the only person who has ever walked this earth who must be spiritually discerned if he is to be known at all." He writes that the way to know him is through God's Word and Spirit.[1] So, this is where I will start: in God's Word, following along the life of Jesus chronologically, as much as possible.

Four very different men write four books about this Son of God named Jesus. All four biographies of Jesus were written within a generation of the time this Jesus lived. We know them as The Gospels—each writer's personality and purpose influence how they tell the story. Before we start, I will share the big-picture basics of who our gospel writers are and why they wrote.

Two of our gospel writers, John and Matthew, wrote from first-hand knowledge; Jesus chose them to be in the inner circle of the original twelve disciples. John, a fisherman by trade, described himself as "the disciple who Jesus loved." His story of Jesus is intimate, passionate, and written by a man deeply in love. We must hold John responsible for this unique idea that "God is love." Before John's story of Jesus, people usually thought of the God of the Hebrews as many things – mainly, Creator of the Universe, Law Giver, Covenant Maker, and The Almighty One to be feared and obeyed.

John tells us about Jesus by reaching back through time to the very creation of the world. "*In the beginning...*" he begins. John wants to make sure we understand this flesh-and-blood man was and is undeniably God. He tells us Jesus used the same name God used to define himself to Moses through the burning bush: the great "I AM." Jesus embraces this name for himself and explains it in physical reminders of provision: *"I am the Bread of Life" (John 6:35), "I am the Light of the World" (8:12), "I am the Gate for the Sheep" (10:7), "I am the Good Shepherd" (10:11), "I am the Resurrection" (11:25), "I am the Way, the Truth, the Life" (14:6), "I am the True Vine" (15:1, capitalization mine).* In those descriptions of himself, Jesus was unmistakably defining himself as God.

The other original disciple who wrote about Jesus was Matthew. Matthew was a Hebrew businessman who decided he could become rich and powerful if he played along with the Roman enemy, who had parked themselves in the defeated world of the Israelites. Matthew set up shop as a tax collector for the despised Romans and had the government-sanctioned opportunity to collect as much tax from his neighbors as his conscience allowed. He had become as despised as the foreign Roman soldiers who stood guard in the Judean streets. Matthew was the last person anyone would expect to follow Jesus. Matthew was the last person anyone would expect to continue following Jesus long after he was executed on a Roman cross.

Matthew wrote to his Jewish brothers to prove Jesus was the long-awaited Jewish Messiah. Instead of judging the people, he was judged on their behalf. Go and tell all the nations the good news: Jesus is King. Come join the kingdom.

Mark probably was a young teenager tagging behind the twelve disciples and Jesus – wanting to hear every word and desperately wanting to be part of their excitement. Rumor has it that he followed them to the Garden of Gethsemane that fateful night. A son of wealth, his finely woven linen garment remained in the hands of a soldier as he ran for his life when Jesus was arrested. As a young man, he continued to follow these disciples of Jesus – beginning with Paul and Barnabas on missionary journeys. Later, he found companionship with the disciple Peter, who told him story after story of Jesus. The uneducated fisherman Peter needed someone to write his story down, and Mark had the advantage of a formal education. When you read the book of Mark, think of the rough-and-tumble fisherman Peter, who was "first out of the boat," dictating his firsthand experiences to an enthusiastic young man who longed to be one of the chosen Twelve who sat at the feet of Jesus.

Mark's writing is quick reading – I imagine him trying to keep up with Peter's storytelling. The story begins in the hometown area of Galilee with fishing boats and teachings by the sea. Jesus tells stories and performs miracles to illustrate that God's kingdom has come near. Mark's destination is Jerusalem, where a suffering servant Messiah celebrates the Passover, dies hours later, and darkness descends; it is a Roman Centurion who first understands that "this man was the Son of God." An angel meets the women at the empty tomb, and Mark abruptly ends his original story as they flee in fear and expectation.

Whew! Mark keeps you on your toes – I imagine Peter had things to do, so he didn't quite finish the story. Later versions add on what we read beyond Mark 16:8.

And then there is Luke. We don't know where Luke came from, but he certainly wasn't one of them, the inside crowd. Luke was probably a Gentile, carefully explaining the Jewish laws and customs as if writing to people who were not familiar with them. He was a coworker with Paul and concentrated on carefully and methodically recording eyewitness accounts.

He had an investigative mind. Determined to explore the story of Jesus, he carefully wrote everything down to send back to his patron, who wanted to know the facts about this man named Jesus. He talked with everyone who had known Jesus, including Jesus's mother and all the women who had cared for him. It appears Luke was a doctor; he called illnesses by their medical names, and he noted Jesus's compassion toward the poor and the hopeless.

The teaching of Jesus was punctuated with healings, and the resulting conflicts with the religious leaders contrasted God's love with the love of power. Luke told the story of Jesus on a restoration mission, bringing justice and mercy. His Jesus embraced the outsider and taught radical generosity, service, and peacemaking.

Luke's writings, between the gospel of Jesus known as Luke and the Acts of the Apostles telling of what happened to transform devout Jews into a new sect known as Followers of The Way, make up the most extensive content of The New Testament. Luke builds the bridge that takes Jesus from Martyr to Messiah King as his life bursts beyond the dusty towns of Israel.

Come walk with me through these Jesus stories. We will be companions as we listen in on conversations, wonder at miracles, ponder difficult teachings, and look closely into Jesus's face. Open your Bible and read each passage at the beginning of each chapter. Nothing will make sense unless you do! I have italicized direct scripture quotes. Otherwise, it is my interpretation. Ask God to give you understanding. Take my hand, and let's see who this Jesus is!

1

Who Is This Man?

Read Mark 1:1; Luke 1:1-4; John 1:1-18

Mark starts simply and directly, as is his way, *"The beginning of the good news about Jesus the Messiah, the Son of God (NIV)."* (Messiah is Hebrew. The Roman term Christ means the same thing.)

Luke starts by explaining why he is researching this man named Jesus in the first place. He is writing an account of the things that have taken place among us—things we have heard about from eyewitness accounts. He has investigated everything carefully. He is making a report so you can know with certainty that what you are taught is true.

And then there is John. Oh my. John describes this Jesus in a way that goes back to before the world began. Back to Genesis and *"In the beginning…"*. There is absolutely no mistaking that John views Jesus as God. As Creator. The beginning statement he puts forth is, *"In the beginning was the Word."* The definition of *the Word* for the Hebrews is the equivalent of Almighty Unknowable Unfathomable Creator God who *spoke* the world into existence. The meaning of *the Word* for Romans was equivalent to knowledge and wisdom— the things they elevated above all else. How brilliant it was for John to describe Jesus as the Word—something holy and highly esteemed in the heart of the Jew and worthy and elevated in the head of the Romans. *"In the beginning was the Word...."*

But John doesn't stop there. He dives deep! Through him – "The Word" – all things were created. He was life. He was light. And this essence of life and light wasn't just here for the Jew. Oh no! He was here for all mankind. Everyone all aboard. And before John even takes a breath, here comes the answer to the question of "why": This light has come to shine into the darkness – and the darkness has not, will not, cannot overcome it.

Darkness. We all understand that. Even this lucky generation knows the wonder of flipping the tiny lever hardwired into each room, and voila, the room is filled with light – even we understand that when we are lost or lonely or heartbroken or terrified, we feel like we are walking in a great darkness. Two thousand years ago, darkness had an even stronger impact on people's everyday lives. Once the sun set, darkness descended, only punctuated by moonlight and starlight. But once you went inside your shelter, the only light was firelight. The idea of light overcoming the darkness was very powerful and extremely real.

But another statement is here: *"And the light shines in the darkness, and the darkness did not comprehend it (NKJV)."* Oh, that sounds different. "Not comprehend." That is the opposite of being "enlightened." It is not seeing, not understanding. The coming of the light lacked meaning and purpose because it was not understood. And suddenly, John brings up another John. This is John the Baptist, John who was sent as a witness before the light showed up here on planet Earth. John cried out, John testified, John told everyone they needed to get ready because this light was coming. And their reaction? The people did not recognize the light. They did not *receive* the light.

A small handful did. And what happened to those who received and believed in the light? *"...he gave the right to become children of God."* This is profound. And it's hard to believe. How did this happen? John hasn't explained it yet, so we must wait for that big picture to come. I think it is perhaps because we don't have a good understanding of who God is yet. But I have a good idea that John or this newly on-the-scene Jesus will explain it to us.

Back to John, the gospel writer. John says that The Word became flesh. That means skin and bones and the ability to feel hunger, thirst, and pain. Flesh means contained and limited. To be born and to die. That means The Word became like us – alive. And The Word lived among us. This means they saw him, talked with him, sat with him, walked with him, and touched him. He was real and knowable. And then, in one amazing sentence, John beautifully describes this person of flesh and bones.

"We have seen his glory;
the glory of the one and only Son,
who came from the Father,
full of grace and truth (NIV)."

A man identified, recognized, and described in no uncertain terms as the only Son of God the Father and filled with the glory of God. He is filled and overflowing with grace (let's go ahead and define grace as unmerited favor or forgiveness) and truth. I don't think I would care for truth if it wasn't accompanied by grace.

John explains this idea of "grace" that has little meaning to me in the twenty-first century. You see, John was a Jew living in a world where every single time you broke God's Law, which had been handed down through Moses, you needed to find a perfect lamb and lead it to the Temple at Jerusalem where the priests could sacrifice it at the altar as a substitute for you. You were saying – I broke God's law and, therefore, broke my relationship with him. I deserve to be punished, but God, through the law, allows this poor little lamb to be "punished" instead. Once his blood is shed, I take on his innocence, and all is good again between me and God. I am forgiven. I am under God's grace. Whew! I better not sin or break God's law again!

In this opening passage, John says—which is utterly shocking to anyone hearing this in that Jewish world—that God gave the law, which defines sin, through Moses, but God has given grace (forgiveness) and truth through Jesus the Messiah. Let me say that again. The law (defining sin) came through Moses. Grace (forgiveness) and truth are coming through Jesus.

Maybe truth means "new truth" or "new revelation." We've got some new information here. This happens all the time. If we didn't accept "new" truth, we would still believe that the earth was flat and that doctors didn't need to wash their hands before surgery.

Here is another little detail: *"Out of his fullness, we have all received grace in place of grace already given (NIV)."* So, God had provided grace (forgiveness) through the law shared by Moses – but it was partial grace and forgiveness. This Jesus is bringing *"full" grace and forgiveness.* Maybe this means we won't need to find the flawless lamb and head up to the Temple anymore. Maybe this Jesus is bringing about a whole new thing?

One last little statement here from our beloved disciple John: *"No one has ever seen God..."* (except for Adam and Eve, I am thinking, and they got that door to innocence and righteousness shut pretty hard on us all!) *"...but the one and only Son (NIV)."* The word "but" means – change that thought - something new is happening here. We are no longer dealing with fallen men and women or prophets or messengers. We are in the presence of a family relationship, Father and Son. Not only that but the one and only Son seems to have a mission. Not only is he God – but he also wants to make God *known*!

This changes everything. Can we really know God? Does he really desire to reveal himself to us personally? And even more unbelievable, is there a way he could come to us clothed in flesh and blood? For the ancient Jew, this is a complete blaspheme. But if you read through their ancient Jewish scriptures, it seems God was always doing this in one way or another. He was always saying, "Hold on here a minute... I see you... I hear you... I know what just happened... Why don't you come to me and we will reason through this situation. I will make your sins of scarlet as white as snow, as white as a flawless perfect lamb. Come a little closer."

This is the God I want to know. Sending himself as his own Son isn't so far out there. Maybe we really needed to see God. To be able to *hear* his words in a softer voice. To be in his presence without burning from his blinding light. Just go ahead and clothe his Living Spirit in flesh and blood and send him down. Let's see what he looks like. Let's listen to what he has to say. Let God speak for himself.

Okay. I'm good with that. Let's do it.

2

In the Flesh

Read Matthew 1:1-17; Luke 3:23-38

We usually rush on by this genealogy stuff. It's just a bunch of names. But these names are important, especially to the Jews. They had been waiting for a long time for God to send a Messiah, his Anointed, to rescue them from captivity. They had been under the thumb – the Romans' sword for a long time. Before that, they were in captivity under the Babylonians and then the Persians. And before that, the Egyptians. For as long as they could remember - and they had incredibly good memories, they had been persecuted by someone bigger and stronger.

God had promised a Messiah to deliver them for a long time. Going all the way back to Abraham. If you look at the fine print, that promise went back to Adam. When the Messiah did show up, most of the people missed it. Because they were looking for salvation from the wrong thing. They wanted military salvation. They wanted to relive their glory days under King David. They conveniently forgot that peace was a temporary band-aid between battles and building projects - even under David and Solomon, their greatest kings.

God had something bigger in mind—and someone bigger. Military deliverance was a small thing. What if God intended to rescue them from something much bigger and more permanent: death? What if he intended to replace death with abundant life? Eternal. What if there was a world, a kingdom beyond what could be seen? What if this world was just a poor reflection of a heavenly kingdom? Now, that would be something worth seeing.

Why do I bring this all up at the beginning of all these names listed as the genealogy of this man named Jesus? Because we need to keep in mind the bigger picture of who Jesus was coming to and through. This line of descendants is traced through the Jewish people who worshipped the One True God. God had chosen them to be his people. And he would be their God. God entrusted them to tell his story. To preserve his history with them. To remember his faithfulness. These people, the descendants of Abraham, had a covenant with God. They had his promise. It was a promise of place, a promise of protection, a promise of life. And that covenant was held together with the assurance of a relationship. Relationship between God and his people.

Here in the list of these names is the reminder, proof, of continued faithfulness, a continued relationship. The people listed here didn't always remain faithful – but God did. Our writer, Matthew, starts with Abraham. Abraham struggled to be faithful – sometimes taking off for Egypt and claiming his wife was his sister. God continued to walk with Abraham and called him friend, and in the end, Abraham trusted God enough to offer his long-awaited son Isaac as a trust offering. God supplied a substitute offering instead, and these Hebrew people suddenly had a story of profound faith and God's provision.

From Isaac, we got Jacob, a complete mess of a man, constantly struggling to be first and have his own way. His twelve sons would become the twelve tribes of Israel and travel from Canaan's famine-parched land to the land of abundant grain, Egypt. This was the great empire of Egypt where God had recently orchestrated Jacob's son Joseph to be ruler over all things—another incredible story of God providing place, protection, and abundant life.

Jacob would lay his hands on his sons to bless them, and oddly, it would be his son Judah who would receive the blessing of the Lion: a coming house of kings, a donkey ride, a scepter, a connected vine, garments washed in wine and blood. It was hard to say at the time how that would play out…

Judah would accidentally impregnate his daughter-in-law Tamar, a Canaanite woman. We didn't see that one coming. She would give birth to twins Perez and Zerah. The meaning of Perez is "breach"-because the infant made an entry into this world that seemed impossible. His birth was a glimpse of what God would do to enter our broken world. He would break through the barrier that separated us from Him, dressed in the soft skin of a human baby.

As we scan the list, we recognize a few other names: Boaz - the son of Rahab, the prostitute who saved the Hebrew spies in Jericho. Boaz became the "Redeemer Kinsman" who married Ruth, the outsider. Ruth, a Moabite, had clung to her Jewish mother-in-law Naomi with the declaration: *"Your people shall be my people, and your God my God."* (Read the story in Ruth 1:1-18 and Ruth 4:1-17.)

Rahab the Canaanite and Ruth the Moabite are odd inclusions in this Jewish line of male ancestry; they are women and non-Jewish outsiders. Perhaps God has a different idea about worth and value than we think.

From Ruth and Boaz would come a son named Obed, who had a son named Jesse, who would have many sons. The youngest son, who watched over the sheep, would be anointed by the old prophet Samuel as king of Israel and kill a giant named Goliath. Ah, here is a very familiar name!

Shepherd David would become King David. He would battle Saul for the throne and seduce Bathsheba, Uriah's wife. Their son, Solomon, would build a stone Temple for God in Jerusalem. But Solomon's many wives would lead him away from the One True God, and everything would gradually fall apart until almost all the descendants of David would be carried off into captivity by first the Assyrians and then the Babylonians.

You can't help but notice that each of these names has the stories of God attached to them. The people often were a mess. Broken. Desperate. Their stories are told without blinking. There is no whitewashing or sweeping their dirt under the rug. Their stories trail along a bramble path, yet there he is – God. In their midst. Or at least nearby as they stride headlong into their futures.

As they ebb and flow in their relationship with him, God continues to call out to them with breadcrumbs of his faithfulness. Even in the depths of their unfaithfulness to him, he speaks to them through his messengers, telling them, "I have a future and a hope for you." "I myself will come be your good shepherd." "I am sending a branch that will connect you to me." "I will give you a new heart to replace your heart of stone." A future, a hope, a good shepherd, a branch, a new heart. God seems to have a definite plan for these broken men and women he created. There is a family line leading up to something good, I think. Our writer, Matthew, doesn't start his story without laying out the family line that traced the generations of God's faithfulness to Father Abraham's descendants.

Our writer, Luke, tells us something a little odd at the beginning of his genealogy. "Jesus was the son, *or so it was thought*, of Joseph." So, Luke's lineage, perhaps, follows the lineage of his mother, Mary, following David's son Nathan rather than David's son Solomon. Matthew traces the line of a King. Luke traces the line of a Priest. Pretty good lineage for a man born to be both King and Priest.

One other thing: Luke doesn't stop at Abraham. He continues back to the very beginning – all the way to "the son of Seth, the son of Adam, the son of God." This Jesus not only had a traceable family line of God's chosen people, but he could also call himself something even better: the Son of God.

One additional little note here on all this genealogical stuff. Throughout the ancient Hebrew scriptures, the scribes meticulously kept accurate lists of families from father to son to the next son, tracing through the 12 tribes of Israel. Even when Israel was divided into two kingdoms of the northern tribes and the southern tribes and captured and dragged off into captivity, the handful of Israelites returning to Jerusalem were still listed out family by family, tribe by tribe. The records of the royal and priestly lines were preserved until Jerusalem and the Temple were utterly destroyed in 70 AD. The city walls were broken down, the Temple completely burned, the people starved and then slaughtered.[1]

From the first-hand account of the historian Josephus Flavius:

"While the Temple was ablaze, the attackers plundered it, and countless people who were caught by them were slaughtered. There was no pity for age and no regard was accorded rank; children and old men, laymen and priests, alike were butchered; every class was pursued and crushed in the grip of war, whether they cried out for mercy or offered resistance.

"Through the roar of the flames streaming far and wide, the groans of the falling victims were heard; such was the height of the hill and the magnitude of the blazing pile that the entire city seemed to be ablaze; and the noise - nothing more deafening and frightening could be imagined.

"The Temple Mount, everywhere enveloped in flames, seemed to be boiling over from its base; yet the blood seemed more abundant than the flames and the numbers of the slain greater than those of the slayers. The soldiers climbed over heaps of bodies as they chased the fugitives."[2]

Why do I share with you such a gruesome description of the fall of Jerusalem? Within the generation that heard the voice of Jesus, the destruction of Jerusalem and the Temple and even the descendants of Abraham as a nation disappeared under the harsh hand of the Roman Empire. The records of genealogies burned in the great fire, and the people scattered or were slaughtered. If God had delayed sending his Son, there would have been no preserved record of a carpenter's son from Nazareth, the descendant of both a royal and a priestly lineage tracing back to Adam and God, showing up to fulfill ancient prophecies of an Anointed One. One who would be both Priest and King. God's timing was perfect. The bloodline was perfect. It will be interesting to see who recognizes this king in priestly robes.

3

It All Started in the Temple

Read Luke 1:5-25

It brings tears to my eyes when I read these words, "*...your prayer has been heard.*" Isn't that enough right there? Do we even need to read any further? How many words, pleas, tears, losses, and joys have been held up to this invisible God – hoping beyond hope that there is a God who hears? A listening, all-powerful God, bigger and better than this small world where we live?

Here is an angel standing at the right side of the altar of incense, starting his message with this reassurance: "Your prayer has been heard." Of course, he also said the usual thing angels say: "Do not be afraid." Obviously, seeing an angel of God is a terrifying sight. And it usually means your world is about to be turned upside down.

God was about to keep his angels busy delivering messages. This angel would show up here in the Holy of Holies, which was pretty much ground zero for Holy Ground, and he would show up again in a young girl's bedroom and then again in a carpenter's workshop. Delivering messages, terrifying the locals, changing the humdrum history of humans.

Back to Zechariah and the angel's conversation. Zechariah is an old man. And his wife Elizabeth is old. God has a history of loving to send babies into the arms of those who had lost all hope. Remember the story of Abraham and Sarah? We have the same sort of story here. This couple, who are descendants of the priestly tribe of Aaron, have been praying for a child for a long, long time. And God has heard their prayers. He has been listening. But he was waiting for the time to be right. And he had decided the time was now.

So "the lot," the roll of the dice, had fallen on this old man Zechariah to have the once-in-a-lifetime honor of taking the burning incense into the Holy of Holies there in the Temple in Jerusalem. All the other priests waited outside. And the angel of the Lord was waiting for Zechariah inside.

A son would be born to him and his wife Elizabeth (I love that God knows our name!), and he will be named John. And he is going to be incredibly special. (I also love that God knows who we will be even before we are born!) And then the angel gives him a list of what this son John (who had not even been conceived yet!) will be like and what he will accomplish:

> He will be a joy and delight to you; many will rejoice because of his birth.
>
> He will be great in the sight of the Lord.
>
> He will never drink wine or other alcoholic drinks.
>
> He will be filled with the Holy Spirit of God even before he is born.
>
> He will bring back many of the people of Israel to the Lord their God.

In the spirit and power of Elijah, he will go before the Lord to accomplish these things:

- Turn the hearts of the parents to their children,
- Turn the disobedient to the wisdom of the righteous,

• Make a people ready for the Lord.

Wow. This is incredible. But we must pause for a moment to look at who this Elijah was and why he would be meaningful in this story. Elijah was a Hebrew prophet sent by God at a time when Israel's King Ahab and his wife Jezebel were contaminating the worship of Yahweh, the One True God, by building temples and places of worship to the Canaanite pagan god Baal.

Insert nature worship, temple prostitutes, fertility rites, and baby sacrifice here. During a God-ordained drought, Elijah had a showdown with 450 prophets of Baal on Mount Carmel to settle once and for all just who was the true God of Israel. To make it even more dramatic, Elijah poured water on the wood that was to burn the sacrifice. As Elijah called on the God of Israel, the fire of the Lord fell, and the altar burst into flames, burning the sacrificed bull, the wood, the stones, the dust, and the water - settling the discussion. Big picture: God sent the prophet Elijah to speak for him, rescue his people from the lies and destruction of paganism, and establish true worship of the One True God.[1] His exciting story unfolds in 1 Kings 17-19 and 2 Kings 1-2.

The spirit and power of Elijah would continue to reach forward into the future according to the prophecy of Malachi 4:5-6.[2]

"Behold, I will send you Elijah the prophet before the great and awesome day of the Lord comes. And he will turn the hearts of fathers to their children and the hearts of children to their fathers, lest I come and strike the land with a decree of utter destruction."

Meanwhile, in the angel Gabriel's presence in the Temple's innermost Holy Room, Zechariah decides to be a little argumentative with this terrifying angel and his revelation. "How can I be sure you are telling me the truth?" Now, we have seen folks question God and his messengers all along the way without being called on the carpet, so somehow I think Zechariah's objections went beyond just doubt.

Gabriel was not having it. And his response is the ultimate slap-down. He doesn't strike him dead – he gives him no room for doubt. Isn't this a great and terrifying response to we humans who decide something is beyond the reach and power of God?

"I am Gabriel. I stand in the presence of God, and I was sent to speak to you." (Translation: Who do you think you are to question God?) "This is good news." (This isn't the last time you will hear this phrase.) "And now, since you did not believe my words, you will not be able to speak until the day this happens."

Outside, the rest of the priests wondered what was taking old Zechariah so long in there. Will they have to haul him out by the cord attached to his ankle in case something happens to the incense bearer in there? When he finally reappears, he cannot speak, and they realize he has seen a vision… or something. When his time of service there is completed, he returns home to Elizabeth. She becomes pregnant, and we hear her reaction to all of this. She immediately knows this life inside of her is from the Lord. He has given her favor. He has heard her prayers. He has taken away her disgrace. In gratitude, she protects herself and this unborn baby; she goes into seclusion.

This is God. When he shows up, our world turns upside down. We doubt. We become speechless. We can see into the future for a moment, but it seems impossible to believe. We receive hope when hope is long gone. We retreat to take it all in and spend time alone with our Creator, our God. This is the very beginning of a new story. This is the beginning of something simply described as *good news.* The Gospel. I hope it will be good news for you.

4

The Fearful Thing of Being Favored

Read Luke 1:26-45

We know this story so well that we no longer hear it. Slow down. Take Mary out of her royal robes, remove the crown from her head, and remove the perfection from her reputation. It is about to be smashed to the ground and into the mud anyway.

Mary is just a young girl. She is not quite – almost, but not quite, old enough to be married. Or she already would be. She is still living in her father's house. She is "pledged to be married" to a man named Joseph, a descendant of King David. She is in agreement with this. But it hasn't happened yet. When it does happen, the whole village will know about it. It will be a big celebration with vows, singing, dancing, feasting, a set-aside time of honeymoon, and seclusion between her and her new husband. But all of that is in the future. It has not happened yet.

This angel Gabriel showing up is a problem. All the beautiful words like "highly favored" and "God is with you" aren't making this an easier problem to deal with. God has a plan, but it appears his timing is off. Gabriel tells Mary she will conceive a son – before her wedding day. All the words capitalized right now - like the Holy Spirit and the power of the Most High - probably felt too unreal to comprehend. It is still a difficult concept for us 2,000 years later.

Why is this illegitimate baby so important? So important he needs to be conceived now, while Mary is still a young virgin, long before her marriage day?

"The child to be born will be holy. He will be called the Son of God," Gabriel explains gently. "He will be called Jesus." (If we were hearing this in the Hebrew voice, we would hear the name as Yeshua, Yehoshua, or Joshua – like the one who fought the battle of Jericho and led the Israelites into the Land of Milk and Honey. But our scriptures came through Greek speakers, so we hear "Jesus" instead.) The angel Gabriel continues,

"He will be great.
He will be called the son of the Most High.
He will be given the throne of his father, David.
He will reign over Jacob's descendants forever.
His kingdom will never end."

Then Gabriel tells her something sweet and equally unbelievable, bringing her comfort and companionship. Her cousin Elizabeth, old and way beyond childbearing years, will also give birth to a God-ordained Holy child. It was a kind assurance in a whisper of truth, "For no word from God will ever fail."

And with that, Gabriel departed.

God favoring you and angels showing up is not necessarily a happy day. It usually means your plans have just changed. Your fiancé may choose to disown you. Your wedding day will be tarnished. You will not be called "favored" by the women who will notice a baby bump appearing too soon. Your son will be whispered about by the neighbors and taunted by the bullies. No, God changing your plans is not the best of news.

Some of us have seen this up close. God rarely asks us to do the easy thing. When God "favors" us, it usually takes us out of our comfortable lives and our comfortable plans. Better to only whisper his name and hope he doesn't notice you too much. Because when Gabriel shows up with a plan, it is going to wreck yours.

Mary packs her bags and leaves town. She shows up at Elizabeth's front door.

We listen in on the most beautiful greeting that has ever been recounted. Mary's young, sweet voice calls Elizabeth's name as she enters her home, and the baby John in Elizabeth's womb dances for joy! The Holy Spirit fills Elizabeth with heavenly knowledge, and Mary does not need to tell why she is there. Elizabeth knows fully and completely! "How can I be so honored that the mother of my Lord would visit me?"

Wait. How could Elizabeth say such a thing? How could she know such a thing? Listen again: "The mother of my Lord?" No one has ever said anything about the Lord God having a mother! Especially a young teen girl! Shhh! Imagine a rabbi overhearing such a crazy conversation! But these two women, both who will carry life impossible inside their wombs, know an unbelievable truth. They know an amazing secret that will change the course of mankind: God is coming into this broken, imprisoned world in the body of a flesh-and-blood human baby.

"You are blessed among women," old Elizabeth assures this young girl. "Blessed is the child you will bear." Mary's response is a song of worship for the God who is merciful to the humble. It is a song of praise to the God who keeps his promises.

Mary stayed with Elizabeth and Zechariah in their small town in the hills of Judea for three months. Count them out: Three months before Mary would return to her hometown of Nazareth and face the scandal of her unmarried pregnancy, three months to be truly known and loved by Elizabeth.

I imagine this was a place of safety and comfort for Mary. I imagine this was a house filled with joy. Preparations were being made for the coming of Elizabeth's baby. Mary could help her older cousin get ready. They could plan together and dream together, each knowing that God's Spirit moved beside them and within them. What a kindness that God gave them one another – one too old, one too young – as they prepared to raise a Prophet and a Messiah.

The Song of Mary

And Mary said:
"My soul magnifies the Lord,
And my spirit has rejoiced in God my Savior.
For He has regarded the lowly state of His maidservant;
For behold, henceforth all generations will call me blessed.
For He who is mighty has done great things for me,
And holy is His name.
And His mercy is on those who fear Him
From generation to generation.
He has shown strength with His arm;
He has scattered the proud in the imagination of their hearts.
He has put down the mighty from their thrones,
And exalted the lowly.
He has filled the hungry with good things,
And the rich He has sent away empty.
He has helped His servant Israel,
In remembrance of His mercy,
As He spoke to our fathers,
To Abraham and to his seed forever."
And Mary remained with her about three months,
and returned to her house.
Luke 1:46-56 NKJV

5

And He Shall Be Named John

Read Luke 1:57-80

This certainly was the talk of the town even before Zechariah and Elizabeth showed up on the eighth day to have their newborn son circumcised. Everyone, far and wide, has been talking about the miracle of Zechariah and Elizabeth having a son in their old age. What a blessing! What a miracle! But things were about to get even better.

Everyone expected the child to be named after his father, Zechariah. Or at least after someone in their family line. But no, Elizabeth insisted his name was to be John. John? There was no John among their ancestors! If only Zechariah could speak, he would put an end to this foolishness. They brought him a writing tablet, and he slowly and carefully spelled it out: His name is John.

Suddenly, the floodgates of praise opened, and Zechariah, unable to speak since his visit with the angel almost a year before in the Temple, immediately found his voice. His tongue had been set free, and he was filled with the words of the Holy Spirit.

He praises the Lord God of Israel, announcing that the long-awaited salvation has come. He speaks of the expected salvation from "our enemies and all those who hate us" and remembers the promise of

God's covenant and the oath He swore to Abraham. Then Zechariah gets specific. He turns the story to this John, whom he holds in his arms. This miracle baby has been born with a purpose: he will be the prophet who will prepare the way for the coming Lord.

This way will be paved with "the knowledge of salvation through the forgiveness of their sins." God will show his people "tender mercy" by the rising sun from heaven to shine on those living in darkness and the shadow of death. This rising sun from heaven "will guide our feet into the path of peace," he proclaims.

God had been quiet for a long time. A prophet had not been sent to the Hebrews for hundreds of years… not since Joel and Malachi. Joel had urged the people to return to their Lord with all their hearts, fasting, weeping, and mourning. To rend their hearts and not their garments (Joel 2:12-17). Joel prophesied that the Lord would pour out his Spirit on all people… and that everyone who called on the name of the Lord would be saved (vv. 28-32).

Malachi had promised to send a messenger, the prophet Elijah, who would prepare the way for the Lord's coming (Malachi 3:1-5; 4:1-6). Could this child, John, be the messenger who would prepare the way?

In rejoicing in this day of small miracles, did the people miss the wonder of the coming miracle? God was speaking again. God was preparing that little world of Judea for a coming Prophet and a coming Savior. The birth of one would appear to be a miracle. The neighbors would crowd into the doorway with celebration. The birth of the other would seem to be a disgrace. The only well-wishers would be shepherds from a nearby pasture. The only witnesses would be a bright and shining star, an obedient carpenter, and the angels.

6

And He Shall Be Named Jesus

Read Matthew 1:18-25; Luke 2:1-20

Two of our gospel writers tell of the birth of Jesus. Matthew, our tax collector, tells the story from Joseph's point of view in a "just the facts, ma'am" style that answers the Jewish concerns. Right up front, he must address this whole problem of Mary turning up pregnant before her wedding day. It was starting to become public knowledge. Not a good thing. And Joseph has no doubt that the child is not his.

Joseph is faithful to the Law of Moses, which gives him the right to have Mary stoned to death for her immorality and her betrayal. A woman – a young girl – "pledged to be married" wasn't what we consider "engaged." In the eyes of the law and the community, she was already "married" to Joseph for all intents and purposes – she just was not living in his house yet. So, this whole problem of pregnancy was his to deal with. The decision that needed to be made was not Mary's problem. It was not her daddy's problem. It was Joseph's problem. But Joseph was also a kind man who did not want to disgrace Mary further, so he decided to "divorce her quietly." She had disgraced herself, her family, and him.

God's angel shows up again, this time in a dream. The message is consistent with what the angel told Mary earlier. The child she carries in her womb is not from man but from the Holy Spirit of God. She will give birth to a son. He is to be named Jesus (Joshua), which means "The Lord Saves." He will save his people from their sins. Joseph is to take Mary into his home as his wife. He will be her husband, her provider, her protector.

And Joseph agrees to all of this.

This was a powerful dream with a powerful message. When Joseph accepted Mary into his home as his wife, he accepted her assumed guilt by the neighbors. He sacrificed his reputation to protect hers. This was no small thing. And the whole story of the virgin girl becoming pregnant through the power of the Holy Spirit – it is still something hard to accept and believe, isn't it? God is always doing this, throwing the laws of nature aside and asking us to believe something outrageous. But making the impossible possible lines up perfectly with God's character and his history with humanity, so I guess we better believe this one. Joseph certainly seemed to believe him.

Since Matthew is writing this all down for his Jewish listeners, he pulls out some Hebrew scriptures to back it all up. He quotes from the prophet Isaiah 7:14: *"The virgin will conceive and give birth to a son, and they will call him Immanuel (NIV)"* (which means "God with us"). You will discover that Matthew does this often; he points to Jesus fulfilling the Hebrew scripture. I like it. It places this unbelievable story on a foundation of fulfilled prophecy.

He adds the intimate detail that Joseph only consummated his marriage to Mary after this son was born. Joseph was a patient man.

Luke tells the story with all the details we love to portray in Christmas pageantry. There is the census. And if you want to look it up in your history book, he connects it to a specific decree under a specific Caesar. Joseph and Mary, who are "pledged to be married," travel to register in the town of David since Joseph is a descendant of

David. This little town of Bethlehem is swollen with crowds beyond its capacity because of the required registry.

There is no mention of being turned away from an inn or a compassionate innkeeper. There is the vague explanation that Mary wrapped her firstborn son in cloths and placed him in a manger – because no guest room was available for them. Now, don't you think God knew Mary was getting ready to give birth? Why wouldn't he have provided a better way, a better place for his son to come into the world?

I know nothing about sheep and shepherds, but God really likes using that analogy to describe his relationship with his people. Through Moses, God taught his people that a blood sacrifice was required to remove the barrier between God and man. The sacrifice was a perfect lamb without flaw. The shepherds who watched over the flocks would carefully wrap newborn lambs in swaddling cloths to protect them from harm and lay them in a manger lined with soft hay. When they were calm and had recovered from the trauma of birth, they would be unwrapped and returned to their mother. These were the holy lambs that would be sacrificed four miles down the road at the Temple in Jerusalem twice a day for the sins of the people.[1]

This son of God, born outside near the fields of the sacrificial lambs, wrapped in cloths, and placed in a manger, was born at exactly the right time, in exactly the right place. And who were the ones who heard the good news of the birth of a Savior? The shepherds who faithfully kept watch over their sheep. The shepherds who were responsible for caring for the sacrificial lambs.

An angel of the Lord appeared to them with the good news of great joy that would be for all the people. Can you imagine the light that overpowered the dark, starlit skies? Can you imagine the sound of angel wings and heavenly song? *"Today in the town of David a Savior has been born to you. This will be a sign to you: You will find a baby wrapped in cloths and lying in a manger (NIV)."* A song of angels filled the air, praising God and his glory, bringing peace to those he favored.

The shepherds left their flock of sheep to find the one. He was not hard to find, for they knew exactly what they were looking for. Mary must have told Luke this story – because we know the little detail that she pondered all of this and treasured it in her heart.

The shepherds could not return quietly to the rolling hills. They spread the word, glorifying and praising God. They told their amazing story of angel song and a baby wrapped as a sacrificial lamb, lying in a manger. Shepherds and sheep and the birth of a sacrificial lamb. Not exactly how we would have written the story of the birth of the king of the world. God is not one for doing things the expected way. But there is no stopping the coming salvation. Jesus. The Lord saves. He has come. God is with us. Immanuel.

7

The Faithful See Him

Read Luke 2:21-40

On the eighth day, the infant was circumcised and given the name Jesus. According to the purification rites required by the law of Moses (Exodus 13:2,12; Leviticus 12:8), Joseph and Mary made the trip into Jerusalem to the Temple. Jesus, their firstborn son, was consecrated to the Lord, and they made a poor man's offering of a pair of doves to God. This is all very normal and expected of every Jewish couple at the birth of their child. But then the unexpected happens.

A devout Jewish man named Simeon is filled with God's Spirit in the Temple courts. Not only is God's Spirit with him, but God has revealed to him that *"he would not see death before he had seen the Lord's Christ"* with his own eyes. And then the Holy Spirit leads him to the Temple courts. Filled with expectation, I imagine God's Spirit spoke to him in some very supernatural way as Simeon saw Joseph, Mary, and this newborn infant. He asks to hold the child in his arms. What wonder! He does not see a mere infant boy – there were probably many there that day. He sees this child as God's *salvation*, prepared in the sight - in plain view – of all nations. How profound that this old Jewish man who had been waiting a lifetime for *"the consolation of Israel"* – for his beloved people to be "consoled" or comforted, did not see a coming Savior for only the Jewish people! He saw in this infant something much more. God's salvation would be *"a light for revelation to the Gentiles, and for glory of your people Israel."*

I can't help but be reminded of the prophecy of Isaiah about the coming Messiah:

"You will do more than restore the people of Israel to me.
I will make you a light to the Gentiles,
and you will bring my salvation to the ends of the earth."
Isaiah 49:6 NLT

This child would become a light to people walking in darkness. God's Messiah would come to restore, comfort, and save both Jews and Gentiles. That pretty much includes everybody—or at least anybody who will accept his gift of salvation.

Isn't that beautiful? But Simeon is not done. He turns to Mary—he must know that she knows this child is God's—and tells her wonderful and hard things.

"This child is destined to cause the falling and rising
of many in Israel,
and to be a sign that will be spoken against,
so that the thoughts of many hearts will be revealed.
And a sword will pierce your own soul too."
Luke 2:34b-35 NIV

Oh my! Perhaps this is more hard than wonderful. This young girl has just given birth under challenging circumstances (ruined reputation for becoming noticeably pregnant by someone other than her intended), traveling a long journey by donkey to pay taxes (while extremely pregnant!), no room in the inn, giving birth somewhere akin to a barnyard with no women folk to help, and a bunch of unclean shepherds showing up wanting to see the baby! And now, at the

Temple, an old man tells you your child will be "spoken against" and a sword will pierce your soul! I'm thinking maybe he could have left that part out.

This is the problem with God. He tells us the hard things.

This infant has come into this world with a profound purpose. Salvation is not an easy thing. If so, it would not be so long awaited. Jesus would be a turning point for many. He still is. He is a rock in your path. Stumbling in the darkness, he is the rock to guide you toward the right path - solid, strong, and foundational. Or he is a stumbling block, causing you to trip, lose your footing, and fall. God's Spirit has revealed these extraordinary and disturbing prophecies in the Temple to Simeon, who has now revealed them to Joseph, the carpenter, and the young new mother, Mary. Baby Jesus, eight days old, has a big future ahead.

Jesus would return to this same Temple as a man, a rabbi who was shaking up the Jewish world. The Jewish leaders would come to him and demand to know by whose authority he spoke. He would tell them a strange parable of a vineyard, the men who rented the vineyard, and the vineyard owner's son who came to collect the rent. The tenants would kill the son. The vineyard owner would come to kill the tenants and give the vineyard to others. The people who heard this story were horrified and protested, "God forbid!"

Jesus looked directly at them and asked,
"Then what is the meaning of that which is written:
'The stone the builders rejected has become the cornerstone'?
Everyone who falls on that stone will be broken to pieces;
anyone on whom it falls will be crushed."
The teachers of the law and the chief priests looked
for a way to arrest him immediately,
because they knew he had spoken this parable against them.

But they were afraid of the people.
Luke 20:17-19 NIV

This baby in Simeon's arms would be that Rabbi who taught in the Temple. He would be that sign, that cornerstone. He would reveal the thoughts of many hearts. And Mary would live to have her soul pierced by the sword of a Roman cross.

But their Temple visit isn't done yet. The 84-year-old prophetess Anna, who never left the Temple day or night, worshipping and praising God, will also speak to them about this mere baby. She will praise God for this child and tell of God's coming redemption of Jerusalem.

These were signs of encouragement to the old faithful believers Simeon and Anna. And these were affirmations of God's promises to Mary and Joseph. They would return to their hometown of Nazareth, where the whispers of their sin would continue. But they would hold onto the shouts of praise they heard in the Temple, God's Holy Place, over the arrival of this infant in their arms.

And what can we say of the child? As he grew up, he was filled with wisdom and God's grace.

God placed his Salvation, his Hope for the nation, his Light for the Gentiles, his Way out of darkness far north of Jerusalem, away from the Holy City, in the land of Galilee, in a humble town called Nazareth. There he is, safely tucked inside a loving Jewish family—an ordinary family doing ordinary, everyday things.

Childhood passes quickly. We have very few words to describe those formative years. He grew. He became strong. He was filled with wisdom. But there was something else; the favor, *the grace of God,* was on him. Sit still with that for just a moment. It is the quiet light filling the skies before the sun breaks through the horizon's hard line. There is the waiting as the darkened earth turns just a tiny bit more, and the light bursts forth, illuminating every created thing. There will be no going back. The sun will rise in its perfect arc. A new day is unstoppably dawning. There will be daylight, undeniable, and those of us living in darkness will see clearly what the shepherds and Simeon and Anna all saw: God's Savior, filled with the light of God's glory!

8

Wisemen and Kings, Angels and Dreams

Read Matthew 2:1-23

Only Matthew tells us of the wise men following the star, searching for the child born to be king of the Jews. And it took a while to unfold; they didn't jump on a magic bus that landed them at the manger along with the shepherds. And this story has a very disturbing story within it of slaughtered babies. Maybe we could have done without this story. But no, God decided it needed to be told.

This story is full of concrete, check-it-out information: specific rulers who placed it in a specific time frame, with very specific places. We follow the Magi from the east to talk with the Roman King Herod in Jerusalem and to visit a toddler in Bethlehem. Then, the family of Jesus escapes to Egypt and finally returns to set up house in the northern town of Nazareth because Herod is dead. Yet, his dangerous son, Archelaus, is in power in Jerusalem. Whew! That's a lot of time and place information.

Matthew also includes two passages of prophetic Hebrew scripture which, in his opinion, is fulfilled. We will get to that in a minute.

Then, this story has spiritual and supernatural elements that cannot be easily dismissed or explained—a new star in the heavens, warning dreams, and instructive angels. I am betting that Joseph was getting accustomed to conversing with those heavenly messengers. He had no doubts when they showed up. He just immediately did whatever they instructed him to do.

Let's start at the beginning of this story. Who are these "Magi from the east"? Some say they were wise men, astrologers, or philosopher-priests, perhaps from as far away as Babylon. We usually call them "the three wise men" although nothing here says "three" other than the gifts they brought: gold, frankincense, and myrrh. This is what we know: they study the stars in the nighttime sky and have seen a star they have never seen before. Something in their star-gazer encyclopedia tells them that this new star is announcing the "one who has been born king of the Jews."

They go to King Herod, surmising that since he is king, he would know about this newly born king. This new-king business is news to him. Unpleasant, disturbing news. Herod is of Jewish lineage, but he doesn't know much about the Jews because he likes the power and authority the Romans can give him. It will be best to find this baby and get rid of him as quickly as possible. Herod is no stranger to getting rid of his competition. Or anyone he perceives as having questionable loyalty to him. Rumor has it that he killed two or three of his sons when he decided they could be threats to his throne.

First, he must find out where this kid is because the star only tells them so much. "Oh yes!" the Jewish chief priests and teachers of the law inform him. "The Messiah, God's anointed king, is to be born in the little town of Bethlehem. He will be a ruler to shepherd the people of Israel" (Micah 5:2, 4).

Herod finds out the wise men have been traveling for many months following this star of the new king. They have come from a great distance and at great cost to bring their treasures and pay homage. But all that means to Herod is he needs to find this toddler and get rid of him before he grows up and becomes trouble. Herod smiles and spreads his hands in a display of humility. "Oh, by all means, as soon as you have found this child, come tell me so I may go and worship him also."

The wise men saddle up their camels, and lo and behold, there that star is again, shining brightly. It went ahead of them, leading them to a specific house. And there it stopped. Have you ever seen a star act like this? It must have been amazing! Sure enough, toddler Jesus and his mother, Mary, are at that house. This must have been much more profound than we can imagine. Think of it; what would it take for you to *bow down and worship* not just a baby – but *a toddler*? I have a couple of those running around my house. They are darling and amusing, but they certainly do not inspire worship, especially from brilliantly educated, wealthy, well-respected men who have traveled over hill and dale looking for a king!

The Jewish shepherds coming to see the Messiah-King was one thing – but what is the deal with these Gentiles from another land? Hmmm. Could it be found in that little detail the angel was talking about, *"good news that will cause great joy for all the people"?* Maybe this is someone more than the king of the Jews. Is there a clue in the treasures the Magi bring?

The men who traveled from afar to honor a new king brought gifts of great worth. Gold was a valuable gift worthy of royalty. Frankincense was fragrant, an incense with a pleasing aroma worthy to offer to a perfect deity. Myrrh was a spice and a perfume often used for embalming. Could this valuable gift be pointing to the death and burial of a Savior sent from God?

Reflecting on the precious gifts brought to a child-king makes me pause when I think of the disposable gifts we offer each other at Christmas time. Are the gifts I wrap in paper and ribbon and offer to the ones I love as thoughtful as these? And even more thought-provoking, what are the gifts I offer this king? How do I truly celebrate the birth of Jesus?

❧

No sooner have the Magi come than they are gone, leaving by a different route from when they arrived. They were warned in a dream to avoid this disingenuous King Herod. An angel shows up in Joseph's dream that night with an urgent warning. "Get up. Now. Herod is sending soldiers to kill the child. Go to Egypt and stay there until I tell you to return." Immediately, Joseph got up in the night; they packed their belongings and were gone before Herod's soldiers were streaming through the streets of Bethlehem.

This is the horror of this story. This is the heartbreak. This is the stuff we wish we didn't have to know about. King Herod sent his soldiers to kill every boy-child two years old and under. Or thereabouts. Who knew how old this child was since it had taken quite a while for the Magi to travel such a long distance? They couldn't know which child could be the coming king of the star, so they tore the children out of their mother's protective arms and killed them all. The prophet Jeremiah told of it long before it happened.

This is what the Lord *says:*
"A voice is heard in Ramah,
mourning and great weeping,
Rachel weeping for her children
and refusing to be comforted,
because they are no more."
Jeremiah 31:15 NIV

Rachel was the beloved wife of Jacob (whom God renamed Israel). She died giving birth to Benjamin, Jacob's youngest son. She was buried just beyond Ramah on the way to a little town called Bethlehem. Presenting Rachel as a representation of mourning Jewish mothers, Jeremiah prophesied the coming time when Jewish young men would be marched past Rachel's grave to captivity in Babylon. Shortly after Jeremiah wrote these words of prophecy, they were fulfilled in 586

B.C. Hundreds of years later, with the slaughter of the innocents, once again, mothers will weep for their sons they will never see again.

God heard those anguished cries long before they happened. Why couldn't he have prevented this part of the story? Why couldn't we have skipped this chapter? We must open our eyes to this world's evil and our people's wickedness. These horrible, unthinkable things still happen today. And yes, even to children. To the innocents. God does not want us to close our eyes, to pretend this isn't real. This is why he came. He hears our cries; he sees the horror against the innocent. He doesn't turn away. He offers a way of escape. He sent his own son to receive the blows, to suffer the injustice, to defeat the terror and darkness of death.

Under Joseph and Mary's protection, Jesus would not stay in the safety of Egypt for long. He would return at the angel's bidding once the danger was past. Bypassing the turmoil of Jerusalem, their little family would return to the land of Nazareth. There, near the sea, Jesus would grow to be strong and wise. We would hear little about this king who had come to be worshipped by both Jews and Gentiles—until the time was right.

9

Lost in His Father's House

Read Luke 2:41-52

This is obviously a story told by Mary. It is the story of a proud momma who knew her son was beyond ordinary. This was probably one of those family stories told over and over again, much to the chagrin of Jesus. Can't you see him looking down with a slight smile and shaking his head as Mary told this story again with a mixture of laughter and exasperation? Everyone in the family and the village of Nazareth knew Jesus was different; this story came the closest to explaining it as any.

Every family would make the yearly journey to Jerusalem for the Passover Feast. The roads that led to the holy city were packed with travelers looking forward to a time of family reunion and religious celebration. Passover. It was a time to remember with joy and gratitude the night God came down to give his last and final warning to the Egyptians to let his people go. The tenth plague was terrifying; the firstborn was suddenly struck dead around midnight unless there was blood spread on the doorframe of the house. Inside, each family ate a meal of unleavened bread, bitter herbs, and the roasted meat of the slain unblemished lamb (Exodus 12:1-32).

Their Lord had commanded that his people always remember this time of deliverance when he passed over their houses with the blood on their doors. It was the Lord's Passover. Every year, Jewish men, as well as many Jewish women, packed their bags and headed to the holy city of Jerusalem for this holy celebration.

The year Jesus was 12 years old was no different. Off the family went on the 75-mile journey to Jerusalem. They walked along with friends, neighbors, and family; the children safely mingled with different groups as they all shared the same destination.

When I was a child, my family loaded up our station wagon and headed to Daytona Beach, Florida, caravanning with my aunt and uncle's family in their station wagon. Returning from our week at the beach, we stopped at the Georgia-Florida state line Stuckey's to gas up the cars and take a restroom break. I was mesmerized by the long shelves filled with pralines and pecan logs, and it took a while for me to notice that the store had gotten very quiet. The aisles were empty of familiar faces. At the front of the store, the station wagons were gone.

I took off running as fast as my little bare feet would go across the gravel parking lot. I had been riding with my aunt and uncle, so my mother hadn't given me a second thought. My aunt and uncle thought I had switched cars. As the caravan picked up speed on the interstate, my mother had playfully called out, "Everyone turn around and wave goodbye to Florida!" She turned to see her seven-year-old daughter far in the distance, racing with all her might to catch up with the already accelerating cars. It became the family story that was told over and over again, in the words of my four-year-old little sister, as "the time we was 'bout to left Georgia." Unlike Jesus, I was pretty traumatized!

But yes, it isn't so hard to leave someone behind... and not miss them for a while.

Back to Jesus's story. The Passover Feast is over, and everyone is heading back home. A day passes, and Mary realizes they haven't seen their oldest, Jesus, in quite a while. They check with his friends and their relatives. No one has seen him… since Jerusalem. They return, retracing their steps, asking everyone along the way if they have seen him. For three days. They finally find him – of all places – sitting with the teachers of the law in the Temple. Asking questions and discussing the fine points of the law. And this is the surprising point of the story; these men who have spent their entire lives studying the law given to their people by Moses are *"amazed at his understanding and answers"!* He is twelve. Still a boy on the threshold of becoming a man. Who were these highly respected men that they would spend days talking in depth with a child about things of God? Stop and think about this. This was not normal. This was incredibly unusual.

Jesus looked at this as if it was the most logical thing ever. Of course, he would be here, *"in my Father's house."* Mary, who has talked with angels about this boy she gave birth to, can only say about herself and Joseph, "…we did not understand what he was saying to us." They did not understand. Of course, they didn't. How could they? They were looking for him to act like an ordinary boy. He was not.

From a distance, Mary looked back on this one story of Jesus as a child that foretold what he would be as a man. The NKJV translation reads, *"Did you not know that I must be about my Father's business?"* Jesus knew his Father. It was not Joseph, the kind carpenter. It was someone greater. And his Father was preparing Jesus for the work he would do.

There's a little postscript here: Jesus returned with Mary and Joseph to Nazareth and was obedient to them. He grew in wisdom and size. He found favor with God and his fellow man. Mary treasured these things in her heart.

This story is significant. His birth was announced by angel song and starlight. His first visitors were the shepherds who kept watch over the sacrificial lambs for the altar in Jerusalem. Devout Jewish worshippers foretold his future as a stumbling block and as a Savior. Gentile wise men sought him as king of the Jews and brought precious gifts to honor him. And the priests and teachers at the Temple were astounded by his understanding of their law and their God. No wonder Mary treasured these stories in her heart. This was no ordinary boy. He will be no ordinary man.

10

A Voice in the Wilderness

Read Matthew 3:1-12; Mark 1:2-8; Luke 3:1-18; John 1:19-28

You have to love John the Baptist. What an outrageous character! We started this story of Jesus with the story of John's father, Zechariah, meeting the angel Gabriel in the Temple. Gabriel had exciting news about a soon-to-be conceived child who would be filled with the Holy Spirit of God even before he was born. This son John would be great in the sight of the Lord, and he would bring many people of Israel to the Lord; and he would *"go on before the Lord, in the spirit and the power of Elijah... to make ready a people prepared for the Lord (NIV)."* And lo and behold, thirty years later, here he is, shouting in the wilderness.

And what a message! He doesn't hold back. He is not polite. He does not give a message of love and prosperity. It is a message with a big capital R. "Repent! Get rid of your sins! Come wash yourself clean in the River Jordan. Be forgiven. Change your ways because the kingdom of God is coming near!" His message would be very unpopular today. I dare say he would be ignored entirely. We like our God messages to be filled and overflowing with joy and encouragement. John didn't have time for that.

Interestingly, the crowds flocked to hear him. They came from far and wide to see this very-unlike-them man dressed in camel hair and animal skins with dreadlocks down to his waist shouting in the wilderness. He wasn't in the Temple courts dressed in fine linen. Heck, no. The people had to make a great effort to get to him. Travel outside the city. Take a right at Jericho. Cross the Jordan River. You'll find him on the west bank in an area known as Bethany Beyond the Jordan.[1] And apparently, everyone who was anyone went to see him.

The leaders were there: the Pharisees, godly Jews who delighted in studying the law of Moses and who taught in the Temple, as well as the Sadducees, who were the wealthiest members of the upper class and served on the Supreme Court as lawyers and the liaisons with the Romans. Soldiers responsible for keeping the peace in this outlying Roman territory were there. Even tax collectors, who were the epitome of injustice and legal thievery, lined up to hear John's warnings. And then there was "the crowd"—basically, everybody else. This was no small thing. This was big. There hadn't been a fearful God-appointed prophet with a message from God in quite some time. Say, about 400 years. Not since the prophet Joel had shouted out his warnings:

"Even now," declares the Lord,
"return to me with all your heart,
with fasting and weeping and mourning."
Rend your heart
and not your garments.
Return to the Lord your God,
for he is gracious and compassionate,
slow to anger and abounding in love,
and he relents from sending calamity."
Joel 2:12-13 NIV

And there had been the terrifying words of the prophet Malachi, who told of the coming day of judgment:

"I will send my messenger, who will prepare the way before me.
Then suddenly the Lord you are seeking will come to his temple;
the messenger of the covenant, whom you desire, will come,"
says the Lord Almighty.
But who can endure the day of his coming?
Who can stand when he appears?
For he will be like a refiner's fire or a launderer's soap.
He will sit as a refiner and purifier of silver;
he will purify the Levites and refine them like gold and silver.
Then the Lord will have men who will bring offerings in righteousness,
and the offerings of Judah and Jerusalem
will be acceptable to the Lord,
as in days gone by, as in former years.
"So I will come to put you on trial.
I will be quick to testify against sorcerers, adulterers and perjurers,
against those who defraud laborers of their wages,
who oppress the widows and the fatherless,
and deprive the foreigners among you of justice,
but do not fear me," says the Lord Almighty.
Malachi 3:1-5 NIV

Was this rough-and-tumble John, shouting in the wilderness, the "coming messenger"? He certainly had the attention of everyone. All four of our gospel writers point to this idea of the "coming messenger" foretold by their greatest prophet, Isaiah.

A voice of one calling:
"In the wilderness prepare
the way for the Lord;
make straight in the desert
a highway for our God.
Every valley shall be raised up,
every mountain and hill made low;

the rough ground shall become level,
the rugged places a plain.
And the glory of the Lord will be revealed,
and all people will see it together.
For the mouth of the L*ORD* *has spoken."*
Isaiah 40:3-5 NIV

This is why John had everyone's attention. He looked like a prophet from God. He spoke like a prophet from God. And he didn't point to himself. He pointed to someone else. Someone who was coming. Someone who had an ax and a winnowing fork. Someone who didn't just baptize with water. Someone who was bringing God's Spirit and God's fire. John's voice was loud and clear, "Get ready. A storm is coming. And I ain't it."

11

A Sign from Above on the Wings of a Dove

Read Matthew 3:13-17; Mark 1:9-11; Luke 3:21-22; John 1:29-34

Poetry. That is the only way I know how to start talking about this. Baptism is the spiritual journey down into the water and up again into new life. This is where it began for me:

The invitation.
The chance to respond.
What if it was never given?
What if the question was never asked?

"Do you want to accept Jesus into your heart as your Savior?"

And I said,
palms sweating against the back of the wooden pew in front of me,
knees shaking and legs like jelly,
pushing past my cousins lined up beside me,
"Yes."

And Preacher Billy Joe Bridwell met me at the front of the church,
his hands reaching out to take mine,

leaning down to whisper
now forgotten words
and sitting me down on that front-row pew.

Surprisingly, others joined me there…
my cousin Jill, my cousin Barry
and that Sunday night, we walked down the metal steps into the
flood-light blue water
of the baptismal at Rock Hill Baptist Church,
once again to take
Preacher Bridwell's hands…

This time to be lowered down,
white dress floating out in the water,
and brought back up again,
alive.

Baptism. I grew up in a church with a baptismal built into the back wall behind where the choir sang and the preacher preached. Baptism was part of the holy ceremony of accepting Jesus as your Lord and Savior. If you said yes to Jesus, Son of God, you also said yes to baptism. It was the outward symbol of dying to self and being reborn into the new life of Christ.

It was simple to me—unquestionable, undoubtable. It surprised me as an adult when I learned there was such controversy about it. It still surprises me, actually. Jesus did it, so I did it. From this simple viewpoint, I approach this beautiful story told by Matthew, Mark, Luke, and John. But my favorite telling is by John the Baptist himself, through John the Apostle's gospel.

John picks up the story apparently the day after he baptized Jesus. He introduces this unknown man, Jesus, with an unusual title: *"The Lamb of God, who takes away the sin of the world!"* Wait. The Lamb of God? These Jews he was talking to knew about lambs. They were slaughtered day in and day out on the altar of the great Temple there in Jerusalem. Every sin of every Jewish person had to be confessed, and their sin atoned for, forgiven, through the blood sacrifice of an innocent, blemish-free lamb. God had given Moses his commandments, his law, on Mount Sinai as he led his people out of the bondage of Egypt and into the Promised Land.

With the law came the warning that every broken commandment must be repaired with blood. From that point forward, the blood of innocent lambs flowed from the altar. Broken law was called sin; it symbolized a broken relationship between the perfect God and his imperfect people. The sin, the broken law, never stopped. Therefore, the flow of blood never stopped. It took an army of priests and the never-ending parade of lambs to get through another day. Do you understand? The blood of the lambs never stopped flowing. Into this world of constant sacrifice stepped Jesus, *"Lamb of God, who takes away the sin of the world."*

The day before, John's ministry had taken a radical turn. Jesus, his cousin from Galilee, had shown up to be baptized. Matthew tells us John protested: "I am the one who needs to be baptized by you, and yet you come to me?" Jesus nodded his head yes. "This fulfills righteousness." This is right.

If we know Jesus, we say we have a "testimony." It is our personal story of when we first knew that Jesus was the Son of God, and we accepted him as our Savior. John the Baptist, who had baptized perhaps thousands of people, tells us this is his testimony: "I did not *know* that Jesus would be the one, but God, who had sent me to baptize with water, told me I would see His Spirit come down and remain on the one who would baptize with the Holy Spirit. This is God's Chosen One. He has surpassed me because he was before me."

What did John see that made him so sure? I love the drama of Mark's words. *"He saw heaven being torn open and the Spirit descending on Jesus like a dove. And a voice came from heaven: "You are my Son, whom I love; with you I am well pleased" (Mark 1:10-11 NIV).*

This story started many years before with angel-song and shepherds watching the flocks at night. But now the hero has been named and the story has a purpose: Beloved Son, Lamb of God, who has come to take away the sin of the world and to baptize with the Holy Spirit.

The dove has landed. God has spoken. John has testified. Things will never be the same.

12

Temptation in the Wilderness

Read Matthew 4:1-11; Mark 1:12-13; Luke 4:1-15

If you want your stories of Jesus to line up perfectly row by row, here at the very beginning, you will start to be a little disappointed. These stories immediately vary in their details and in their timeline. John tells his stories as if he is filling in between the gaps of what the others are telling. He entirely skips the forty days in the wilderness, yet he will state, as if looking at his calendar, "The next day John saw Jesus… and the next day John was there again… on the third day a wedding took place…" What's up with this?

These variations of eyewitness accounts make complete sense to me. When I was growing up, if you had gathered my mother, my sisters, and me together in a room and asked us to tell you about a specific event in our lives, you would have heard multiple versions of the same story. And one of us wouldn't have remembered the event at all. Or wouldn't think it needed to be told. I love this. It tells me that the story is accurate because each person experienced it through their point of view and brought their own interpretation to it. These variations add credibility to the telling of the story.

John completely omits the wilderness story. Mark, who gets his information from Peter, bottom-lines it with two sentences. Matthew and Luke tell us the same story, but the order differs. I am looking at Matthew's telling as I think about what happened.

The first thing you cannot miss is that the Holy Spirit led Jesus into the wilderness. This immediately dismantles the naïve assumption that if you are obedient in following God, he will guide you down a rosy path. Apparently not. And it wasn't just an outward-bound, get-away-from-it-all for a little alone time with God kind of retreat. No. Jesus's camping companion was the devil. Satan. The Serpent. The Tempter. And this enemy of God had plans of his own. He planned to stop God's plans.

Forty days, forty nights, no food. The first temptation would be so easy to fall for it would be child's play: "If you are the Son of God, tell this stone to become bread."

The first part of the challenge is an accusation: "God's Son? So, you claim to be God's Son? The God who created heaven and earth? The God who rained down manna for the Israelites for forty years? Then this will be easy for you…" The stinging word here is the word if. Every challenge will have this little accusing word at its center. "If you are who you say you are, then you certainly have the power to do these little tricks. If you are who you say you are, you can do anything you want… Show me. Prove it, Son of God. *If* you really are…"

Turn stone into bread. Stones surrounded Jesus. Turning stone into bread was going from hunger and want to fulfillment and abundance. The devil's first attack was on physical need. The weakness of the fleshly body influences our thoughts and our feelings. Jesus responded by quoting Deuteronomy 8:3, which teaches that the material provision of God didn't compare to the spiritual provision of God. *"Man shall not live by bread alone, but on every word that comes from the mouth of God" (Matthew 4:4NIV).*

If you read this verse in context, it is a beautiful reminder from Moses to the Israelites preparing to enter the Promised Land, a good land flowing with abundant streams, rich with wheat and barley, fig trees, and pomegranates. It is a land where they will lack nothing. It is a reminder that God has been with them as they traveled through hardship and wilderness for forty years. God had humbled them to test what was in their hearts. He humbled them, allowing them to hunger so that he might teach them that the words of the Lord are more valuable than bread. (Read Deuteronomy 8:1-10.)

How perfect that Jesus would refer to the encouragement of Moses and this specific time of God's faithfulness in the wilderness. Jesus didn't need bread to sustain him; he needed the bread of life—God's own words. The temptation was physical provision, but Jesus knew God's spiritual provision was more important.

"Oh, you want to play that game," the devil muses. "Okay, I can quote scripture, too." And so, he does:

"For he will command his angels concerning you
to guard you in all your ways;
they will lift you up in their hands,
so that you will not strike your foot against a stone."
Psalm 91:11-12 NIV

The devil's challenge to Jesus, from the highest point of the Temple in Jerusalem, was, "If you are the Son of God, throw yourself down." In other words, "Jump. God will protect you, right?"

Psalm 91 is one of the most beautiful songs of God's protection ever written. Perhaps it was written by Moses, who learned well the protective character of the God who rescued his people from the mighty Egyptians and led them through a stone-filled desolate land. Or perhaps it was written by David, a warrior king who knew the terror of facing the enemy. The psalm writer describes God as a refuge and a fortress, his faithfulness a shield. He is a God of rescue, protection, deliverance, and salvation. "If you are the Son of God, do you believe this?" the devil asked. "Do you trust your God to save you? Prove it."

The temptation here was trusting God for physical *protection*. Could his God protect him from all harm?

Again, Jesus quotes Moses from Deuteronomy 6:16, *"Do not put the Lord your God to the test...(NIV)"* but the rest of the passage is unspoken by Jesus in Matthew. It continues, *"...as you did at Massah."* Well, you may ask, what happened there?

Remember those grumbling Israelites whom God had rescued from slavery in Egypt? God was leading them to a new land, but they must learn to trust him along the way. They had been on the road for a while, and we catch up with them in Exodus 17. Right before they camp for the night in Massah (which wasn't named Massah yet), they had been concerned because they had no bread. God had provided bread from heaven, called manna – but they were to only collect enough for each day's needs. If they tried to hoard it, it rotted and bred worms overnight. They were to collect double the day before the Sabbath because God was resting on that Holy Day, and they all needed to do the same. Some people went out to collect manna on the Sabbath and were surprised to find none. Trust. God was teaching them to trust him.

So, not too long after the manna trust lesson, they set up camp in this new place that doesn't appear to have water. Immediately forgetting God's provision of manna, they begin quarreling with Moses, asking, "Why did you bring us up out of Egypt to kill us and our children and our livestock with thirst?" God instructed Moses to gather the people. He would stand before Moses there at the rock of Horeb, and Moses was to strike the rock with his staff. Water flowed out to quench the thirst of those complaining untrusting Israelites, their children, and their livestock. Moses named that land Massah, meaning "testing," and Meribah, meaning "quarreling," because the people had doubted the Lord, asking, "Is the Lord among us or not?"[1]

Jesus referenced this story as he called to mind that God was with him, protecting him with an angelic guard lest he fall. Jesus trusted God. There was no need for a test for God to prove himself trustworthy.

But the devil isn't through with Jesus. Let's try another one. One that has an almost irresistible allure for every human: wealth and power. Listen to the devil's description of what he is offering from Luke: "I will give you all the world's authority and splendor; it has been given to me, and I can give it to anyone I want to. All you need to do is bow down and worship me."

I think this is true. The devil may hold the power of the earthly governments and the illusion of wealth in his hand. Our earthly kingdoms are glittering and appear to be made of gold. Yet, somewhere in my heart, I know that underneath it all, there is only emptiness and the rot of death. What Satan offers as a great prize is a great lie. Jesus didn't fall for it. He knew who owned the cattle on a thousand hills (Psalm 50:10). His Father had no deficiencies. All of creation was already his. God the Father was immeasurably rich in mercy, rich in love, rich in grace, rich in kindness (Ephesians 2:4-8). What could the devil possibly offer beyond what God could freely give?

This is always the test, the temptation, the trick: Satan desires to be worshipped and placed above God the good Father, but all he can offer is smoke and mirrors. He is the original Wizard of Oz instructing Dorothy to "pay no attention to that man behind the curtain."

Jesus again turned to Moses's instructions as he sent God's children into the Promised Land. Jesus stated it simply: *"Worship the Lord your God, and serve him only (NIV)."* But the original passage has quite a wallop of power behind it:

"Fear the Lord your God, serve him only
and take your oaths in his name.
Do not follow other gods, the gods of the peoples around you;
for the Lord your God, who is among you, is a jealous God and his
anger will burn against you, and he will destroy
you from the face of the land."
Deuteronomy 6:13-15 NIV

Wow. We don't think of God this way anymore. Fear God. He is a jealous God. His anger will burn against you, and he will destroy you. This was coming from Moses. Moses had met with God on the mountaintop, where God spoke from the midst of the fire. Moses had encountered this Holy God. In light of this surreal conversation with Satan, I think it is safe to say Jesus had, too. He would not be deceived. He would not bargain with the devil. He knew his Father was jealous for us. He knew his Father demanded an exclusive relationship. There was no room for the devil and his lies.

The only thing left to say was, "Get away from me, Satan!"

This is the only thing we need to say: "Get away from me, Satan!" There is no discussion worth having. There is no bargain to be made. His ultimate purpose is this: He desires to be worshipped by you. And he will stop at nothing to steal your heart. Jesus will teach that the devil was a murderer from the beginning and the father of lies. There is no truth in him. He is the prowling lion waiting patiently for weakness. His favorite approach is to make you doubt the goodness of God. And then he pounces. Jesus knew his enemy. "Get away from me, Satan!"

Satan left him. The angels attended to him. Tempted, tried, and tested, the anointed Lamb of God emerged victorious from the wilderness, filled with the power of the Holy Spirit. He would begin teaching in the synagogues. God's power and truth would begin to spread throughout a barren land.

In my mind, I picture Jesus taking off his family responsibilities and carpenter's apron and slipping on the spiritual responsibilities and robe of the Rabbi and Priest. Soon, more than only John and the devil will know who he is.

13

The Seekers

Read John 1:35-51

The invitation of Jesus seems simple. "Come. Follow me." And apparently, people do. There is something powerful and magnetic about him. Something fascinating and worthy. And he comes with the highest recommendation. From, of all people, John the Baptist, who had been shouting about the coming Messiah and his coming kingdom from the beginning. John points out this dove whisperer to two of his own disciples and calls him *"the Lamb of God."* The disciples immediately follow him.

They spend the day with him. They call him "Rabbi," which means teacher. We get the strange little note of the time: 4:00 in the afternoon. Why? What is the significance of this? I thought surely there must be something symbolic here. Nope. Apparently not. The time was meaningful to John, a fisherman, disciple of John the Baptist, and soon-to-be disciple of Jesus. It was a moment when his life became something different, something more. It became the touchstone to look back on and whisper to himself, "My life before Jesus, my life after Jesus." Much like John Newton, who also wrote about his first encounter with Jesus:

’Twas grace that taught my heart to fear,
And grace my fears relieved;
How precious did that grace appear
The hour I first believed.[1]

One of the other men, Andrew, who spent that afternoon with Jesus, was so excited about the conversation he could not keep it to himself. He immediately went to find his brother Simon with the announcement: *“We have found the Messiah!”*

The simple conversation between Jesus and Andrew’s brother, Simon, is key to understanding what made Jesus so appealing. Jesus looked at Simon and knew him. He saw who he was and who he would become. “You are Simon, son of John. You will be called Cephas (Aramaic). You will be called Peter (Greek). You are rock. Foundational. Dependable. Trustworthy.” Now, that is my expansion of what Jesus said to Simon Peter – but that is what we will see to be true about this Simon, son of John.

Simon Peter will be the one who takes the step out of the boat to join Jesus on the water. Simon Peter will be the first to state that Jesus is the Son of God. Simon Peter will be there on the mountaintop to see Jesus transformed into his spiritual self as he is encouraged by Moses and Elijah. Simon Peter will follow Jesus into the courts of the Sanhedrin on that last night. Simon Peter will race John to discover the tomb is empty, and he will be the first to enter. Simon Peter will walk alone with Jesus on a lonely beach, and Jesus will leave with him the responsibility to feed his sheep - his followers. Simon Peter’s testimony will be the rock, the firm foundation of the church to come. Simon, who will be called Peter. Jesus *looked at him* and *knew him.*

Jesus packs his bag to head back north to his hometown area of Galilee. He knocks on Philip’s door with an invitation: “Follow me.”

Philip, Andrew, and Peter are all from the same little town of Bethsaida, on the edge of the Sea of Galilee. They are buddies. But apparently, there is someone else Philip has to tell about their discovery:

Nathaniel. Nathaniel's first reaction is to scoff. "Jesus of Nazareth? Can anything good come from there?"

Isn't this little detail of Nathaniel's reaction of immediate dismissal so very real? We all carry in our pockets our own idea of who God is and how he acts and what he reveals. God certainly wouldn't send his Chosen One from somewhere as rinky-dink and disgusting as Nazareth. That place was not just the wrong side of town – it was the wrong town. Unfazed, Philip continues his invitation, *"Come and see."*

Before Nathaniel reaches Jesus, Jesus already knows him. He describes him as an Israelite who is honest and forthright, one who would never stoop to deceive another. (A very different description from the original Israel – Jacob, son of Isaac, who was quite the deceiver!) And Jesus tells him he saw him before Philip went to him under the fig tree. Why was this such a powerful revelation?

This power of Jesus to see beyond what could be seen was so convincing to Nathaniel that he declared new titles on this man who, just moments before, disgusted him. Jesus of Nazareth is now *"Rabbi," "Son of God,"* and *"King of Israel."*

I imagine Jesus laughed here. A great joy-filled laugh before telling his new friend, "So you believe because of something as simple as my seeing you earlier under a fig tree? Oh, you just wait! You will see much greater things than that! You will see heaven open and the angels of God ascending and descending on the Son of Man!"

Flip back in your Bible to the story of Jacob sleeping out under the stars, fleeing from his home, and his brother Esau, who threatened to kill him for "stealing" his blessing of the firstborn son by deceiving their father (Genesis 28:10-22). Jacob was on the run. His head on a rock. His destination was an unknown future in an unknown land. In the night, Jacob dreamed of a ladder, or a flight of steps set up on the earth, and the top reached into heaven. Angels were ascending and descending on the ladder. The Lord stood at the top, foretelling the blessings he would give Jacob: the land on which he was lying, offspring as numerous as the dust of the earth, and all the families on earth would be blessed through his offspring. Oh, and God would be with him and would not leave him—quite a promise! Jacob awoke and declared that place the house of God, the gate of heaven, named it Bethel and worshipped God there.

What in the world does Jesus mean when he tells his newest friends that they will see heaven open and the angels of God ascending and descending on the Son of Man? Would they receive a blessing similar to what Jacob received from the Lord? Were those angels treading on an open gate that connected earth-bound man to the heavenly Lord God? And what is the meaning of describing that ladder or open gate as the "Son of Man"?

Again, we need to flip open those ancient scriptures of the Hebrews, this time to the outrageous stories of a young man held captive in the royal courts of Babylon. His name was Daniel. One night, during the first year of the reign of King Belshazzar, he had a dream filled with visions of the coming future.

He foresaw four terrifying beasts that symbolized four kingdoms that would rule over the earth for a time, and he also saw into the kingdom of heaven, where the Ancient of Days sat on his throne in judgment. Approaching his fiery throne came one who could stand in the presence of the Lord, and he was given *"dominion and glory and a kingdom that all peoples, all nations, and languages should serve him."* His kingdom would be everlasting and one that would never be destroyed (Daniel 7:13-14). The one who was given this kingdom was called by Daniel "one like a son of man."

Jesus would often use this description of himself as the Son of Man, pointing to a king of redemption. But you would have to have spiritually attuned ears to hear this meaning. Now, the phrase "son of man" is also just a simple description of a human being born of man. Which Jesus was. Or you could call him the Son of God, which he was. But he didn't agree to that description of himself until he was ready to be crucified. Because those were fighting words. Son of Man. Son of God. Jesus was "guilty" on both counts.[2]

Putting these pieces together, do you see how very profound this little conversation was? *"You will see much greater things... You will see heaven open and the angels of God ascending and descending on the Son of Man."* So, what do you say? Do you want to come along to Galilee with us? It just may be the adventure of a lifetime!

Before we walk away from this conversation, there may be one little, tiny question at the beginning that we have overlooked. Jesus asks those curious followers, *"What are you seeking?"* It is a simple but profound question. It reminds me that I must ask myself this question: What am I seeking? What do I want to find? What am I looking for in following this Lamb of God? Do I want to be fully known? Do I want to know God fully? Is such a wonderful thing even possible?

14

Just One More Glass of the Good Stuff

Read John 2:1-12

My cousin Meadors is an incredible storyteller. I love to see him get tickled with delight in the middle of telling his story. It is just so good. The Tanners were not big drinkers. As an adult, I found out my daddy had a drink occasionally (apparently a gin and tonic) with my mother after we kids had gone to bed, but I never saw him do anything of the like personally. My cousin told me he not only never saw his parents have a drink, but his mother was entirely against alcohol of any kind. Kidding her, he said, "But Momma, what about Jesus turning water into wine? If Jesus did that, it couldn't be such a bad thing." She leaned in close to tell him, "Well, I would have thought more of him if he hadn't." Meadors had tears of laughter rolling down his cheeks by the time he finished the telling. It completely cracked him up that his mother would have felt better about the character of Jesus if he hadn't had anything to do with wine!

Alcohol became an explosive subject in the early 1900s with Prohibition. There certainly have been many whose lives have been destroyed by alcohol. And I do not buy the idea that wine during the time of Jesus was grape juice. If that were the case, the Proverbs writer would not have said, *"Be not drunk with wine."* (I have heard it taught that wine of that time had perhaps a 3% alcohol content.) Personally, I prefer the instruction that *"wine makes the heart glad."* And I like to be glad. So, I guess you know my thoughts on the first miracle of Jesus. Bring it on.

Galilee. Cana. A wedding. A celebration of marriage, family, promises, and provision before God, family, friends, and neighbors. I love that God loves a good celebration! Everybody was there, including those new disciples of Jesus. His mother must have had some close relationship with the newly married couple since she knew the wine had run out. This was an embarrassment. This was a social catastrophe. This threw a big wet blanket on the party. Mary turns to her son. Unusual. But she knows something about her son that makes her think this situation can be turned around.

He seems disrespectful. Dismissive. He calls her "woman." I have a friend who sometimes calls me "Woman!" I don't mind. It is a little endearing in that I don't think she uses that term with just anyone. Anyway, we see that Mary, his mother, is not offended. Nor is she disheartened. She tells the servants to do whatever he asks.

He asks for something highly unusual. He points to the ceremonial jars that usually hold ceremonially clean water—pure water for washing, blessed water that will change the unclean to clean, water that will allow a devout Jew to partake in the meal.

Jesus instructed the servants to fill the six giant stone water jars. With water. To the brim. They obey him. "Now take some out and present it to the banquet master for approval." Can you imagine all the objections going through the minds of the servants? They know with absolutely no doubt – that all they will be presenting is plain old water. What would be their punishment for something as outrageous as offering water as wine? Don't you know they held their breath? Don't you know they tensed, waiting for the head of the banquet to spit the ordinary lukewarm water back in their faces?

Instead, the banquet master nodded. He smiled. He went to the young bridegroom to pull him aside and whisper, "Everyone brings out the best wine first, saving the less expensive wine until after the guests have had too much to drink and will not notice. But you! You have saved the best wine until now!"

John explains this is the beginning of Jesus revealing his glory. Jesus didn't just turn water into a bottle of wine as a party trick. He turned gallons and gallons – an enormous abundance of water – into the best wine. A wine that a seasoned banquet manager would be impressed by. And those ceremonial pure pots for holy water would never lose the red stain. They would need to find a new purpose. And the groom, who stood to carry for the rest of his life the embarrassment of not honoring his new bride and their wedding guests because he scrimped on the wine, was seen instead as a man of generosity and abundance, offering his best.

Watching this first miracle unfold, his disciples believed. They believed what? That Jesus was a most unusual man. There was something about him that pointed to glory. Something that pointed the way to something much bigger, much better. He produced abundance in the valley of emptiness; he offered redemption when it looked like there was no hope. Here in their midst was something they had never seen - only heard about from the prophets and the ancient prophecies. Something that felt like it would never come. But here he was without fanfare, instructing that the empty ceremonial jars be filled. Wine flowed. Come! Taste what is good! The banquet has begun!

Could it be? Could this be the One they had been waiting for?

15

Clearing the Temple: Take One

Read John 2:13-25

The beloved disciple John writes as if he is writing in chronological order, flipping through his mental calendar. He starts new stories with phrases like "the next day," "the third day," "after this," and "when it was almost time for the Passover." Okay, I will play along. After all, he was there.

After the wedding at Cana, he notes that Jesus spends time in Capernaum with his mother, brothers, and disciples. Obviously, there was a good family relationship there. And suddenly, we are approaching the time of Passover, when everyone Jewish (especially the men) made the trip to Jerusalem. It may surprise you when you read that Jesus traveled "up to Jerusalem" since he was hanging out around the northern vicinity of Galilee and Jerusalem is far, far south. Honey, I grew up in the South, and it is always "down" from pretty much everywhere else. So, what is going on with this "up to Jerusalem" talk?

Jerusalem was a city on a hill – that is why it was such a valuable city for King David to establish as his capital; high, raised up, you could see your enemy coming from a long way off. And then you have Jericho. It is north of Jerusalem, but everyone refers to going "down" to Jericho. The road to Jericho is steep and dangerous, running down deep into the valley. So, there you go, a little description of the lay of the land. Up to the heights of Jerusalem, down into the valley of Jericho. Jesus, like every other Jewis man, was headed up to Jerusalem because it was the time of Passover.

We know this story. The courtyards of the Temple look and sound like a world bazaar. There are bulls. And sheep. And doves. I imagine the smell of manure was pretty strong. The days of Moses are long gone, and Rome has realized the potential wealth of thousands and thousands of people needing to make sacrifices. And quite honestly, the priests have gotten a little greedy.

The Temple makes it so much easier for everyone: you don't have to risk your precious little lamb not meeting the requirement of "flawless." Buy from us, and we will guarantee a perfect, high-quality little lamb. Plus, you don't have to travel from Timbuctu dragging your sacrifice behind you. We can provide a "fully guaranteed" sacrifice for a very reasonable price. Just bring us your money.

And you don't even need to worry about having the right change! The Temple now provides the correct currency for you! This is where we find the small print most of us aren't aware of: you couldn't use just any old money from anywhere, oh, no ma'am! You were required by the Temple authorities to use the currency they designated. It was yet another opportunity to make a little more profit. For the Temple. All good.

Well, not really. Jesus is not amused. He actually gets pretty violent. This may not match up with the gentle Jesus picture you have in your head. This is where you must remember God is a God of justice. The Temple was his house, a place to come and worship him. It was a house that accommodated not only the men of Israel but also outer courts to welcome the women and the "outsiders" – the Gentiles. But space was limited, so those outer courts were utilized for commerce. The Temple priests didn't think the Jewish women and the Gentiles would notice. Jesus does.

He is angry. He makes a whip. He is driving the animals out of the Temple. He is overturning the table of the money changers. His disciples, who are probably a little terrified, quote the words of his ancestor David from Psalm 69:9: *"Zeal for your house will consume me."* And then the Jews show up.

Of course, the Jews are already there, so I think John is referring to the religious leaders of the Jewish people. The ones who have much to lose if the status quo is disturbed. These Jews are the ones in power. And they have a question for Jesus about power. "Who has given you the authority to come here and do this? Prove to us you have more authority, more power than we have. Give us a sign that points to your authority." That's really the name of the game here: power.

And Jesus says the craziest thing: "Destroy this Temple, and I will raise it again in three days."

Don't you know his disciples silently groan? "Oh, come on, Jesus! We have been watching you do amazing things. Why do you have to say something crazy now? Show them who you are!" This is the problem with being the smartest person in the room. Jesus was saying something entirely true. His listeners just had no clue what he was talking about. They couldn't. They wouldn't. Until years later.

Jesus had come to change everything. Including the Temple. And sacrifice. And worship. Everything. There was no way these Jewish leaders could understand that the Temple, which had been the center of all God worship, was getting ready to change from a building of stone to a flesh-and-blood body with a heart. And God's Spirit would live *there*. The sacrifice of one perfect lamb would fulfill the ongoing, never-ending sacrifices of bulls, lambs, and doves. Worship would no longer need to take place in Jerusalem; it would be in the humbleness of the bowed knee of any believer, anywhere. The Temple Jesus referenced was his own physical body; it would be destroyed on a wooden cross, and God would raise it back to life in three days. "Destroy this Temple, and I will raise it again in three days." Oh, yeah, he would - because he was God. It was better that they didn't understand. Yet.

Somehow, everything settles down. He isn't arrested, fined, stoned, or even run out of town. Many people listen to him teach throughout the following days of the festival. They see signs that help them believe in him. Signs that point to some sort of authority from above. He certainly is unusual. He has a powerful quality that is mesmerizing. And appealing. But he doesn't get carried away with his success or growing fame. John tells us what we are already figuring out: he knew what was in each person. Although he possessed a rock star magnetism, Jesus seemed interested in them. He really saw them – and knew who they were – through and through. This ability will make him very attractive to some. And very dangerous to others.

16

A Little Late-Night Conversation

Read John 3:1-21

One of the most well-known scripture passages about Jesus is within this little story. You will see people at baseball games holding up a sign with "John 3:16." Many years ago, during a meeting, the man I was working with who owned an advertising agency randomly stated that example, with the question attached, "What does that mean? John 3:16?" Being the good Christian girl that I was, I immediately started rambling off, *"For God so loved the world..."* And he cut in, "I know, I know. But what does it mean?" He wasn't asking for the scripture. His point was that even non-Christians are aware that simply the notation of this passage points to the heart of Christian belief. It is an interesting intersection between Christianity and the rest of the world.

The profound and direct proclamation of *"For God so loved..."* took place in an intimate setting. I imagine lamplight and one-on-one deep conversation. It is hard for us to hear just how revolutionary this conversation was and how disturbing these ideas were. We get our first clue in the first paragraph of this little story: when it took place and who was there. John is the only gospel writer who tells us this story. I wonder if he was there? Or did this story possibly come from Nicodemus himself?

Nicodemus is a man of great authority. He is a Pharisee. When we hear that today, we don't understand that the Pharisees were the ultimate religious leaders within the Jewish community. We think, "Oh. *Pharisees* equals *bad*." No. The Pharisees had the education, time, devotion, and opportunity to study the Torah and teach it. The priests were tied up with making never-ending sacrifices and fulfilling the requirements of worship in the Temple according to the religious law; the Pharisees were the ones who connected the Temple and the teachings of Moses to the people.

Nicodemus is even more than a devout Pharisee. He is also a member of the Jewish ruling council. Just insert "Supreme Court" here. Much of the Supreme Court of the Jews was made up of the Sadducees, the Jewish upper class who had one foot in the Jewish world and one foot in the Roman world, but there were also Pharisees there, and Nicodemus was one of them. And he is curious. About this guy, Jesus. But he also doesn't want everyone in town to know he is interested in what this outsider Jesus is teaching, so he shows up after the sun has gone down and most folks are tucked safely away in their little homes. There is no crowd here. Just one-on-one, he can ask some questions. And he starts with words of respect.

"Rabbi, (teacher), we (is he representing other Pharisees?) know you are a teacher *who has come from God* (really?) because no one could do the (miraculous) signs you are doing if God were not with him." This is the whole purpose of miracles. They are signs that point to God. It is not so much the lame man walking or the tasty wine from the water, but the intention is, "Look at God! What is he up to? What does this unusual thing say about him?"

Immediately, Jesus jumps off the diving board and into the deep end. Way over Nicodemus's head. It's like Jesus is saying, "Good! Now that you understand that, let me tell you about God and his kingdom.

You need to know this truth to see into his kingdom: You must be born again."

Wait. What? We have been concentrating on honoring God's Law. What in the world are you talking about, "Born again?"

Jesus begins describing the essence, the nature of God. He is Spirit. He is like the wind, which cannot be seen but affects where it is. You cannot tell where it is going, but you can hear it passing by. No one can control it or contain it. God is Spirit; to enter God's world, you must become Spirit. You must be born of his Spirit and of water.

Then Jesus includes someone else in his explanation: "*We* speak of what we know. *We* testify of what we have seen. But still, you do not accept *our* testimony." He lays out who he is, where he comes from, and why he comes. "No one has gone into heaven (God's kingdom) except the one who came from heaven (that would be Jesus, that "Son of Man" Daniel described as someone who would be given an everlasting kingdom). And I will be lifted up, just as Moses *lifted up* the snake in the wilderness so that everyone who *believes in him* may have eternal life."

We must remember that Jesus is talking to a scholar of God's scriptures. Nicodemus knows the story of the Israelites traveling through the wilderness for forty years. In Numbers 21:4-9, you can read the story of people being snakebitten. The people were traveling toward Canaan, but the people of Edom refused to allow them to travel through their land. God directed them to do no harm to the Edomites and to go the long way around. The people didn't like this solution and started cursing and grumbling against God and his provision. He sent snakes among them. A little painful reminder of their sin against him. Uh-oh. With the snake's bite came an agonizing death. The people repented of their sin and asked Moses to go to God for them. God's solution to the snakes was very strange. He didn't remove the snakes. He had Moses create a bronze snake and raise it high on a pole. Whoever was bitten by a snake only needed to look at this bronze snake, and he would immediately be healed and live.[1] It was that easy. Simply look.

Jesus is comparing himself to this holy, lifted-up snake who brought life where there was painful death. And the salvation he is offering is as simple as that: "Look at me, and you will be healed. Instead of painful death, you can have life."

I just recently became aware that the conversation may have ended there. Jesus had probably blown Nicodemus's mind. Think of all he had heard that night: "I have come from God. God is Spirit. If you want to know God, you need to be reborn: physical birth is only physical; you need to have God's Spirit if you want to know God." There's some little unexplained connection here with water. And then he continues, "You may know good works and God's laws, but you are still dead inside. You have been snakebitten. You must look at the life-giving bronze snake that will be lifted up and exalted." Jesus had laid it all out. It was too much to take in.

In some translations, the quotation marks continue, as if Jesus is still speaking. But in others, they end, and perhaps it is John who is giving his own commentary and understanding of what Jesus was saying that lamp-lit night. "For God so loved the world..." There it is – that profound thought. People didn't always think of God as love way back then. They thought of a holy taskmaster who had high expectations. There was a lot of respect – but also a lot of fear-based obedience going on. Break one or two of God's laws, and you are unclean and tossed out of the community unless you make a sacrifice. Grumble against God, and venomous snakes show up at your door. The people of God had seen what it was like to go against God. It was easy to forget that this God loved them with an everlasting love. Until Jesus showed up wearing a flesh-and-blood body and reached out to touch them. Our disciple John, the writer of this story, had seen and touched this flesh-and-blood God. And what he saw was love.

Love that reached down and gave a great and costly sacrifice. "For God so loved the world that he gave his one and only Son... (NIV)."

God is the only deity who makes a sacrifice for his people. Let that sink in.

Next, we must remember what Jesus just said about the bronze snake being lifted up: *"that whoever believes in him shall not perish but have eternal life (NIV)."* Here is another new and unbelievable thought: eternal life! Who ever heard of such a thing?

John had seen it. He had watched in agony as Jesus was tortured on a Roman cross, a spear thrust into his side to confirm his death, his bloody body wrapped in burial cloths and sealed in a stone grave - only to live again. Then he watched this born-again Jesus ascend into the heavens, accompanied by a band of angels, those terrifying ones God had sent to communicate with ordinary men and women. John had seen something that made him believe in this whole born-again business and the very real possibility of eternal life.

Let's put it all together: this one statement that tells everything about Jesus and why God sent him: *"For God so loved the world that he gave his one and only Son, that whoever believes in him shall not perish but have eternal life (NIV)."*

And then we get the bad news: we are condemned. This is the little truth in the fine print at the end of the story. We are all already condemned. We don't like to think about that one. No one gets out of here alive. We are all condemned to death. But God. God sent his Son into the world to save those who would look on him and *believe* in the name of God's one and only Son.

John uses an interesting word: verdict. *"This is the verdict (NIV)."* There is a judge and a trial, and the verdict is always the same; we are found guilty of evil, of darkness, slated for death. God offers something very different through his one and only Son: a pardon bathed in light and truth with the opportunity to stand in the sight of God instead of hiding with fear in darkness.

I don't know about you, but I'm accepting the pardon.

17

Mission Accomplished

Read John 3:22-36

I wonder how John the Baptist felt after Jesus showed up. His whole life had been in preparation for announcing the coming of the long-awaited Messiah. He had shouted repentance and preached for a life of righteousness and justice. He had built a reputation as the man to see to wash your sins away in the waters of the River Jordan. And suddenly, there is Jesus, Son of God, baptizing just up the river from him. What was his purpose now?

After an argument over ceremonial washing, we hear John's new career plans: "He must become greater, I must become less." If we, like John, accept that this Jesus is indeed Son of God, Messiah, the Christ, we must do the same. Jesus must become greater; we must become less.

Why? Because why would we settle for things and thoughts and words of the earth when we could have the things and thoughts and words of God instead? Why wouldn't we choose what is better? This passage tells us some beautiful truths about God and heavenly things. Jesus came from above and, therefore, is above all things. He has eyewitness testimony and, thus, is trustworthy. God has sent him, and he speaks the words of God. God gives his Spirit without holding back.

God has placed everything in the hands of his Son, whom he loves. Belief in the Son brings eternal life. All of this is amazing! Why wouldn't we want this - more of Jesus and less of us?

Ultimately, this is the whole purpose of the coming of Jesus. Our hearts have become hardened, our souls prefer the darkness of secrecy, our brains justify our selfish actions, and our tongues spin lies and deceit. Jesus shows up with a big scrub brush to wash us clean and a brilliant light to expose the stains in the corners. This entering in of Jesus is not easy because he also throws all the junk we have been hoarding out onto the street. Stuff we usually don't want to let go of. He cleans up our inner house. He fills up the emptiness and loss with peace and wisdom. For him to do his work, we must allow him to have full authority over our lives. He must become greater; we must become less.

"But," we may think to ourselves, "I like how I am. I don't want Jesus messing things up with all his cleaning. I don't really want to change. There is nothing wrong with the way I am. If I ignore him, maybe he will look the other way." Then there is the splash of icy water with the chilling reminder at the end of this little story in verse 36: God's wrath (something we don't talk about these days!) *remains* on us if we reject God's Son.

Take a look at that word: remains. We haven't done anything to deserve God's wrath, we think to ourselves – that's for those other people. Those bad people. Think about this for just a moment: if you have a child and someone mistreats, insults, rejects, or even ignores your child, how do you feel about them? It is as if they are harming you personally, right? Since you have great love for your child, it may even hurt you worse. Here we are, barely into the ministry of the Son, and we are already being warned that our rejection of Jesus brings about our rejection by God. Maybe it would be wise to at least listen to what he has to say. And then decide.

Before we leave John the Baptist standing in the river, let's listen to his response to this newly arrived Messiah. John compares Jesus to the bridegroom who has come for his bride. John has had the honor of being the bridegroom's best man. He has gone ahead to alert the bride of the coming of her groom. It has been a trusted responsibility. The bride has not been caught unaware; she has dressed in her finest, her maids have lit their lamps in the darkness, and the wedding feast has been prepared. There is excitement in the anticipation. The best man listens carefully, waiting. Then he hears the voice of the groom calling out as he comes through the streets; soon, he will arrive to knock at the door of his betrothed and ask for permission to enter. "I am the Messiah's best man," John explains. "I was sent ahead of him. He has safely arrived at the door of his bride. My mission is accomplished, and my joy is complete. He must become greater; I must become less."

If we have welcomed this Messiah into our lives, we are much like the bride accepting the bridegroom. Interestingly, in this male-dominated culture where the family arranged marriages, the future bride still had the option to reject the marriage when her betrothed arrived. She could simply refuse to open the door.[1] When Jesus called out to the church with the lukewarm heart that had locked the door against him, needing nothing he offered, he used the inviting words of a generous bridegroom.

"Behold, I stand at the door and knock.
If anyone hears my voice and opens the door,
I will come in to him and eat with him, and he with me."
Revelation 3:20 ESV

It is an offer of fellowship and intimacy, a holy union, a commitment of love and provision, a marriage.

God has sent his own Son as the Messiah Bridegroom. John the Baptist came as his most trusted friend at night to tell us he was on his way. Do you hear his voice calling your name? Do you hear his knock on the door? It is your choice: do you let him in?

18

Who are the Samaritans? A Sort of Short History Lesson

Read John 4:1-6

Jesus learned that the Pharisees had heard he was making and baptizing more disciples than John the Baptist. However, John the Disciple clarified that the disciples were doing the baptizing, not Jesus. Instead of hanging around to argue with the religious leaders of Jerusalem, Jesus sees this as the time for him to return to his hometown area of Galilee. This journey has only one problem: the most direct path leads straight through Samaria. Samaria is a problem for a devout Jew because Samaritans live there.

Who are these dreaded Samaritans who were "unclean" in the eyes of every Jew? It is time for a short history lesson so we will have the same knowledge that everyone who initially heard this story immediately drew from.

Long, long before, a God-fearing man named Abraham had been called by God to follow him into a land he promised would one day belong to Abraham's descendants. Jacob, the grandson of Abraham, had also received this promise as he traveled around this area near

Shechem, pitching his tents and digging wells for his flocks. Jacob, on his deathbed, gave his grandson Ephraim, son of Joseph, the land near Shechem (Genesis 48:22). The little problem here was that all the family had up and moved to the land of Egypt, where Joseph was currently the leading man in charge of everything, as they waited for a seven-year famine to end. They were far, far away from their promised land, which held the graves of Sarah, and Rachael, and Leah. They were far away from the wells that marked their land.

These early descendants of Jacob (renamed Israel by God) did not expect to be away for so long, but they found themselves enslaved by the Egyptians and ended up hanging out in Egypt for hundreds of years. God delivered them from the Pharoah's iron hand through Moses, the ten terrible plagues, and a miraculous, deadly evening called Passover. After crossing the Red Sea and receiving God's instructions from the mountaintop, they headed into the wilderness, grumbling over every challenge and doubting God's protection. Refusing to follow God's leading into the Promised Land (the land originally promised to Abraham; the land Israel and his twelve sons had lived in earlier), they spent the next 40 years in the wilderness learning God's laws – especially the one about not worshipping any gods of the pagans around them.

Finally, after all the old doubters (including faithful Moses) had died, Joshua led them across the Jordan River and into the Promised Land. You could think of it as a baptism of sorts. The twelve sons of Jacob had become the twelve tribes of Israel, and they divided the land among themselves and promptly forgot all about their promise to love the Lord their God with all their hearts and not bow down to idols. Those native gods were just so enticing! And there was sex involved in worship – so who wouldn't be attracted to that?

Eventually, God lost his patience with their constantly burning fires on the hilltops and their dance of idolatry. He sent the mighty Assyrians to the northern part of the Promised Land (The Northern kingdom of the ten tribes, also referred to as Israel) to destroy everything. He sent everybody packing in chains of captivity into a foreign land. For the same reasons, God would later send the Babylonians to the southern part of Israel (The Southern kingdom of the remaining two tribes), known as Judea, since the tribe of Judah primarily settled that land. In the meantime, the king of Assyria sent people he had captured from other foreign lands into the now-abandoned city of Samaria (the previous capital of the Northern kingdom) to live in the buildings and farm the land. They intermarried with the handful of the poorest Israelites left behind.

But then the lions showed up. Yep, they did. And they started eating people. The solution to this problem was to send a Jewish priest back to Samaria to educate these foreigners about *"the law of the god of the land."* (All of this is found in 2 Kings 17:24-41.) He taught them how they should fear the God of Israel. And they did, sort of. But it was just so much more fun to dance around the poles in the high places and sacrifice their children in the fire to Adrammelech and Anammelech, so they combined a little of this and a little of that. They feared the Jewish Lord *and* served their own gods. Samaria became the Wild West, where everyone did their own thing.

The Babylonians, who had carted off the southern tribes of Israel (including Daniel and Shadrach, Meshach, and Abednego), were overtaken by the Medes and Persians one night as they slept. (This is an excellent story about reading the writing on the wall in Daniel 5.) The new Persian King Cyrus opened the door to allow any Israelites who wanted to leave Babylon and return to Jerusalem to go and rebuild the altar and Temple with his blessings.

The returning Israelites had learned under Babylonian captivity what they would not learn under their previous freedom in the land of Judah: to fear the Lord their God. As the Jewish Temple was rebuilt and the walls around Jerusalem resurrected, the people once again were taught the laws of God and were humbled by their disobedience. Let's quickly examine the fundamental truth they had just experienced. This was Moses's long-ago warning to them before they entered the long-awaited land of promise:

"Hear, O Israel: The LORD our God, the LORD is one.
Love the LORD your God with all your heart
and with all your soul and with all your strength.
These commandments that I give you today are to be on your hearts.
Impress them on your children.
Talk about them when you sit at home
and when you walk along the road,
when you lie down and when you get up.
Tie them as symbols on your hands and bind them on your foreheads.
Write them on the doorframes of your houses and on your gates.

When the LORD your God brings you into
the land he swore to your fathers,
to Abraham, Isaac and Jacob,
to give you—a land with large, flourishing cities you did not build,
houses filled with all kinds of good things you did not provide,
wells you did not dig, and vineyards
and olive groves you did not plant—
then when you eat and are satisfied,
be careful that you do not forget the LORD,
who brought you out of Egypt, out of the land of slavery.

Fear the LORD your God, serve him only
and take your oaths in his name.
Do not follow other gods, the gods of the peoples around you;
for the LORD your God, who is among you, is a jealous God and his
anger will burn against you, and he will
destroy you from the face of the land.
Do not put the LORD your God to the test as you did at Massah.
Be sure to keep the commands of the LORD your God
and the stipulations and decrees he has given you."

Deuteronomy 6:4-17 NIV

The Jews had returned from Babylonian captivity to their homeland again after being almost entirely destroyed by their idol worship. God had kept every promise he had made to them. Good and bad. You better believe they were going to keep his laws and decrees. Or at least make the appearance of doing so. The priests burned incense and offered sin offerings at the rebuilt Temple. Devout Jews traveled from far and wide to worship within the gated city of Jerusalem. But now, dividing the once united nation of Israel, the constant reminder of their idolatry and captivity lived smack-dab in the middle of their land: the Samaritans. Those misplaced foreigners easily crossed the line between their evil little gods and the One True God. They were best avoided. Many good Jews bit their lip and traveled the extra mileage around the area of Samaria instead of stepping foot into that polluted land.

But here is a weary Jesus, resting at a well that once belonged to his ancestor Jacob. His disciples have gone to buy food in the nearby city. And along comes a lone Samaritan woman, carrying her water bucket in the heat of the day.

19

A Long Story About Water

Read John 3:22-26; 4:1-29

This is a story about water. Water in the wilderness. In a barren land, water is precious. We, Jesus's followers, know well that Jesus defined himself as the source of water that can quench thirst forever; water freely given that will well up as a spring of eternal life. We forget that he claimed such an outrageous thing in a religious wilderness to a shunned woman forced into her own private wilderness. If this were the only story ever told of Jesus, it would be enough to define who he was and why he came.

Let's back up a few verses to understand who was where and why. John the Baptist was baptizing in a place with deep and plentiful waters; Aenon means "springs." Biblical scholars place this site west of the Jordan River in the northern area of Judea, closer to the Sea of Galilee.[1] Jesus has remained closer to Jerusalem. Both camps preach a message of repentance, and people seek out both to be washed of sin in the waters.

John's disciples have a discussion – or a dispute with a Jewish leader concerning their preaching of needing to be washed in water as a symbol of repentance. There was a Jewish practice of water submersion – but it was a ceremonial washing for purification, which seems slightly different in the fine print. That discussion opened the door for John's disciples' concern that more people were heading to Jesus than John for baptism.

John 4 begins with this same thought. Not only have John's followers started questioning the rise in popularity of Jesus, but apparently, the Pharisees in Jerusalem are concerned about the same thing. It seems Jesus knew it was a waste of time to start tangling with the Pharisees over the pros and cons of ceremonial washing. Perhaps he knew others would be more open to the idea of needing to be washed in the cleansing water of forgiveness. And so, he leaves. He heads north toward his home area of Galilee, taking the most direct route leading straight through the center of Samaria. He rested near Sychar at a well that once belonged to Jacob.

Women usually had the responsibility of drawing water for their families, and they usually did it early in the morning before the sun was high and the temperature hot. And you know women - if we get a chance to gather together, we do. Drawing water at the well was more than a daily chore; it was a social gathering. It was a time to connect and catch up with the neighborhood news. This woman was here at an unusual time and alone. Perhaps she was avoiding the knowing looks. Perhaps she was avoiding the latest gossip. Perhaps she was the latest gossip.

Jesus, a very Jewish man in a very Samaritan village, asked her to give him a drink of the water she was drawing from the well. She was taken off guard that he would speak to her. In one sentence, Jesus had broken every barrier: Jews did not speak to Samarians, men did not speak to women, and strangers did not speak to one another.[2]

Without missing a beat, Jesus compared the water from the well to the spiritual living water that only God can give. And he called it a "gift," something both valuable and free. He invited her curiosity about *who* she was speaking to.

Trying to get her head around who this unusual Jewish Rabbi could be, she simultaneously challenges and attempts to insult him. "Where do you get that 'living water'? Are you greater than *our father, Jacob*?" It is a not-too-subtle reminder that the Samaritans traced their ancestry to Jacob through Joseph and his sons, Ephraim and Manasseh. She, a lowly Samaritan, and this Rabbi share the same bloodline.

Jesus isn't insulted, and he isn't deterred. He explains the difference between the water she speaks of and the water he offers: her water's ability to quench thirst will last for a little while, and the water he can give will become a living spring of water welling up to eternal life. "Okay," she agrees, "give me this water so I won't need to come here daily to draw water for my family."

"Okay," Jesus agrees. "Go. Call your husband and come back."

Is this ancient trolling? With one mention of her *husband*, the conversation takes a left turn. I think this odd back-and-forth agreement and sparring of Jesus is because of what we have observed in Jesus before; he *knows* us. It is relatively easy to say, "Yeah, yeah, I hear you – I'll go along with what you are offering," knowing that we will quickly forget about this bumping shoulders with a religious man by tomorrow. But if we are confronted by a living God who knows us and still wants to continue the conversation despite who we are, that is pretty exciting!

"Yeah, I know about you," Jesus tells her. "Five husbands and even more relationships with men that aren't exactly kosher... but the offer still stands." He continues to sit there in her presence. Waiting to see if she will open the door. Waiting to see if she will accept the gift. Waiting to see if she desires the living water.

Now that she understands he is someone extraordinary—perhaps even a prophet, she can't help but bring up the whole problem with "religion." It is the rules that no one can agree on.

> "You like po-tay-to and I like po-tah-to.
> You like to-may-to and I like to-mah-to.

Po-tay-to, po-tah-to, To- may-to, to-mah-to.
Let's call the whole thing off!" [3]

This old disagreement continues today: "Where do you go to church? What songs do you sing? How do you serve communion? Obviously, you aren't doing it right because you aren't doing it the way we do it!" Religion concentrates on physical actions instead of spiritual worship.

Jesus tells her absolutely everything. He holds nothing back. "Neither place matters – the Temple in Jerusalem or the traditions on the mountain of your forefathers. It doesn't matter where… let's talk about who and how. The time is coming – the time is actually here – when people will know they only need to worship the Father in spirit and in truth. God is Spirit and desires to be worshiped in spirit and truth."

I imagine her almost wistfully hoping for what she has perhaps heard from the reading of Deuteronomy 18:18. *"I will raise up for them a prophet like you from among their fellow Israelites, and I will put my words in his mouth. He will tell them everything I command him (NIV)."* Her longing response to Jesus is, "When the Messiah comes, he will tell us all things."

"I, the one speaking to you—I am he."

Their conversation ends suddenly with the interruption of the return of the disciples.

Those of us listening in on this story of water are left shaking our heads. Wow. This outsider woman by the well heard the complete revelation of the identity and purpose of Jesus. God's Messiah, God's Anointed One, was sent to speak the words of God. Jesus was sent to explain that God, the One and Only God, is Spirit. And he was seeking – looking for people who would worship him fully and completely in spiritual truth. Did she understand what she had heard? Did she look at him and believe?

She was gone… but she had left her water jar behind. Something tells me she will be back. And she won't be alone.

20

She Believed, They Believed, He Believed

Read John 4:28-54

Is it this simple: *"Come and see... Can this be the Christ?"*

The woman Jesus met at Jacob's Well experienced something extraordinarily different about this Jewish Rabbi. He had seen her and known her in a way she had never experienced before. I think this is so powerful and appealing—to be known. What would our world be like if each person was really seen by those around them? Really seen and known?

In 2015, I started collaborating with a woman on a film project. She had written a script based on a true story of a young man who went into an elementary school in Decatur with a gun and an announcement that everyone was going to die that day. Moments before he entered the school office, the school bookkeeper relieved the receptionist to go to lunch. Between rounds of gunfire exchanged with police, it was this woman – the bookkeeper - who convinced the troubled young man to lay his gun down and surrender to the SWAT team as helicopters circled overhead.

As soon as I heard the story, I knew it was God's story. It was. The bookkeeper gave all the glory to God. So did the 911 operator who had stayed on the phone relaying messages from the police negotiator. The bookkeeper looked at the terrifying young man and endearingly told him she loved him – and it wasn't too late to lay his gun down. And he did. I didn't know of any other school shooter story that had ended with everyone still alive to tell their story. What was the shooter's story?

Getting permission to visit him at Philips State Prison took almost a year. Navigating through security clearances, razor wire, and metal doors, I sat shaking in the visitation room, waiting to speak with this young man who terrified a community one afternoon with promises of death.

Michael had been in and out of residential psychiatric facilities since he was a child. His mother taught him how to steal from the local grocery store. He maintains that an older brother had molested him. Another brother accused him of threatening to kill him. Mainly, Michael tried killing himself: drinking household cleaners, overdosing on pills, slitting his wrists, and setting his apartment on fire. The voices in his head told him to do it. The school shooting was his intention to end his life – suicide by cop. But God had given him the gift of someone who looked at him and saw him: the Jesus-following school bookkeeper.

I had never met someone utterly unloved before, and it shook me to my core. Michael had no one. There was not a single person who looked at him and knew him. After the headlines were over, he was invisible to the world. Sitting on that plastic chair across from him, I began to understand that God had placed me in Michael's life to see him and to know him.

The woman at the well explained the power of Jesus as someone who knew her. He knew her better than she knew herself. And she believed. The whole town of Samaritans came out to investigate her claims. They invited Jesus to spend the night. Or two. They came away with the same conviction: here is someone greater than anyone else – someone who has the power to save the world. "We believe this man is from God – and he has come to save the world. We believe he is God's Savior." What happened to make them believe that? He didn't put on a show or perform miracles. What happened to make many say, "We believe"?

Jesus continues northward. He arrives in Cana of Galilee, where he is welcomed because many there had seen *"all that he had done in Jerusalem at the feast."* Yet there is a little disclaimer here that a prophet has no honor in his own hometown. In Cana, Jesus is approached by an official from the town of Capernaum, about 13 miles away. He has traveled a great distance in great haste, desperate to ask Jesus to heal his dying son.

On the surface, it seems that Jesus just callously dismisses him with an accusatory, "Unless you (plural tense) see signs and wonders you will not believe." This is written so very matter-of-factly. It sounds so uncaring. What was the tone of his voice? Yes, we do have trouble believing! I wonder what God thinks about our doubt and inability to understand his power. If he knows us – then he understands we need something much bigger than us to explain the bigness of him.

It isn't written this way, but for this begging father, there must be fear and tension wrapped tightly around a very slim hope for salvation for his son from death. I imagine the father of this boy is desperate. What would you do if there was the slightest possibility to save the life of your dying child? You have heard rumors of a man of miracles. You have traveled far to find him. The man asks him again, *"Sir, come down before my child dies."*

And with one command, *"Go; your son will live,"* the man believes. I think he believes more than the miracle that his son will live. I think he believes, like the Samaritans, that this man is more than ordinary. He is someone sent by God to save. A Savior. Someone who has power over life and death. The man leaves – because he believes. He believes

- for some unexplainable reason - the unbelievable. He believes that sickness and death will flee with the command from Jesus.

And it is true. When Jesus speaks in Cana, the boy's fever disappears in Capernaum. It was the "seventh hour" – 1:00 in the afternoon. The official's servants, who have traveled many miles to intercept him with the good news that the child lives, confirm the time of the miraculous healing. The unnamed official of Capernaum believes. And so do all the people in his household.

Sandwiched in the middle of all this believing, Jesus has a teaching moment with his disciples. It parallels his conversation about water at the well with the woman. Remember how their conversation began concerning the physical need for water and transformed into a discussion about spiritual thirst? The disciples returned from the town of Sychar after buying food, and Jesus changed the conversation to spiritual food. *"My food is to do the will of him who sent me and to accomplish his work."* Jesus spoke of fields ripe for harvest. He spoke of gathering fruit from seed that someone else had sown. He spoke of the joy of eternal life and the combined efforts of those who planted the seed and those who would reap the fruit. "You have entered into the labor of those who came before you," he taught. (My paraphrase.)

This is something amazing and mysterious. God's Spirit prepares hearts to listen and receive his words. When we tell of God's wonders and his Son's story, we are allowed to "enter into the labor" of those who came before us. It is a humbling experience to enter into God's field and see what he has already been preparing. He allows us to share in his glory when we tell his story.

I am betting the disciples were confused at the time. They would begin to understand later. As the story continued, they would have time to see that this coming of Jesus would be the turning point—from a long history of seed sowing to arriving at fields ripe for harvest.

One last little bit about my first conversation with Michael: schizophrenic, suicidal, headline-news, school-shooter. That first time I met him in the visitation room, he had pointed to the still-healing red wounds on his wrists from a recent suicide attempt. He had pointed to the indentation of the tracheotomy scar at his throat as he explained, "The doctors at the hospital said I wouldn't remember some things after the fire..." Brain damage from smoke inhalation when he had attempted to set his apartment on fire. He had admitted he had hoped the police would kill him that afternoon at the school. But he had gotten scared – like he usually did when it became hard to breathe and the desire to live overpowered the desire to die.

"Michael," I began hesitantly, "the bookkeeper believes God placed her in that room that day at that moment because he had a plan to save you. The 911 operator believes the same thing. And I don't know you very well – but I think God did not want you to die that day – that he had some bigger purpose for you."

"Yes, ma'am. I believe the same thing."

"Michael, do you believe in Jesus?"

"Yes, ma'am. I do."

I left that day after reaching for Michael's clammy hands and praying for him. I knew I would be back. And I would go back again. And again. Somewhere in Michael's lonely past, someone had planted some seeds, and he had heard the words of Jesus. Those words become muffled sometimes by the voices of the demons. He is a broken child whom no one ever loved in the body of a mentally ill man. But somewhere along the way in his troubled life, he experienced the knowing look of Jesus, and he believed.

21

An Unexpected Place to Begin

Read Matthew 4:12-17; Mark 1:14-15;
Luke 3:19-20; 4:14-15; Isaiah 9:1-7

John is arrested.

Herod, the tetrarch of Galilee, Roman ruler over the Jews, can do what the Jewish priests Annas and Caiaphas were powerless to do: shut John up. John's constant voice, crying out in the wilderness, had people thinking about their God and what he desired of them. But John wasn't content to only prick the conscience of the ordinary people – he had also become a thorn in the side of Herod by publicly condemning his relationship with Herodias, his brother's wife. And there were a few other touchy things that probably were also being pointed out. John didn't know when to keep his mouth shut.

Roman soldiers marched out to the Jordan, handcuffed John, and threw him behind bars without bail. With this, Jesus withdrew or returned to Galilee and started his public ministry, announcing, "The time is fulfilled, and the kingdom of God is at hand: repent and believe in this good news." Before John's arrest, all of Jesus's conversations were private with specific individuals or selected groups (other than that Temple-clearing escapade). John's arrest is a turning point. It kickstarts the crowd-following ministry of Jesus.

Why didn't Jesus go straight to Jerusalem, the epicenter of Jewish religion, if he had come as God's Anointed Messiah? Why "withdraw" to Galilee? How was the kingdom of God coming near or arriving "at hand"? Repentance? Aren't the Jewish people already following God's commandments and making daily sacrifices at the Temple for their sins? And what in the world is this good news? John was saying the same kind of stuff and look where that got him.

Matthew, our good Jewish boy, sends us to the Hebrew prophet Isaiah for explanation. I love that God has been dropping bread-crumbs all along the way for his people to follow. Isaiah was another loudmouth prophet God had sent 700 years earlier to warn the people of Israel to turn their attention and hearts to God. Isaiah told them God was jealous and judgment was coming their way. He also told them that in the future, God would be sending them (actually, the world) a Savior through their bloodline and that they had better pay attention so they would be able to relay the message. Here is a little of what Isaiah said the Savior would look like:

"Nevertheless, there will be no more gloom
for those who were in distress.
In the past (God) humbled the land of Zebulun
and the land of Naphtali,
but in the future, he will honor Galilee of the nations,
by the Way of the Sea, beyond the Jordan—
The people walking in darkness
have seen a great light;
on those living in the land of deep darkness a light has dawned."
Isaiah 9:1-2 NIV

When the prophet Isaiah wrote this, the people of northern Israel in the tribal areas of Zebulun and Naphtali were under the oppressive threat of the mighty Assyrians. By the time Jesus showed up, this area was under the tyrannical rule of the Romans. It was no longer divided into tribal regions but was collectively considered Galilee. There were many Gentiles in this area – people who lived in darkness because they didn't have the light of God. Galilee was on the outer fringe of Israel, easily rubbing shoulders with the rest of the world. If Jesus was this long-promised Messiah-King, the Royal Son of God, isn't it interesting that his ministry would explode in an area inhabited by both Jews and non-Jews? Could Jesus be this dawning light to illuminate the darkness?

And every good Jew hearing this prophecy would also know the promises that followed in this passage:

You have enlarged the nation
and increased their joy;
they rejoice before you
as people rejoice at the harvest,
as warriors rejoice
when dividing the plunder.
For as in the day of Midian's defeat,
you have shattered
the yoke that burdens them,
the bar across their shoulders,
the rod of their oppressor.
Every warrior's boot used in battle
and every garment rolled in blood
will be destined for burning,
will be fuel for the fire.
Isaiah 9:3-5 NIV

"You have enlarged the nation." Could it be that the Jewish nation, those chosen people of God, would enlarge beyond Jewish blood and the sign of circumcision? Could outsiders be invited in? There is coming joy as "people rejoice at the harvest." Is this what Jesus explained at the well in Samaria; was the harvest ready?

Midian's defeat? Shattered yokes, the shattered rod of their oppressor; was this a reference to the burden of outside oppression, or was it referring to the burden of the law? Could there be an easy yoke? Lighter? Jesus would reassure his followers that *his* yoke would be agreeable and his burden light. We will have to wait to see what this will mean.

Isaiah's words about the evidence of conflict are poetic; battle-worn boots and bloodstained clothing will be burned into ashes. I am reminded of the spiritual song of slaves working in ancient fields, words made popular to our generation by anti-war protestors: "I ain't gonna study war no more." This song, published in 1918 in *Plantation Melodies: A Collection of Modern, Popular and Old-time Negro-Songs of the Southland,* was an encouragement. God promised a time when swords would be beaten into plowshares and spears into pruning hooks (more harvest imagery!), and *"Nation will not take up sword against nation, nor will they train for war anymore (NIV)."* Again, the words of the prophet in Isaiah 2:4. This is beautiful and hopeful! Could the time be here when enemies would be defeated and peace would descend from the throne of God? Could that ever be possible?

The prophet Isaiah wasn't finished describing this coming Messiah who would deliver his people. We know the remainder of this passage in Isaiah from yet another song, Handel's Messiah:

"For to us a child is born,
to us a son is given,
and the government will be on his shoulders.
And he will be called
Wonderful Counselor, Mighty God,
Everlasting Father, Prince of Peace."
Isaiah 9:6 NIV

Every Christmas the world hears the prophecy foretelling God's Messiah through Handel's glorious music. Only one person comes to mind: the illegitimate carpenter's son and short-lived rabble-rouser known by one name: Jesus.

If John's arrest signaled the beginning of Jesus's ministry, you may wonder what the end would look like. Interestingly, God gave Isaiah the story's ending and the beginning. Well, it's not exactly the ending since "forever" has no end!

"Of the greatness of his government and peace
there will be no end.
He will reign on David's throne
and over his kingdom,
establishing and upholding it
with justice and righteousness
from that time on and forever.
The zeal of the Lord Almighty
will accomplish this."
Isaiah 9:7 NIV

John has been arrested and silenced in a dungeon in Jerusalem. Jesus has set up base camp in Capernaum. He is a descendant of the warrior king David, but he isn't singing songs of war. His message is one of repentance - turning away from the darkness and to the light of God. He brings good news. The kingdom of heaven is near. The king has arrived. And his name is Jesus.

22

Kill the Messenger

Read Luke 4:16-30; Isaiah 61:1-2

At first, it all sounded like good news. Jesus showed up in his hometown of Nazareth and went to church on Sunday. His family filled the pew, and he was surrounded by friends and neighbors who had known him since he was a little boy clinging to his momma's skirt. There was Miss Florine, who had taught him in Sunday school. And Deacon Clark Howell was always the first to approach with a big smile and a welcoming handshake. Oh, wait a minute – that's my hometown church. But I bet the synagogue where Jesus went on that Sabbath morning had much of the same welcoming atmosphere.

They were excited to have him there. Rumor was that he was teaching with unusual authority and performing miraculous signs. Surely, he would do the same thing here. The rabbi invited him to read from the scroll of the prophet Isaiah. He stood before them, honoring the words of their great prophet, and read.

> *"The Spirit of the Lord is on me,*
> *because he has anointed me*
> *to proclaim good news to the poor.*

He has sent me to proclaim freedom for the prisoners
and recovery of sight for the blind,
to set the oppressed free,
to proclaim the year of the Lord's favor."
Luke 4:18-19 NIV referencing Isaiah 61:1-2 (Septuagint) and 58:6

Ah! What a beautiful passage of hope and redemption! Good news for the poor, not just the economically unstable, but perhaps also the poor in spirit who haven't heard good news in a long time. Freedom for the prisoners, those who are locked behind dungeon doors, and maybe even those who are restricted by religious or societal mandates. Recovery of sight for the blind, those who cannot see physically, and perhaps even those who are blind spiritually. It is the time of Jubilee when God recommends that all debts be canceled and all oppression be lifted. What a wonderful message!

Then, the story builds as we wait for the scroll to be rolled and returned to the attendant. Jesus sits to teach, as is customary in Jewish worship. All eyes are on him—expectant and hopeful—and he begins.

"Today this scripture is fulfilled in your hearing (NIV)."

Hallelujah! Glory to God, can it be? But wait a minute, is he also claiming the status of the great prophet Isaiah; is he telling us he is filled with the Spirit of the Lord? Is he anointed by God to speak for him? His words are gracious and powerful – but we have known him his whole life. He is one of us. He is just the son of Joseph, the carpenter. Maybe he could perform some miracles to prove himself. You know, turn water into wine or heal a sick person. Come on, Jesus, we're waiting.

The people like Jesus's message but are confused that this man who grew up among them could be the Messenger. He knows what they are thinking. He doesn't ignore it – he confronts it with the statement that introduces his authority over justice and his understanding of sin and doubt: "I will tell you the truth that you do not want to hear. Listen to this…"

Jesus uses two examples of God performing a miracle, blessing people who were not "good Jews from the neighborhood" but outsiders. When God sent Elijah to the people of Israel, there was a drought for three and a half years, causing a horrible famine. Why didn't Elijah feed the poor Jewish widows there? Instead, he went to the Gentile widow in Zarephath in the region of Sidon and multiplied her oil and her meal to make bread (1 Kings 17:8-16).

Why did God allow Elisha, the prophet, to heal Naaman, the Syrian, of leprosy? (2 Kings 5:1-14). Weren't there plenty of good, law-abiding Jews who had this debilitating skin disease?

Why did Jesus throw these two examples in their face? And why are they infuriated? They were angry enough to go from sitting at his feet, listening with excitement and anticipation – to seizing him immediately and taking him to throw him off a cliff! What happened?

We humans like our elevated status and being favored above others. The Jews knew they were God's chosen people. He loved them and told them repeatedly that he was their God, and they were his people. It is easy to take that kind of love for granted. Maybe God won't notice if I don't care about what he cares about. Maybe he won't see what's in my heart if I go through the motions of being good. Maybe it's too hard to care about the widows, the imprisoned, and the blind man on the street. They are outsiders anyway, and obviously, God doesn't care about them because he certainly isn't blessing them with his favor! Maybe it would be much more enticing if God would do some magic tricks to entertain me.

Jesus looked at them and knew them. They thought they knew him, but they did not. He was not there to prove himself worthy of their esteem. He was there as a Messenger. "God has anointed me to proclaim good news. Good news for the poor, the prisoners, the blind, the oppressed." All of them – including those who stood outside the favored status. God's message of good news might embrace both the Jew and those outsiders, the Gentiles.

They think this Messenger must have gotten the message wrong. The emotional solution is to kill the messenger. They will tar and feather him. They will hang a noose around his neck. They will make sure he doesn't insult them again. They drive him to the edge of the cliff and press forward to throw him down. Furious faces lean close to his.

What happened? Was his composure too powerful to overcome? Was his peace stronger than their anger? Was his love more appealing than their hatred? We are missing exactly how it happened, but Jesus walked through the great crowd and went on his way.

Kill the messenger. It will take a couple of years, but the crowd will eventually have their way.

23

Full Nets

Read Matthew 4:18-22; Mark 1:16-20; Luke 5:1-11

They had seen him before. First at the Jordan with that fire-and-brimstone preacher-prophet John the Baptist proclaiming him *"the Lamb of God, who takes away the sin of the world."* They spent an afternoon sitting with him and listening to teachings they had never heard before. He seemed to know with certainty things about God that no one else knew – even the most educated rabbis. He had been there in Jerusalem at the Passover, clearing the merchants out of the courts of the Gentiles, teaching in the synagogue, and healing the sick and broken. There was just something about him that was… different. It was hard to put your finger on it, but one thing was sure – this was no ordinary man.

Jesus came for them. I don't think he was wandering around and just happened to see them. I think he went to the Sea of Galilee specifically to call them. *"Come, follow me."* It was a simple request. It was a direct command. It had a purpose attached: "I will send you out to fish for people." What a strange mission statement! But they got it. The descriptions of the call and their responses are "at once," "without delay," and "immediately." There was no hesitation in getting out of the boat, leaving their nets, walking away from the family business, and saying goodbye to their profession. It sounds so very simple: drop everything and follow Jesus. Done.

But it also sounds just so… implausible. Impossible. Our investigative writer, Luke, tells us this story of "Follow me" a little differently. People were already flocking around Jesus in these early days, pressing in close to hear him teach. Two boats were on the edge of the Sea of Galilee (the Lake of Gennesaret), their owners on shore cleaning their nets after a long night of unsuccessful fishing. Jesus stepped onto one of the boats and asked the owner to push him out into the water. I love reading this detail. Voices travel well over the water's surface – it naturally amplifies sound. Jesus sat down to teach, and the crowd gathered there on the shore could clearly hear his words.

When he had finished speaking, he instructed Peter, the boat owner, to put out into the deep water and let down his nets. This was no small thing. Peter and his buddies had been out all night fishing. Their nets had come up empty. They had pulled the nets out of the boat and onto shore to clean them as they did each morning. This Rabbi, who knew nothing of fishing, asked him to do it all again. And the sun was high in the sky, which meant the fish would be deep in the water. Peter voiced his objections but agreed to go out again for some reason.

I imagine this was a half-hearted gesture. The nets were dropped into the water. Ripples began as the fish filled the nets. The weight of the catch strained against the side of the boat. It quickly became impossible to pull in the nets from the tremendous weight of the fish. Peter and his brother Andrew urgently called James and John to help them bring in the nets. The catch was so full and heavy that both boats began to sink from the weight.

Peter sank to his knees at Jesus's feet. His eyes were opened to the glory of this man sitting in his boat, and it devastated him. The bounty of Jesus contrasted deeply with Peter's sudden awareness of the brokenness and sin in his own life. "You must leave me…" was Peter's desperate response.

"You must come with me," was Jesus's response. "Follow me – and you will fill your nets with something much more valuable than fish."

When they brought their boats to the shore, they left everything and followed him. No longer casual observers or interested listeners, these four fishermen—Simon, who would become Peter, his brother Andrew, and James and John, sons of Zebedee—would become *followers* of Jesus. His purpose would become their purpose.

This invitation to follow still happens today. Now. People hear this simple call from Jesus, "Come, follow me," and they do. When people say yes, they are not content to stay sitting in their boats, repairing the same nets they repaired yesterday and the day before. Their eyes are opened to larger seas and bigger fish. They hear in the voice of Jesus something more true and more real than anything they have ever experienced. It is as if a light has been turned on in the darkness. It is as if true life has overtaken dullness and death. It is a powerful call.

It all started with the unlikely call of a Jewish man who had laid down his carpentry tools. He seemed to have something more in mind than an ordinary life. He seemed to have something more in mind than simply teaching the ancient scriptures of God. Is it an invitation? Or a command? It is something you will have to answer for yourself. *"Follow me."*

24

Demons and Declarations

Read Matthew 4:23-25; Matthew 8:14-17; Mark 1:21-39; Luke 4:31-44

It appears Jesus begins his ministry with a healing frenzy. As he travels from town to village, he does more than teach. Matthew tells us he is busy *"healing every disease and every affliction among the people."* That would certainly get everyone's attention!

They made their way to Capernaum. It was the Sabbath, and Jesus taught in the synagogue. This was no ordinary teaching, telling the same old stories with the same old explanations. His teaching was new. Different. Jesus spoke as if he knew God personally. He spoke as if he had been there at the Lord's right hand and knew what God was thinking. Jesus spoke with authority, without doubt, as if he was absolutely sure. He spoke as if he were a son in his father's house. He spoke as if he were a king describing his kingdom.

And then the demons spoke. This was terrifying! The peace of Jesus's voice was interrupted by the terrifying shrieks from a man possessed; *"What do you want with us, Jesus of Nazareth? Have you come to destroy us? I know who you are – the Holy One of God! (NIV)"*

It is fascinating that the demons immediately recognized Jesus for who he was. They recognized him with fear. They knew he had come to defeat their master and to destroy their power over mankind. They knew where he had come from. And they knew who he was: The Holy One of God.

Jesus did exactly what he had been sent to do: Silence them. Free their captives. The demons were helpless before him and did exactly what he commanded. They departed.

This became front-page news. No one had ever seen anything like this! It was undoubtedly a miraculous sign to heal the sick – an excellent trick indeed – but to order evil spirits to depart was something else. This Jesus seemed to have power, not only over physical illness but also the illness of the mind and soul. Our very best doctors still struggle to do this today. Jesus healed the mind as easily as he healed the body. Jesus did good. Jesus defeated evil.

Matthew, Mark, and Luke all tell us the little story of going to Peter's house for lunch after church. But the roast isn't cooked, and the potatoes are not peeled. Peter's mother-in-law is sick in bed with a fever and is unable to do anything. Jesus touches her hand, and it is enough. The fever immediately leaves her. It seems a little thing after the big event in the synagogue, doesn't it? Is it to tell us that nothing is too small for Jesus to touch and heal? He doesn't need a big audience or an incurable malady; he is there to touch and heal the small things as well as the big ones. Dinner is ready. Let's eat.

The house is filled with people as the sun gets low in the sky that evening. The whole town comes to the door with their sick and their mentally ill. Jesus lays his hands on each one, healing them, casting out their demons with a word. Matthew, our meticulous record keeper, reminds us of the prophecy of Isaiah being fulfilled: *"He took up our infirmities and bore our diseases" (Isaiah 53:4).*[1]

That Sabbath in Capernaum was a busy day. I am sure everyone slept well that night. The Holy One of God had brought healing and peace. His reputation was rapidly growing as the people from all across the Jordon gathered up their loved ones who suffered from illness. Hope was in the air. Everyone had the same destination in mind: seek this miracle worker Jesus.

But Jesus was nowhere to be found. While it was still dark, he had risen and gone away to a solitary place. There, he spent time in prayer, talking with his Father. When he was found by two of his disciples, he explained, "It is time for us to travel to other places, to other villages. I must continue telling others about the good news of the kingdom of God. That is why I have come."

Jesus had come. He had good news to share. God's kingdom was drawing near. The king had arrived; he had touched down on planet Earth. Angels and shepherds had announced his arrival, and now even the demons couldn't help but declare his name. He taught about God with authority. He reversed the effects of physical illness and released the captives of spiritual oppression. And most unusual for a devoted man of God, he didn't hesitate to reach out and physically touch the sick and the unclean.

I am sure there was much discussion about the identity of this teacher and healer. He had yet to explain just exactly who he was. But the enemy had already figured it out. There was a new sheriff in town. And his name was Jesus.

25

Healing The Unhealable, Touching the Untouchable

Read Matthew 8:1-4; Mark 1:40-45; Luke 5:12-16

Speaking of healing, there was a disease that struck terror in every soul: leprosy. That word has little meaning to us. We sanitized people living in a world of cleansing soaps and medical advances know next to nothing about this dreaded disease that rots the skin and devours the tissue. It spreads with a touch. It destroys physically, alienates its host religiously and socially, and torments them emotionally. It was, and still is in some places, a terrifying disease.

God included in his law ways to deal with skin disease; they were lumped together under the catch-all of leprosy. The priests were responsible for keeping the community safe from this contagious disease. These instructions are listed, step by step, in Leviticus 13 and 14.

The passage in Leviticus begins with great detail on diagnosing the white skin and open bleeding that characterizes leprosy. Instructions for treatment follow. First, the leprous person is to be quarantined for periods of seven to fourteen days and then reassessed. If eruptions on the skin continue, the person is declared unclean and banished from the community. This is not a quiet affair. It is almost a death sentence. The affected person is required to wear torn clothes, let their hair hang loose, cover their upper lip, and cry out, "Unclean, unclean!" It is a terrifying warning to everyone to stay far away. Clothing that has touched this person is to be burned. From then on, they will live alone, outside the camp, outside the warmth and love of their community and family.

If, for some reason, the disease abates, the person must go to the priest to be cleansed. This will take place outside the community encampment. The person will be reexamined; if his skin is healed, two live, clean birds will be offered; one killed over an earthenware vessel of fresh water, the other bird dipped in the blood of the dead bird along with cedarwood, scarlet yarn, and hyssop. Then, this blood is sprinkled on the one healed of leprosy. But we are not done yet! The living bird will be released in an open field, free to fly away, while the healed person is to wash his clothes, shave off all his hair, and bathe in water. Declared clean, he will be allowed to return to camp but must live outside his tent for seven days. On the seventh day, again, he is to shave off all his hair, including his eyebrows, wash his clothes and body with clean water, and then be deemed clean.

But he still isn't done! He is then required to take two unblemished male lambs, one unblemished young, unweaned female lamb, and a grain offering to the priest. Before the entrance to the tent of meeting, the priest will make atonement before the Lord as a guilt offering ("sin offering" is used interchangeably) and a burnt offering. The blood of one of the sacrificed lambs will be placed by the priest on the lobe of the right ear of the cleansed person, on the thumb of his right hand, and the big toe of his right foot. The same shall be done with the oil from the grain offering: right earlobe, thumb, and big toe. There are options for substituting turtledoves or pigeons if the person is poor and cannot afford the great expense of lambs.

You must know all of this to understand the severity of the story of this leper coming to Jesus. This is no small thing. This is not a case of topical eczema that needs a little cortisone ointment. This man has been declared unclean and has been cast out: his skin, his hair, and his clothing are warning signs that forbid any interaction with any other human. "Stay away from me. I am unclean." Yet he has heard stories of this man Jesus. Desperate, yet with boldness, he approaches Jesus with a forbidden request and a statement of faith: "If you are willing, Lord… you can make me clean." The man has fallen to his knees with his face to the ground. He is in no position to ask for favors; he is begging for mercy.

Jesus looks at him with compassion. Jesus reaches out his arm, leans down, and *touches him. "I am willing. Be clean."* Immediately, the leper's skin is healed and cleansed of disease.

What is the meaning of the word choice "If you are *willing*"? The leper believed Jesus could… the question was, would Jesus heal him? *"If you are willing…"* This may be where you are. You look at the stories of Jesus and believe he has the power and might to heal – but would he look at you in your deep distress and brokenness and decide you were worth healing? Worth cleansing? Worth saving? Are you willing, Jesus, to heal *even me*? With nothing to offer in return, all bargaining, all convincing, all advantage is off the table. You are totally dependent on the kindness and compassion of Jesus, who can heal *if he is willing.*

"I am willing," he answered the leper, face down in the dirt.

And this is where we find the powerful word *immediately*. A trademark of miracles is that they happen immediately. There was no "wait for seven days and check back with me." All three gospels use the same word: *immediately*. And there followed a simple, direct instruction that Jesus gave the miraculously healed leper: "Go to the priests, and under their supervision offer the sacrifices ordered by Moses so that this will be a testimony to them." Jesus knew that for this man to be re-established within the community as clean and whole, he needed the sanction of the priests. Jesus also sent an undeniable message to the religious leaders: he was there to heal what was diseased. He had come to make clean that which was declared unclean. They would be very interested in healing a person with leprosy – something only done by Moses for Miriam (Numbers 12:10-15) and Elisha for Naaman the Aramean (2 Kings 5:1-14).

But you know how it is – when something unbelievably good happens, you just can't help but go and shout it from the rooftops. This is precisely what happened. The ex-leper was so overwhelmed with receiving this gift of life that he couldn't keep his mouth shut. Who knows if he ever made it to the priests to be declared legally healed? This miraculous private healing of the very obviously unclean man opened the floodgates. The crowds started seeking the miracle worker; the streets were overflowing with people filled with hope, seeking a miracle for their own hurt and pain. The secret was out. Jesus would need to tint his windows dark and hire a few bodyguards before venturing into the streets again. Rock star mania had begun.

What in the world was Jesus up to? He had healed one who was unhealable. He had touched one who was untouchable. The religious leaders were undoubtedly going to have something to say about this. Healing was under the purview of the priests. There was a prescribed order to things. You can't just go out there willy-nilly and do whatever you want, however you like! Can't you just hear their outrage? Jesus is going to be in big trouble now. Just wait until your daddy gets home, young man, and we will see what he has to say!

26

The Tricky Problem of Forgiveness

Read Matthew 9:1-8; Mark 2:1-12; Luke 5:17-26

Jesus returned to Capernaum, and the crowds found him there. They squeezed themselves into the house where he was staying, looking in through the doorway, straining from the street to catch any word that would drift their way. People had come from all over to hear the teaching of God's Word by God's own Son. They didn't realize that was what they were experiencing – they only knew this Jesus knew things they didn't know; he understood meanings they had never grasped. In the front row sat a handful of their religious leaders, the Pharisees and the scribes. They had come to hear this man's teaching for themselves. Some of them came from as far away as Jerusalem. The crowd pressed in, and there was no more room. It must have been hot in there.

There was a scraping noise above them as roof tiles were lifted away. Sunlight poured into the room; dust drifted down in a soft cloud illuminated by rays of light. From above, a paralyzed man was carefully lowered down into the room before Jesus. I imagine Jesus looking at the man and then looking up to see his four friends' expectant and hope-filled faces. And he saw faith. Great faith. They believed in the power of this teacher Jesus. They were convinced that Jesus could and would heal their friend. And Jesus looked back at the paralyzed man and said the strangest thing:

"Son, your sins are forgiven."

What? Wait a minute, Jesus – you misunderstand what we hope for here! We want the man to walk again! We want the muscles to regain their strength! We want his brain to transmit the message through those damaged nerves to move! That's what his friends are thinking.

What are the religious leaders thinking? They are not even interested in the possibility of physical healing because they are so offended by Jesus's outrageous statement that he has just forgiven the sins of this man! How dare he! It is the responsibility of the priest to go before God with great sacrifices and offerings and ask for forgiveness that only God can grant. This Jesus is claiming the ultimate ability of God alone! The Jewish priests are the closest ones to God, and they wouldn't dare even think such a thing.

Jesus knows exactly what they are thinking. This is the beauty of Jesus: He sees into our secret hearts and reads our thoughts as if they are words on a page. He knows our intentions. He knows our motives. And our flawed reasoning. We think if someone has something horrible happen to them, maybe God is withholding his blessings and his protection. "What great sin brought on God's punishment?" they silently wonder about their afflicted neighbors.

Jesus knows this. He goes to the heart of the matter. Sin. *"Son, your sins are forgiven."* That didn't go over well. He directs his following words to the unhappy scribes: *"Which is easier, to say to the paralytic, 'Your sins are forgiven,' or to say, 'Rise, take up your bed and walk'?"* Don't you love this? Both are impossible! With Jesus in town, people were hoping for a miracle; they were expecting a miracle… a physical one. But a spiritual miracle of forgiveness? Who would have possibly expected something like this? Nobody. Yet Jesus knew we needed an outward sign to tell the story of inward spiritual healing. "So you will know that the Son of Man has authority on earth to forgive sins," and with this, he turns to look into the eyes of the paralyzed man on the mat, "I say to you, rise, pick up your bed, and go home." And he did.

Slow down a moment and think before you start celebrating this glorious miracle with the crowd. Look closely at what Jesus said about himself: *"The Son of Man has authority on earth to forgive sins."* Each word here is a powerhouse filled with meaning. Jesus was referring to himself as the *"Son of Man."* He is referencing Daniel's vision of One who looked like a Son of Man who was able to stand before the Ancient of Days and was given all power and all of God's glory (Daniel 7:13-14). Remember that guy? Jesus claims to have *authority on earth.* That will be something those religious leaders will be asking Jesus about later: "Who has given you this authority?" They weren't going to like the answer. And here's the kicker: Jesus has come to do more than make a paralyzed man walk. He has come to heal the ultimate problem – the problem of sin.

Remember that pesky proposition Satan had enticed Eve with: "Take a little bite of this pride… It is just so good! You won't be able to take just one bite. Never mind all that stuff God said about it being the death of you. He is just trying to keep you under his thumb. Go ahead, try it! You'll like it." And it has been a problem ever since.

Sin: it becomes death embedded deep within our souls, and there doesn't seem to be any way to get it out. God had provided a release from the guilt and sorrow – the blood of an innocent animal instead of our own blood – but it was always a temporary fix. Give us a few days, and we'll be right back at it. Sin. Yep, it was a problem. And forgiveness? Standing righteous in the presence of a righteous God? He could always see into our hearts and read our thoughts, and there was no hiding our separation from him. But here is Jesus saying something so outrageous: "*But that you may know* the Son of Man has authority on earth to forgive sins, I will do something equally outrageous you can see with your own eyes. I will make a paralyzed man walk just by saying the word *rise*."

Luke tells us they were seized with amazement. Everyone glorified God. They were filled with awe. "*We have seen extraordinary things today.*" And what was unseen was even more impressive.

If you hear folks say that Jesus was a "good teacher," a "moral man," or a "prophet of God" and leave it at that, they couldn't be more wrong. Jesus seemed to be convinced he was more than that. He wasn't content to entertain the crowds with magic tricks and physical healings. He seemed to have something much bigger in mind. If he kept this up, those Jewish priests were going to be out of a job.

27

Guess Who's Coming to Dinner?

Read Matthew 9:9-17; Mark 2:13-22; Luke 5:27-39; Hosea 6:6

The Pharisees and the scribes weren't the only ones starting to have a problem with Jesus; the disciples who followed John the Baptist were also confused by what they saw. Before John was arrested, he had spent time separating himself from anything extravagant or worldly. He lived in the wilderness, choosing a tent instead of impressive architecture, rejecting designer clothing for sackcloth. He dined on locusts, and his lips never touched fine wine. He shouted warnings of coming judgment and the heat of hell's fires. Jesus was an unsettling contrast to John.

Hanging out with those Galilean fishermen was pretty innocuous. But then Jesus chose a questionable companion: Matthew, the tax collector. He was also known as Levi, the son of Alphaeus. Tax collectors were despised for the authority the Romans granted them: "Set up a booth on the main street and charge your fellow brethren a Roman tax of your choosing. If you want to charge them more than what is due and slip the extra coins into your pocket, the officials will easily look the other way." A tax collector was a traitor. A tax collector took the hard-earned money from the working man's pocket and became arrogant and wealthy from another man's sweat. It was government-sanctioned stealing. No moral Jew would associate with these unscrupulous men. With their ill-obtained wealth, they wined and dined with others who had found a way to prosper outside the moral law of Jewish society.

And this is where we find Jesus hanging out with the wrong crowd right in the middle of the party. And he's not standing on the tabletop, sweeping their delicacies to the ground and shouting for them to repent. No – he is reclining beside them. I imagine him laughing and telling a good story as he takes another sip of fine wine. The hardened men around him are smiling back, relaxing in the warmth of their new friend.

It sort of makes you uneasy, doesn't it?

The good moral men look on with one big question – well, actually, multiple questions buzzing in their brains: "Why are you here hanging out with these men and women? Their reputation is evident. They delight in broadcasting their bad behavior. We avoid them at all costs. But look at you! You are shamelessly sitting in their midst! You are eating their feast – purchased at a high price with stolen wages. You are sharing their cup. You are relaxing in a compromising situation. What in the world are you thinking? We thought you were one of us – not one of them!"

This is another interesting trick Jesus does. He turns outsiders into insiders while the insiders stand outside looking in. And the ruckus he causes doesn't seem to bother him one little bit.

Instead of being shamed, Jesus replies to their indignation with surprising images. He speaks of a doctor healing the sick, not the well. He responds that he has come for the sinners, not the righteous. It is easy to hide under this diagnosis with our own self-righteousness. "Oh… okay, because I am not sick. I am just fine, thank you. No need for repentance here. I certainly am not sick like these people. I'll just wait over here and keep my hands clean, thank you."

Jesus isn't done explaining what he is doing and why he has come; he asks the grumblers a question: "Do wedding guests fast while the bridegroom is with them?" Not only is Jesus the great physician of healing who has come to heal the sick, but he is also the bridegroom celebrating the joy of his union with the bride. Feasting? Celebration? These are not things you think about when you try to imagine God's promised Son arriving – and especially that the guest list would include these sorts of lowlifes! And he continues with, "There will be plenty of time for fasting when I am gone." Gone? You just got here. Yet Jesus knows his time is limited, and his purpose is great. I am betting that most of this went right over their heads at the time.

Here, Matthew adds the warning from Hosea that God desires mercy, not sacrifice.[1] During the days of the prophet, God had mourned the unfaithfulness of his people and the evil schemes of his priests. He compared their love to the fleeting morning dew that disappears with the rising sun. "You are busy with your show of sacrifices," God told them, "yet you forget to acknowledge my presence." Mercy. Surely, Jesus was not saying that upright religious leaders should lean in close to *these people* with mercy. They were already busy enough keeping the Temple fires burning brightly.

Then Jesus tells them short parables about repairing an old garment wearing thin by tearing up a perfectly good new garment of unshrunk cloth and sewing that new piece onto the old. It would be a waste of the new and would not match or improve the old. It actually would make the tear in the old garment worse. And everyone understood the mess that would be created if new wine was poured into old stretched-out wineskins; new wine needed fresh new skins stretching and growing to accommodate the expanding wine as it fermented.

What was Jesus saying? Was he bringing to them something new that would stretch their understanding of who God was? Were their perceptions of God and worship old and worn out? Could he possibly mean that he was a new garment that wouldn't simply be a patch on the old? Was he saying he was a new vessel containing the new wine of God? His listeners shook their heads and said to themselves, "Our old wine is good enough."

Their conversation was interrupted as they were still shaking their heads in disagreement. Something about a dead daughter. Well, good luck with that. This Jesus may be entertaining and a bit of a charlatan. He may be a fascinating miracle worker. Maybe even a prophet of God. But he's too unorthodox to have the power of a great prophet like Elijah, who raised the widow's son – so don't get your hopes up. But before they could get these words out, Jesus was already up, out the door, and on his way.

28

To Touch His Hem

Read Matthew 9:18-26; Mark 5:21-43; Luke 8:40-56

The party is interrupted.

Matthew tells us that Jesus suddenly left his house at the request of a synagogue leader, who was insisting that Jesus could bring his dear daughter, who had just died, back to life. Mark and Luke place this story at another time, but I am going with Matthew's timing since I believe if the guest of honor left the party at my house, I would remember it!

The urgent interruption was caused by a man named Jairus, whose 12-year-old only daughter was either on the verge of death or had just died. The thing to hold onto here is Jairus, who was a respected Jewish leader, believed that his only chance to preserve the life of his daughter lay in the hands of this new Rabbi who had been doing miraculous healings. I imagine he rushed through the streets with his heart in his hands, hoping to find this Jesus. It wasn't hard since the gossip in town centered on the outrageous sight of Jesus at the house of Matthew, the tax collector.

And off they go, Jesus at the lead, matching the stride of a dignified but desperate father. The crowd presses around them, growing larger as they go – after all, who wouldn't want to see this teacher Jesus heal a young girl? Or better yet, see if he possibly had any power over death.

Can't you see them in their urgency—robes flowing out behind them, dust kicking up from their sandals, jabbing elbows as the people push closer, moving faster, trying to keep up as they jostle against the stream of people moving in the opposite direction, and suddenly the teacher Jesus comes to a complete and total stop. He turns. He looks behind him. His eyes search the crowd. "Who touched me?" he asks gently.

And suddenly, the world slows down. It comes to a grinding halt as Jesus stands, refusing to move forward until his question is answered, until this person who has touched him comes forward. If I were shooting this, we would have a curved dolly track. We would circle Jesus as he turned, searching the crowd. We would reverse the shot, looking deeply into each face.

Peter is the first to speak – of course! He is in a hurry to be on their way because Jesus has something incredibly important to do. "It's just the crowd pushing against you!" he explains. You can almost see him rolling his eyes impatiently and tugging Jesus by the arm.

No, Jesus stands his ground. "It is much more than that. I felt power leave me when I was touched." And they wait.

How long did it take her to get her nerve up? To humiliate herself in front of this crowd of neighbors, acquaintances, and strangers? She had dared not even to touch him… just the edge of his robe… yet here she is exposed, trembling, and healed.

"I touched you," she tearfully admits as she steps away from the cover of the crowd and toward this healer, Jesus. Her eyes are locked with his until she falls at his feet and gives her reason. "I have bled for twelve years." There is no need to explain. Everyone in that crowd knows precisely what that means. She is unclean. Untouchable. Unacceptable. Unwelcome. Un-whole.

She couldn't go to the synagogue. She couldn't be touched by her husband, her sisters, her friends, her children. She was unclean, and whoever she touched became unclean. She had hired doctors, nothing. She had made the prescribed sacrifices. Nothing. Her money was gone. Her hope was gone. Her life was gone. She was dead in her own small world.

And there he was: Jesus. She saw him moving quickly through the street and thought, "If I touch him… maybe… I can be healed." She held her breath, reached forward, and hoped.

And Jesus stopped. He stopped and searched the faces in the crowd for her. In front of God and everyone, he called her "daughter"; he declared her faithful, forgiven, and clean. He reached down and lifted her to her feet – this is my addition because we do not know since the story is suddenly interrupted.

"While he was still speaking…" we read, a servant came from Jairus's house. "Your daughter is dead. There is no need for the Teacher to come anymore."

Oh, isn't this exactly like us? Time has run out. It is too late. Don't bother. But this is not our God. Time doesn't run out on God's timing. God's timing – whether it is too early or too late in our minds – always brings glory back to God. Jesus stopped to seek out a woman who needed to be publicly healed. And that will allow him to do something much more wonderful than healing the daughter of Jairus. He will have the opportunity to prove he not only can heal the sick but also has the power to raise the dead back to life.

The mourners are already there, encircling the house, wailing their grief song. By all accounts, Jesus rebukes them: "Why all this commotion and wailing? The child is not dead but asleep." They scoff at him. They know dead when they see it. This is not a culture that calls for the mortician - and stands at a distance from their dead. The women have been with the child, tending her; they have heard her take her last breath; they have closed her unseeing eyes. They have touched her cold skin. She is dead. There is no doubt.

Jesus leaves the crowds behind him. He clears the house except for the child's mother and father and his inner circle of Peter, James, and

John. I am sure the room was quiet. The voice of Jesus could clearly be heard as he took the girl's hand in his and commanded life back into her body. "*Talitha cumi!*" ("Little girl, I say to you, get up!") And she did. Can you imagine her inhaling that first breath? Can you see her eyes open – perhaps surprised to be awakened all at once? She stood, holding Jesus's hand. She walked around the room. I am guessing she fell into her mother's waiting arms; she looked up into the eyes of her adoring father. She smiled.

And there are the strange little details. Give her something to eat. Do not tell anyone. Good luck with that last one. The whole town is waiting just outside the door. Don't you think this news is going to travel fast? Jesus just publicly acknowledged and healed an unclean woman who, for all intents and purposes, was invisible. He made her very visible. He had just raised from the dead the daughter of a well-known synagogue leader while the whole town waited outside. How did he possibly think this would all be kept quiet? I have a feeling this secret has already been told.

29

Blind Men and Demons and Shepherd-less Sheep

Read Matthew 9:27-38

Our storytellers fan out in different directions, sometimes recounting one of the healings of Jesus as of one accord, with one voice; other times, only one of them will talk about a specific healing or parable that the others fail to mention. As I said before, it reminds me of how we humans tell our stories; one incident will be profound and meaningful to one, while another who was there doesn't even remember it at all.

Our tax collector, Matthew, tells little stories of healings that happened right after Jairus's daughter is read a bedtime story and is safely tucked back into her bed that our other writers don't mention at all. I wonder why these healings stood out to Matthew. They are short little stories – barely worth a paragraph – yet, in his mind, they needed to be recorded. And they are filled with the little details that make them ring true.

Two blind men follow Jesus, crying to him, *"Have mercy on us, Son of David."* Mercy. My goodness, that is something we all need more of, isn't it? Mercy. What is the meaning of mercy? It is compassion or forgiveness shown toward someone from another who has the power to punish or cause harm to them. It is a cry of humbleness. It is a request for kindness. It is a hope for generosity. It is a definition of grace. This is how we see our God: He is a merciful God. He doesn't have to be merciful – he chooses to be. He sees us clearly as we are, torn and broken and helpless and blind, and he reaches out to us with mercy.

Mercy means little without power. If one is powerless to touch, to heal, to grant pardon, or to forgive, then there is no reason to ask them for mercy. So here they come, two blind men, desperate and hopeful, asking for mercy. Jesus, this traveling healer, already knows what they need and what they think of him, but he asks the question that he asks all of us: "Do you believe I am able to do this?" Their answer is two simple words, "Yes, Lord."

Two words that change the world. Two words that open eyes to see and ears to hear. Two words that open the door to new life. Yes. Lord. Yes, I believe. Yes, I trust. Yes, I want what you want. Lord, I lay down my objections. Lord, I place my life in your hands. Lord, I give up my will for yours. Two words that don't roll off the tongue easily if they truly come from the heart. Two words of great personal cost. Two words of surrender. Two words that I need to remember to say at the beginning of each day. Two words that lift the heavy weight of the world from my shoulders and place the responsibility on God instead: Yes, Lord.

And then Jesus placed his hands on their eyes. This is what Jesus does. He knows the hurt, and he reaches out to touch us *there*. There can be no relationship with this man, this Son of David, this Son of God unless we get close enough to allow him to touch us.

His words tell us our battle with lost sight is more than a physical ailment; it is also spiritual. *"According to your faith be it done to you."* Your faith is the conduit that flows healing into your life. Oh, no. What will happen to those of us with little faith - faith as small as a mustard seed? And how big is a mustard seed anyway?

When I was a little girl, I tormented my older sister Ann, who was eleven years older than me. I idolized her and wanted to be near her and in her stuff. I wanted to listen to her Elvis records and try my hand at putting on her eyeliner. I was locked out of her room a lot! She had a necklace that was a simple gold chain with a glass globe locket dangling from it. Encased inside was a little speck of a yellow seed. A mustard seed is the smallest of all seeds, yet when planted, it grows into a bush so large that birds can rest in its branches. Faith doesn't start out as big as a full-grown bush. It starts out teeny tiny, small enough to be worn around a teenage girl's neck.

Yet, teeny tiny faith is enough to open eyes that are blind. It is enough to see a whole new world.

It is always confusing when Jesus does this little disclaimer after a miraculous work. "Hey, I know it will be obvious to everyone who knows you that you have been blind, and suddenly now you see – but don't tell anybody about this. Okay?" Of course, it doesn't remain a secret for more than two seconds. Of course, they have to tell the story of Jesus healing them. Of course.

The once-blind-now-seeing men are barely down the road before a demon-oppressed man is brought to this healer Jesus. The demon has tangled his tongue so that he cannot speak. We don't know the details of how Jesus healed him, but we know the response of the onlookers: "He is doing miracles that have never been seen in all of Israel." In other words, "God must be at work here among us!" But there is also the opposing reaction: "The Prince of Demons must be at work here!" Ah, ha. This may be our clue why Jesus does not want a fan club formed in his name yet. He is moving among the people, touching and healing, but it is one-on-one and personal. Too much power shown too quickly, and you can bet your bottom dollar the officials are going to show up with lots of questions, and it won't be long before he will be perceived as a threat to both the Jewish leaders and the Romans. Best to start slow and easy and build his message within the hearts and lives of the common people first.

Matthew tells us this is what Jesus did: he continued teaching in the Jewish synagogues, talked about the good news of the kingdom of God, and healed people of every disease and affliction. He did all of this with great love and compassion. Can you imagine how irresistible this combination was? Great power mixed generously with great compassion? Matthew, the once hard-hearted tax collector, was touched by how Jesus viewed this crowd that surrounded him: they were like sheep without a shepherd – harassed and helpless.

God had sent a great prophet named Ezekiel about 600 years earlier to warn the once-holy priests of Jerusalem. At that time, Jerusalem was being dismantled by God through the Babylonians. God's chosen people had chosen to rebel against him, enticed by their neighbors and foreign gods, confident in their strength. God's priests, his shepherds, were ignoring the needs of their people. God had called for them to come back to him. They had ignored his cries. So, God sent the mighty Babylonians to bring his people to repentance and humility. Their hearts were cold, and it would require burning the Temple, destroying Jerusalem, and marching them off to a foreign land of captivity to get their attention. Ezekiel was the voice calling out to them, warning the priests of their selfishness, reminding them of God's holy nature and his concern for his lost sheep.

"Son of man, prophesy against the shepherds of Israel;
prophesy and say to them:
'This is what the Sovereign Lord says:
Woe to you shepherds of Israel who only take care of yourselves!
Should not shepherds take care of the flock?
You eat the curds, clothe yourselves with the wool
and slaughter the choice animals,
but you do not take care of the flock.
You have not strengthened the weak or healed
the sick or bound up the injured.
You have not brought back the strays or searched for the lost.

You have ruled them harshly and brutally.
So they were scattered because there was no shepherd,
and when they were scattered they became
food for all the wild animals."'
For this is what the Sovereign Lord *says:*
"I myself will search for my sheep and look after them.
"I will place over them one shepherd, my servant David,
and he will tend them;
he will tend them and be their shepherd.
I the Lord *will be their God, and my servant*
David will be prince among them.
I the Lord *have spoken."*
Ezekiel 34:2-5,11,23-24 NIV

Was Jesus this long-promised shepherd who had come in God's name? Had he come to strengthen the weak, heal the sick, and bind up the injured? Had he come to bring back the strays and search for the lost? Could he be the servant David pointing the way back to God?

Without a pause, Jesus launches into a new thought: "The harvest is plentiful, the workers few. Pray earnestly for the Lord of the harvest to send workers into his harvest field." This thought is familiar; we heard it when Jesus saw the people from Samaria coming to him after his conversation with the woman at the well. Why was he concerned about "the harvest"?

These are three small stories filled with big ideas, big requests, big proclamations. How do we jump so quickly from one revelation to the next? Are we any closer to discovering who this Jesus is? Is he a merciful healer who knows that his touch can heal our sight and heal our hearts? Is he an encourager who opens doors according to our small and hopeful faith? Is he filled with the power of God? Or could he be doing these wonderful things through the power of evil? Is this Jesus, a descendant of David, the compassionate shepherd who has come to care for his lost sheep? Is he the vineyard owner's son, aware that the grapes are ready to be harvested, who has come to look for willing workers?

It may be too soon, but I have to ask the question, "Who do you think he is?"

30

The Problem of the Sabbath, the Problem of a Miracle

Read John 5:1-15

We will walk with the disciple John for a while as he tells us stories of conflict brewing between Jesus and the Jewish leaders. It is easy to group these stories together because they have one unresolvable issue at their heart: keeping the Sabbath holy. It is an issue I have watched play out in various ways during my short lifetime 2,000 years later. Who would have ever thought the Sabbath would be such a problem?

My nephew practices Orthodox Judaism. If he is staying in town with me over the weekend or during the Jewish holidays, he stays in the homes of other Orthodox Jews in a neighborhood near me that is within walking distance of the synagogue. I love how these people are so hospitable and open their doors to a stranger for the 24 hours of Sabbath rest – from sundown on Friday to sundown on Saturday.

Keeping the Sabbath holy for the orthodox Jew involves many rules that sound very unusual to me, including not riding in or driving a car and not turning on or off lights (which includes unscrewing the lightbulb in the refrigerator beforehand!). One Friday afternoon, as I drove Ian to the home where he would be staying, I watched as gray rain clouds moved across the sky. "Oh, I should have thought and given you an umbrella!" I exclaimed. Ian laughed, "Oh, it doesn't matter - I couldn't use it anyway. It's considered work to carry or open an umbrella." Well, I'll be!

When we Christian followers of the Jewish Messiah Jesus changed their holy day from Saturday to Sunday (because Jesus rose from the grave on that day after being crucified and buried on Friday afternoon), we carried some of the Jewish traditions over into Sunday with us. As we did, we brought along some of the sticky problems of keeping one day of the week set apart and holy from the other days.

Growing up in the South, my family treated Sunday differently from every other day. We put on our "Sunday best" and spent the morning in Sunday school, then filled the wooden pews for the hour-long church service afterward. Sunday dinner was a big meal that Momma usually had cooking in the oven and ready to be served when we got home. The table was set with her best china, including crystal glasses and silverware. The menu included roast beef or chicken, lots of vegetables, rolls, dessert, and plenty of iced tea. After the table was cleared, it was a lazy reading of the Sunday newspaper and a nap. Then, my aunts, uncles, and cousins met at my grandparents' house to sit on the porch and visit until nightfall. It was very much a day of rest.

Stores were closed. No one I knew drank – but of course, alcohol wasn't served on Sunday anyway if you went to one of the few open restaurants. On Sundays, people didn't cut their grass, and thank goodness those noisy leaf blowers had not been invented yet. Overall, across our town, Sunday took on a very relaxed, very restful atmosphere that was very different from any other day.

Today, it is a different story. We go to church on Sunday mornings and try to spend the afternoon at a slower, restful pace - perhaps napping, reading, or gathering with family, but everything else in our city is going full-guns. Every store is open, and almost every restaurant is. There are a few reminders that this is Sunday: Grocery stores and restaurants can only sell alcohol after a set time - which I find odd and archaic. My husband will not cut grass out of respect for the neighbors. Otherwise, this day seems much like any other day.

Keeping the Sabbath holy. What does that mean? Sabbath means "rest." Rest that is holy. What does that look like? Why did God think including it in his top ten laws was so important? I think contemplating this whole idea of Sabbath Rest is good to consider as we go into the following few stories – because there is a great problem here with Jesus breaking the laws of the Sabbath. What did Jesus say about the Sabbath? What did he do to observe this day of rest? Why did he blatantly disregard some of the "regulations" of his culture? Do I need to observe the Sabbath? Why? What should that look like for me? All these questions come first as I think about this story of Jesus encountering an invalid at the pool of Bethesda. Let's look at this story and what Jesus teaches about this holy day of rest.

Jesus is in Jerusalem for one of the Jewish festivals. It is a time of celebration, so Jerusalem is filled beyond capacity with Jews who have come into the city to worship at the Temple. He is going into the city through the Sheep Gate on the north side of the city wall (Nehemiah 12:38-39), where five covered colonnades surround a pool. There is an explanation in many manuscript translations that was common knowledge; many paralyzed, lame, blind people waited here for the "waters to move" – stirred by an angel of the Lord, or more likely by the springs bubbling up from beneath. The first one into the pool after each disturbance would be cured of whatever disease they had. Wow. Did this happen often enough that it was considered accurate? This sounds a little hocus-pocus to me. But here he is - Jesus. And he notices one invalid among all the others. He has been an invalid for 38 years. This man has been waiting for a long, long time for a miracle from the stirred waters.

Jesus asks the man a question that has nothing to do with faith or righteousness. It almost seems ridiculous to me: "Do you want to get well?" It sounds like an accusatory question, doesn't it? It's sort of like he is saying the guy isn't even trying to be healed. And the invalid's explanation is nothing profound either – he has no one to help him get up and into the pool, and someone else always receives the healing instead of him. It is hopeless, really.

Do you ever feel that way? You have shown up at the place of miracles. You are there – waiting. You see others receive a blessing that changes everything. But you are alone. There is no possibility of moving just a few feet into the moving waters of healing. But you are still there, waiting, hoping. It occurs to me that the invalid never answers the question – maybe because the answer is so obvious.

With absolutely no fanfare, Jesus tells him, *"Get up! Pick up your mat and walk (NIV)."* Boom. Done. And the man does. And Jesus disappears into the crowd and is gone.

But the Jewish leaders are there. They don't see a man who has been waiting for 38 years for a miracle and who can suddenly walk; they see a man who is breaking the law. And they see themselves as enforcers of the law. Do you remember God's accusations through the prophet Ezekiel?

"Woe to you shepherds of Israel who only take care of yourselves!
Should not shepherds take care of the flock?
...You have not strengthened the weak or healed
the sick or bound up the injured."
Ezekiel 34:2, 4 NIV

How concerned had these shepherds, the Jewish leaders, been about this man when he was lying on his mat? How concerned were they when he suddenly had the strength and the ability to pick his mat up and carry it? They did not see the person – they saw *the action* that offended them.

This is where I must slow down for a moment and look at myself. Do I look for the person who needs my help? Or do I only see the action that offends me? What little laws have I created that separate me from my neighbor who needs help getting into the healing waters?

This story has a very odd ending. Jesus finds the healed man at the Temple. Okay – stop right there. How long had it been since this man could choose where he went? Thirty-eight years. And the place he chooses to go is the Temple! That tells me right away his priorities – he is there to worship, praise, and glorify God. Jesus finds him. Strangely, the conversation does not address the Sabbath rule breaking or his questioning by the leaders. Jesus addresses this new life of the once-invalid and his future: "See, you are well again – stop sinning, or something worse may happen to you." What? Is Jesus implying that the man's physical condition is related in some way to his spiritual condition? Is he saying, "You have been given a second chance… go and sin no more?"

This sounds harsh, doesn't it? Perhaps that is what Jesus wants for all of us. Now that you can walk – walk away from things that harm you. Walk away from the life that held emptiness and hurt. Walk away from a life steeped in darkness and sin. I think Jesus knew things about this man that we do not. I think Jesus knows things about us that casual observers do not. The religious leaders looked at this man; all they saw was an illegally carried mat. Jesus looked at this man and saw a broken man – physically and spiritually. "I see you," Jesus said. "I healed you physically. but you need spiritual healing; get up and walk away from your sin."

It is offensive, isn't it? Jesus doesn't seem to play by the rules. He doesn't care if he offended the religious leaders. He doesn't seem to care if he offends the now-walking lame man. He doesn't seem to care if he offends us. Do I need to examine my heart and motives more closely than I think about my physical limitations and the barriers standing in my way? Is this what Jesus is more concerned with? That thing hidden away in my heart that is making me lame? Perhaps there is no need to stare into the waters, waiting for the miracle.

"Do you want to get well? Do you believe I can heal you? Get up, pick up your mat, and walk. Don't wait another day. Look up. Stand up. Watch carefully where your feet are taking you. Now that you know me, keep walking – into a new life – and away from your sin."

31

Like Father, Like Son

Read John 5:16-47

This is where John often confuses me. The miracles I get. The teaching moments of Jesus sometimes lose me. Since I seek to understand this Jesus better through his own words, I need to dig in and go deeper. And who better to take me there than John?

We are looking closely at the conflict over the Jewish Sabbath and healing; apparently, the two are not supposed to go together because the Jewish leaders consider healing "work." The Sabbath is set apart for rest. There are six other days for work. But no. Jesus shows up all around town, and on just any day of the week, he causes an uproar by healing yet another person. This has got to stop. Everyone knows that healing is work. Tensions are running high.

Yes, they are because this very Jewish man named Jesus is out of control. He is out of control of the Jewish religious leaders and their respected interpretation of the Jewish law. To make matters worse, Jesus explains it this way: "My Father is working now, so I am working." Like Father, like Son. Now, doing work isn't the only problem – Jesus claiming God as his Father opens another can of worms. It's just a skip and a jump from God being called *Father* to Jesus claiming himself as Son. That is entirely not allowed! No one can be the Son of God! That would impart some sort of holiness and divinity to a mere human. Bingo. I think we have a winner here. Jesus cannot be God's Son – he just can't. This whole idea is preposterous. But Jesus keeps wading in deeper and deeper. It is best if we just stand quietly in the corner as the bombs drop.

"The Son (that would be me)," Jesus explains, "can do nothing on his own – he only does what he sees the Father doing. My Father loves me and shows me what he is doing – and I do the same thing. He will do even greater things than you have already seen so that you will believe in me."

Don't you know that by now, the Jewish leaders are bristling – everything Jesus is saying offends them. But he doesn't pause; he continues with even more outrageous revelations.

"The Father can raise the dead back to life; he will give his Son the same ability. The Father can judge, but he has given that responsibility to his Son. In the same way you honor the Father, he desires that you honor his Son. If you don't honor the Son of God, you are not honoring the Father. If you believe God sent me, you will have eternal life. You will not enter into judgment; instead, you will pass go, collect $200, and enter eternal life." (That last part is mine. But, like me, are you feeling Jesus is in it to win this game? I think he just swooped up all the blue and green properties, and the religious leaders are still waiting over by Baltic Avenue.)

My goodness, give us a moment to catch our breath! I am sure all that was more than those poor, negligent shepherds could absorb. By now, they have decided this charismatic man parading around in Rabbi robes and healing a handful of lame and blind must be certifiably crazy. But wait. Jesus isn't done yet. He has more to say. Let's listen to him through the ears of the Jewish leaders.

"Wait!" they think as they cut sidelong glances at each other. Now Jesus is talking about the dead hearing the voice of the Son of God and rising to live again! He says this will happen soon – oh wait, he is saying the time has come! Did you hear that? Yes, we agree that God is the source of life, but now Jesus asserts that our great Creator has given his Son this same ability – to be the source and the creator of life! Complete blasphemy! And God has given him – (now he is calling himself the Son of Man, like in the vision of Daniel!)—the authority to execute judgment! He says he has the ultimate authority to raise the dead to face either judgment or resurrection of life!

As we take a breath and a step back, Jesus pauses and looks into our faces. He reads our expressions and acknowledges the doubt. Yes, he is correct; we marvel at his words! Yes, we are pretty sure he is crazy!

However, if we can think clearly, we must acknowledge something. Slow things down and look at him *closely*. He is calm. He is self-assured yet reverent in every word he says about God. He is gentle in his demeanor, although his words are so disturbing. He does not rave or wind up the crowds surrounding him into a frenzy. He isn't manipulating their emotions. There is a peace and a directness about him that is very… we can't find the right words for it… possibly righteous? He seems so *different* from any other man we have ever known. What is it about him?

Jesus continues, telling these Jewish listeners in the holy city of Jerusalem more about *who he is* and *where he has gotten this authority and power* that they see in him; it comes from the One who sent him. Jesus listens to God's voice. Jesus follows God's will. Jesus judges by God's justice. And in this culture that demands two testimonies to corroborate the truth, others testify about the truth of Jesus.

"Remember John the Baptist?" he asks. "You yourselves saw his light. He was a burning bush, a shining lamp to your feet; he brought joy to your hearts and *testified about me.*

"Remember the miraculous works you have seen me do? Those works could only be done through the power and might of God himself; they are a great testimony, a great proof of evidence pointing back to God, testifying for me.

"Remember the scriptures – the holy words of our history and our God? You know well the Laws given to us by God and taught to us by Moses. Look at them carefully, for they are also *testimony* about *me.* You think those words will give you eternal life. They will not. Those words only point to eternal life in me. Moses told the story of my coming! If your hope is in Moses, yet you refuse to believe in me, it is the very words of Moses that will accuse you before my Father.

"Three testimonies speak for me: John's prophetic words, these miraculous signs, and the writings of Moses. Do you still have trouble believing? Do you still refuse to come to me that you may have life? Do you seek the glory of God, or do you seek the glory of each other? Do you have the love of God within you? Do you see the love of God in me? This, my friends, is love; I have come in the name of the Father that you may have life."

I may have paraphrased these words a little softer than Jesus intended. There it is, staring back at me in black and white. *"But I know you, that you do not have the love of God in you" (John 5:42 NKJV).* Ouch. Here it is again. This unavoidable problem with Jesus: *"I know you...."* These religious leaders are not going to shake this off so easily.

All of this started with a little conflict over healing a paralyzed man on the Sabbath. I think it is beginning to be undeniable: there is a bigger issue at hand. Resting or working on a Holy Day may be the tip of the iceberg. Our little boat has just crashed against an ancient rock, and I don't think we will be sailing merrily on our way anytime soon.

We need to look closely into these words of Jesus. Two thousand years have come and gone since they were spoken to the hearts of religious Jewish men in the heart of the holy Jewish city of Jerusalem. Perhaps they were even spoken there in the courtyards within the holy Jewish Temple. We don't know for sure. But we know this: these words are outrageous, offensive, and downright shocking. Don't let them pass you by without knocking you off balance. They are meant to.

These are words of undeniable boldness. These are words of profound accusation. These are words of a man claiming unabashedly to be the Son of God – equal with God! These are fighting words. These are words of deep love. Jesus does not kneel down before you with a gentle offer; he stands firm and looks deep into your eyes with a challenge. It was a challenge then. It is a challenge now. He still asks the same question: "Do you believe *in me*?"

32

The Sabbath Turned Upside Down

Read Mathew 12:1-14; Mark 2:23-28; 3:1-6; Luke 6:1-11

We are back with our trio of Matthew, Mark, and Luke as they continue exploring the ongoing problem of keeping the Sabbath holy. We are looking at these events right behind John's telling of Jesus healing the invalid at the pool since, once again, we are tangling with the Sabbath and the scholars of the law.

When I was a little girl, and my parents packed us into our station wagon for a trip to the mountains or the beach, the red Coca-Cola ice chest was always wedged in the floor between the front and back seats. The white tray at the top was packed with egg salad sandwiches wrapped in wax paper, which my mother had prepared earlier that morning before we got on the road. It was the 1960s, and fast-food restaurants had yet to be built on every street corner, so you always took the food you needed. There was nothing better than those cold sandwiches made on white bread!

I can't imagine the difficulty of finding food when you were traveling 2,000 years ago. Sure, you could have bread in a knapsack, but how long would that keep? We don't know how far Jesus and his buddies traveled on this Sabbath, but I am betting no restaurants were nearby. As they walk through a grain field, his disciples reach out to pluck the head of the grain and rub it together in their hands, separating the wheat from the chaff and then eating the grain. According to Jewish law, there was nothing wrong with this form of casual gleaning as they walked through someone else's field (Deuteronomy 23:25), but the problem was the day of the week: the Sabbath.

This is what was judged work on this Sabbath day of rest: They were guilty of reaping by breaking off the head of wheat, they were guilty of threshing because they rubbed it in their hands, and they were guilty of winnowing as the wheat separated from the chaff. And they were guilty of preparing a Sabbath meal from the whole process – which should have been prepared the day before. So they were in a whole heap of trouble for working on the Sabbath.[1]

Those pesky law-keepers, the Pharisees, are walking with Jesus and his disciples, and they immediately call it to his attention. Jesus reminds them of two little items in their scripture. The first is found in 1 Samuel 21:1-6 when David and his men fled from King Saul. Arriving at the Tabernacle at Nob, David negotiated with the priest Ahimelech for the holy bread on the altar. David and his men needed food– although it conflicted with their Jewish law for him to take it.

Matthew adds the exception of how priests are allowed to eat the bread offered to God on the Sabbath yet are held guiltless (Leviticus 24:5-9). Jesus boldly concludes that *"something greater than the temple is here."* I am pretty sure this set the Pharisees back on their heels. Jesus has just deftly compared himself to David, the rejected King of Israel, to the priests who are guiltless before God, and to the Temple, where God meets with his people. *"I tell you, something greater than the temple is here."*

Are you starting to think Jesus is pushing their buttons? You may laugh to yourself at how easily he sends them into a spin. Or you may be quietly whispering to Jesus in your best parent voice some good advice along the lines of, "Just stop annoying them with the Sabbath issue!" I have a feeling Jesus has a much bigger story to tell than the low-hanging fruit of a broken law concerning work on the Sabbath. In this casual stroll through the wheat field, he is offering why he has come – wasn't that really what they wanted to know? "I have come as King, as Priest, and as something even greater than the Temple."[2]

And if that isn't enough to blow their minds, our friend Matthew, whose principal audience is Jewish, shares that Jesus reminds these keepers of the law of what the prophet Hosea had warned previous priests about: "For I desire mercy, not sacrifice, and acknowledgment of God rather than burnt offerings" (paraphrased from Hosea 6:6). Was Jesus saying it was relatively easy to routinely bake the bread and offer it on the altar, yet more pleasing to God to go look for your burdened neighbor and share your bread with her?

Take note, you rule keepers. This is what tripped the people of God up again and again. Often, they were careful to keep the letter of the law. They kept their eyes peeled for those around them who broke the law and delighted in correcting them. But where was their heart? Were they elevating God by humbling themselves? Or were they elevating themselves by humbling others?

This conversation ended with Jesus declaring himself as lord of the Sabbath. Mark 2:27 explains it in a way that I can understand: "*And he said to them, 'The Sabbath was made for man, not man for the Sabbath.'*" Yes! This is the heart of the whole commandment, isn't it? God, from the very beginning, decided that rest was good. He rested after spending six days creating this world. He wanted the same thing for us: rest. Rest is a holy thing. It is not tied up in knots that are difficult to discern and untangle. It is simply this: rest. It is not to be a heavy burden or a harsh difficulty. God did not create man to honor the Sabbath. God created the Sabbath so that man could rest from his work and glorify God. It is good.

Was there a thoughtful silence as they journeyed on to their synagogue? Or was resentment brewing at their authority being challenged? The question they ask once they arrive tells the story. *"Is it lawful to heal on the Sabbath?"* Everyone is aware of the man in the corner with the withered hand. Jesus, in true rabbinical teaching form, answers their question with his own questions: "Which one of you will rescue his sheep from a pit where he has fallen on the Sabbath? Is a man more valuable to God than a sheep? Is it lawful to do good on the Sabbath or to do harm? Is it lawful to save life or to kill?"

He looks around the room at their hardened hearts. He sees their anger. He sees their lack of mercy. They stand arrogant and proud, heartless shepherds who ignore their distressed sheep. Jesus alone looks at the man with the withered hand. *"Stretch out your hand."* The man lifted his hand for all to see, and it was restored.

This is all we need to know about the Sabbath and holiness. It was created for us. It was created for rest. For restoration.[3] It was created to honor God the Creator. It was created for good. If we get caught up tying the Sabbath in red tape and regulations, we may find ourselves judging others and challenging the authority of the Son of God.

If it is the Sabbath, then rest, my friend. And give thanksgiving and honor to our good God, the Creator, who created the Sabbath for you!

33

The Surprising Servant

Read Matthew 12:14-21

The Pharisees are angry. They are on a path of destruction. They think they need to destroy this messenger. They don't realize they are destroying themselves.

Only Matthew, our messenger who will concentrate on telling the story of Jesus to his Jewish brethren, will connect the dots from this story of healing on the Sabbath down the road to additional healings and then back to the Jewish prophet Isaiah. Matthew tells us that because Jesus was aware of the Pharisees' conspiracy to kill him, he withdrew from that place.

But that didn't stop the crowds of people. They followed him. He healed them. And once again, he ordered them not to make a big racket about it. Matthew tells us this is precisely how the Messiah had been described many years before.

We modern-day followers of Jesus desperately need to understand God's history with the Jewish people. I know how confusing the Jewish scriptures can be; the laws there seem harsh and without reason, and there are stories of people who often prosper despite their selfishness or cruelty to others. And then there is all the war and the killing. I mean, really, who wants to read about all of that? I encourage you to find a good Bible study and dig in. God, who created the world and everything in it, also chose to have a deep relationship with one man (Abraham) and his descendants. He promised them that he would be their God and they would be his people. It was a very messy relationship. Exactly like most relationships.

Yet God entrusted them with telling his story and writing a good record of their history together. Because of that relationship, they held not only the record of their past – but they were also given the story of their future. And one common little theme that continued to reoccur over and over and over again was that God would be sending a Messenger. A Messiah who was chosen and anointed by God. A Savior. A Branch that would connect them to him. He would look like a good Shepherd. He would be a righteous Judge. He would be a mighty King. He would be a Priest who would make the ultimate sacrifice. He would be a Servant. He would contain the very Spirit of God. He would be as beloved as an Only Son.

His purpose would be to cross the barrier that separated a Holy God from his unholy people. He would accept the punishment for all the sin against a sinless God; he would ransom—buy back—the captives held in captivity by their enemy. He would come to defeat death, to crush the serpent, to shepherd his sheep through a narrow gate, and to prepare a kingdom yet to come for those called the children of God. It was a mighty task.

God gave his chosen people the responsibility of carrying his words forward into the future. That is why we have access to them now. That is why Jesus quoted those words. And that is why Matthew turns to them now: "Listen," he tells us, "this is what God told us long ago through the man he sent named Isaiah."

"Here is my servant, whom I uphold,
my chosen one in whom I delight;
I will put my Spirit on him,

and he will bring justice to the nations.
He will not shout or cry out,
or raise his voice in the streets.
A bruised reed he will not break,
and a smoldering wick he will not snuff out.
In faithfulness he will bring forth justice;
he will not falter or be discouraged
till he establishes justice on earth.
In his teaching the islands will put their hope."
Isaiah 42:1-4 NIV

There are so many beautiful promises here that we must pause and look carefully. This is written in the voice of God. These are his own beautiful words. "Look! Look closely!" he says. "Look at my servant – someone who does my will without question. I *chose him.* I hold him up. His strength comes from me. I *delight* in him! I will put my own Spirit within him. He will be one, united with, inseparable from me. And his purpose? He will bring justice – my justice – to all the world." Now, that is an undeniable recommendation. It is a complete endorsement. There is not a single doubt or question. "This man is mine; this man speaks and acts for me." Period.

What does this Servant's conduct look like? Is he marching through the streets with a fist raised in one hand and a protest banner in the other? Is he shouting hell and damnation from the street corner? Is he crying "foul play" and "it's not fair" to the news reporters? My golly, he isn't. He is moving among the people with compassion and gentleness. The crowds are not of his own making – they are there because they see something of God in him that is glorious and wonderful, and they can't help but tell their neighbors, family, and friends. They see a sure hope in him. He looks into their eyes and sees them; he reaches out and touches them. He tells them of a God beyond the law. He tells them of things of the spirit and reaches out to touch the heart. He is unlike any man they have encountered.

There are those in this world who are always looking for the strong and the powerful. If you want to get to the top, look for those people who can pull you up the ladder. This Chosen Servant seems to be searching for the broken ones. The ones who have been bent over by a heavy load. The ones who once burned brightly but have encountered a sudden stormy wind and are in danger of losing it all. He would later explain that he had come for the sick. The lost. He would define himself as the physician who had come to heal and bind up the broken.

We learn something else about him: He is faithful. Faithful means loyal, constant, and steadfast.[1] Faithful also means a true, accurate adherence to the original. Could this mean that this Servant accurately portrayed his Master? Could this mean that in seeing him, we see God?

He will be bringing forth justice – but I don't think it is what we call "social justice." Why? He also said the poor would always be with us. He also said the world would hate us if we followed him. I think he is talking of God's justice, which is much more significant and longer lasting. It isn't limited to this time and place. I believe this justice must have something to do with peace between us and God. It must be connected with God's righteousness—and God's mercy. When we take God out of the equation of justice, we spiral way off course. Yet – we read he will not falter or lose courage until justice on earth is established.

If we skip forward to one dark Friday afternoon before the Jewish celebration of Passover, was justice established on a wooden cross? Was that justice - when one chosen servant took the punishment for a world's bucketload of sin? Is that what God's version of justice looks like? Did God declare me guilty yet send his guiltless son to pay my fine? Is this justice in God's eyes?

If you want to read more about this servant, open your Bible and read Isaiah 42:6-9.

"I, the Lord, have called you in righteousness;
I will take hold of your hand.
I will keep you and will make you
to be a covenant for the people
and a light for the Gentiles,
to open eyes that are blind,
to free captives from prison
and to release from the dungeon those who sit in darkness.
"I am the Lord; that is my name!
I will not yield my glory to another
or my praise to idols.
See, the former things have taken place,
and new things I declare;
before they spring into being
I announce them to you."
(NIV)

In addition to reminding his listeners that he is telling of a new thing that is coming, God also promises that this servant will be protected by him and called forth for righteousness. The beloved servant will be given as a new covenant for the people, a light for the nations, to open eyes that are blind and free those in darkness. I think this perfectly explains our promise in verse 4: *"In his teaching the islands will put their hope."*

The islands? We see this clarified here with the description "Gentiles." That would be me. And probably you. We were the outsiders. In the ancient Jewish world, there were the Jews and everybody else. The Jews were the center of the world. Everybody else was off on their own little island, doing their own little thing. Blind. Unseeing. Sitting in darkness. Far off from God – who was light. But this is what is really cool – God was doing such a great, unbelievable thing that it was too good to offer it only to his Jewish people. He was going to open up his offer to the whole world. All of us. Even the Gentiles. Let's sing hallelujah!

My ESV version of Matthew 12:21 reads this way: *"And in his name the Gentiles will hope."* There you have it. This trusted servant has a name, and it can be none other than Jesus. He is the one the prophet Isaiah wrote about. He is the one who didn't see the rules if they became more important than the person. He is the one who didn't hesitate to heal the body but was more interested in the health of the soul. He is the one who didn't ignore the hurt or the sin. He is the one who was on a mission and would not be slowed down by established traditions or a handful of religious leaders determined to shut him up.

Jesus was not what they were expecting. He still isn't. Who would have ever thought God's Chosen One would look like that?

34

Jesus Calls His Disciples

Read Matthew 10:1-4; Mark 3:7-21; Luke 6:12-16

Word has spread. The crowds come from all over. Galilee and Judea, Jerusalem and Idumea, from beyond the Jordan and around Tyre and Sidon. Get out your map and take a look. This was no small thing. These folks were not zipping down the highway for a little day trip. They were packing their bags and tying up their walking shoes. Pitch a tent or stay with a family member? How long would it take them to get there, and how would they find him? Everything was happening by word of mouth. They have become a "great crowd." And he has become their rock-star healer. And they all want to touch him. He knows he could be crushed by their need to be near him in their hope of healing. We forget how human he is – walking around in that fragile suit of skin and bones.

His disciples prepared a boat for him so he could speak from the safety of the water. The loudest voices, though, are the voices of the demons who cower before him. They know exactly who he is: the Son of God. It always amazes me that they recognize him so quickly, and it takes us so much more convincing.

He moves from teaching and healing the crowds to the quiet of the mountain. Luke tells us he prayed all night, and when morning came, he called his disciples (followers) and chose twelve. There are twelve men – just as there are twelve tribes of Israel. The Gospels name them differently, but don't let that worry you too much. Many people in this world walk around with variations of their names. I think of my uncle, who gave all of us special names: Lil'Red, Snake, Annie-Lauri, and Skeeter. Few outside the family would be able to decipher those. Jesus did the same sort of renaming occasionally. Simon became Peter. James and John became known as the "Sons of Thunder." You have another Simon who was called the Zealot. And then there is James, the son of Alphaeus or James the Less (not to be confused with James, the brother of John, or James, the brother of Jesus, who was not one of the twelve but became a prominent leader in the early church and wrote the book of James). Okay, did I just thoroughly confuse you?

Here, we are given their names: Simon, who became Peter, and Andrew, his brother. James and his brother John. These four will become the ones in the inner circle. Philip and Bartholomew (also called Nathanael), Matthew (also called Levi), and Thomas are in our second group of four. The next four we are less familiar with: James (the lesser or, the younger - son of Alphaeus), Thaddaeus (also called Jude or Judas, son or brother of James), and Simon the Zealot (perhaps because of his religious zeal – he was too early to be associated with the political group of the same name), and Judas Iscariot who betrayed him. Judas would always be listed last and wear that disclaimer: *the one who betrayed him.*[1]

Judas is obviously a complicated man. We wonder why Jesus chose him as one of his closest – if Jesus was God and knew all things – why would he embrace a betrayer? I don't have the answer. Is it as gloriously profound as this: we all are chosen, yet we are given the freedom to choose back? Does Judas mirror our own ability to sell our Savior out for a handful of silver? Judas being fully embraced into this inner circle is such a conundrum. I don't have the answer here. So, I take note that we are forewarned - we best keep an eye on this one.

We are told they were not only disciples – followers – but also *apostles*. If I look at the meaning of *disciples*, I find the description of a dedicated follower and student of a teacher, a mentor, or a leader.[2] In his last instructions, before ascending into heaven, Jesus would charge his disciples to go out into the world and *"make disciples"* – find others who would also agree to follow and learn in dedication. But what is an apostle?

An apostle is a messenger, one who is sent out to deliver those teachings to others. Within the early Church, the twelve original disciples became known as the apostles - but then Saul showed up. He was on his self-appointed mission to destroy those followers of Jesus until Jesus appeared to him on the road to Damascus. He knocked him off his high horse, blinded him with light, and invited him to join the band. Jesus is always doing these unexpected sorts of things. Saul became known as Paul and took on the title of "Apostle" since he was chosen directly by Jesus and sent out to deliver the teachings of Jesus to others.[3]

Here in Mark, these Twelve were "appointed" to be with Jesus – in an inner circle kind of way, and he would send them out to preach, and they would be given authority to cast out demons. (Matthew notes they were also able to heal every disease and every affliction.) Apparently, casting out demons is the most profound and challenging responsibility. Here in the generally safe land of the free, we don't pay too much attention to this demon business. If we traveled just a little outside our comfort zone into other worlds where people commonly believe in evil and supernatural beings, it wouldn't take long to hear the description "demon possessed."

It hides out in the stories of Catholic exorcists and in the religion of vodun, also known as voodoo, commonly practiced in Haiti, Jamaica, Nigeria, Brazil, and many other countries.[4] A friend of my nephew's, who was from Ghana, shared with me one evening her terror of demons. She was adamant that her grandmother had placed a hex on her, which was manifesting itself in anxiety attacks. "She is living in my father's home in Ghana and sleeping in what once was my bed," she whispered. "She is a priestess of voodoo, and she would easily have access to my hair from my hairbrush. She is very angry with me for becoming a Christian and coming to America." It was the first time I had met someone who believed in the reality of this kind of power. Since then, I have met other people I highly respect who share this conviction. Maybe this idea of evil spirits didn't die out so easily a couple of thousands of years ago.

Before we slip past this little passage listing these men who were called to be apostles, I want us to go just a little bit deeper. These men would not only walk, talk, eat, and sleep with Jesus for his few short years in ministry – but they also would be so convicted of Jesus's identity that each would face extremely dangerous futures to fulfill their responsibility to be his messengers. When I read Lee Strobel's book *The Case for Christ,* I was struck by his realization that these apostles not only faced a life of ridicule and torture because they were convinced "Jesus was the Messiah of God who died on a cross, returned to life, and was seen alive by them," but they were also publicly executed – except John who, despite torture and imprisonment, would die in his old age. Strobel concluded with this thought: They knew for sure Jesus rose from the dead – they had seen him with their own eyes, touched him with their own hands. "If they weren't absolutely certain [Jesus had risen from the dead], they wouldn't have allowed themselves to be tortured to death for proclaiming that the Resurrection had happened."[5]

Before we get on the road, let's look at some of these apostles more closely. I think it will help us appreciate their journey with Jesus – especially since, in these stories, Jesus is preparing them to carry his message of God's kingdom beyond their little circle and into the world. What an incredibly overwhelming responsibility! Lord, may we be tender with these mere men as they struggle along this challenging path to belief!

Simon Peter was the first to profess Jesus as the Messiah and Son of the Living God. His confession will become the rock, the foundation the coming church will build on. Married, his home becomes headquarters for Jesus when he is in Capernaum. The Talmud described Galileans as "…more anxious for honor than for gain, quick-tempered, impulsive, emotional, easily aroused by an appeal to adventure, loyal to the end."[6] This certainly sounds like Simon Peter!

He will be quick to ask questions (the meaning of parables, how often one must forgive), and he will be one of the few who will experience Jesus's transfiguration on the mountaintop with Moses and Elijah. Peter is brave and enthusiastic; he will get out of the boat to walk with Jesus on the water, and he alone will follow Jesus on the night of his trial. He will be well remembered for denying Jesus three times that evening. Yet, we will also overhear the sweet conversation between Jesus and Peter as they walk together on the beach after Jesus is resurrected. Jesus will ask Peter three times if he loves him – allowing Peter to be forgiven for his three denials – and he will be given the specific responsibility to *"feed my sheep."*

Peter will step forward after Pentecost and the arrival of the Holy Spirit to boldly explain the life, death, and resurrection of the crucified Jesus to the crowds in Jerusalem and to the very Sanhedrin who had condemned Jesus to death. He quickly became the leader of the Jewish followers of Jesus, known as followers of *The Way.* He will be given a vision concerning clean and unclean food from God, telling him that the unclean Gentiles are also invited to accept Jesus as their Messiah. This will be revolutionary and ultimately turn this little Jewish community upside down!

Peter will write the books of the Bible which we know as 1 and 2 Peter, and he will dictate his experiences with Jesus to the Gospel writer Mark. This uneducated fisherman from Galilee will get himself in so much trouble, boldly proclaiming the story of the crucified

Jesus, that he, too, will find himself on a cross. Legend has it he would insist that he was not worthy to die as his Lord had, and some say he was able to convince his executioners to crucify him upside down. This is Peter, called away from his fishing boat to "catch men" for this unusual rabbi named Jesus. Oh my! To have his enthusiasm and passion for Jesus!

James, John's brother and the son of fisherman Zebedee, will also be included in Jesus's inner circle. He will often appear with Peter and John. He will be the first of the disciples to be martyred for his faith in Jesus, beheaded by Herod in AD 44 (Acts 12:1-2).

John, his brother, will become known as the Beloved Disciple because he will write the story of God's great love and how Jesus fulfills that love. He didn't start that way; with their explosive tempers, Jesus called John and his brother James the *Sons of Thunder*! Since his father had servants to help with his fishing business, he may have been raised in a wealthy family.

John's best buddy will be Peter, and after Jesus's resurrection and ascension, the two of them will become outspoken enough to find themselves in prison in Jerusalem for preaching Jesus as the risen Messiah and inciting the crowds. Angels will show up to rescue them! John will eventually be sentenced to the mines on the prison island of Patmos, where he will write the prophetic book of Revelation. He will also write the Gospel which bears his name, as well as 1 John, 2 John, and 3 John. Later freed, he alone, of all the original disciples, will die as an old man of apparently natural causes.

Andrew, Peter's brother, was originally a disciple of John the Baptist (Mark 1:16-18). When he encountered Jesus, he immediately sought his brother Peter to bring him along. Andrew will be the disciple who tells Jesus about the boy with the loaves and fishes, and when certain Greeks want to see Jesus, they will first go to Philip, but Philip will take them to Andrew. It is church tradition that he traveled far to tell the story of Jesus. Russia, Scotland, and Greece will claim him as their patron saint. According to tradition, he was crucified – bound, not nailed on an X-shaped cross in Achaia, Greece. His crime? The Governor Aepeas's wife and brother converted to Christianity, enraging Aepeas. He preached to his tormentors for two days until he died.

Bartholomew Nathanael may have been descended from royal blood. He was a scholar of the law and the prophets. Jesus referred to him as *"an Israelite indeed, in whom there is no deceit" (John 1:47).* He would venture far, telling the story of Jesus with Philip in Phrygia and Hierapolis, also in Armenia. Church tradition says that he also preached in India, and his death seems to have taken place there, the results of having been flayed with a whip or with knives.

Matthew, our tax collector from Capernaum, was perhaps our most unlikely apostle. In the eyes of a Jew, God was the only one to whom it was right to pay tribute. To pay it to anyone else was to insult God. Mathew, employed by the Romans, was an enemy the moment he showed up. Yet he was perhaps the first to present the story of Jesus in Hebrew to the world. Tradition holds that he died in Ethiopia.

The apostle we know of as doubting **Thomas** (since he insisted he would not believe Jesus was alive unless he could place his hand in his wounds) died in India from a sword or spear wound. The apostle who replaced the traitor Judas Iscariot, **Matthias** (Acts 1:15-26), was stoned and then beheaded. The apostle who met Jesus on the road to Damascus, Saul, who would be better known as Paul, would be tortured and then beheaded by Emperor Nero in Rome. These details are not in the Bible but are accepted as early church tradition.

Stop here with me for just a moment. This is not child's play. Jesus told those who were considering following him to "consider the cost." If you want a reality check, skip ahead to Luke 14:26-33. This discipleship decision has a sharp point: *"Those of you who do not give up everything you have cannot be my disciples" (v. 33, NIV).* Jesus knew – and knows the hearts of those who say yes to him. It is a free offer of salvation through the sacrifice Jesus made– yet there will probably be a cost to you. You will not be able to follow Jesus as his disciple and follow the ways of the world at the same time. If you choose to become like Jesus, you will become unlike the world around you. You will think differently. You will speak differently. You will act differently. You will love differently. You will let go of things, people, and places that pull you away from a life with Jesus. You will choose to hate the things God hates. And the world will hate you for it. It is a lot to ask, isn't it? That is why we took the time to look at those ordinary men who chose the hard path behind Jesus. After Jesus was crucified, they could have easily run away and gone back to their everyday lives. But they didn't. Something held them tight. Something about Jesus was more real, true, and worthy than their lives. I hope we can say the same.

35

From One Mountain to Another, From Moses to Jesus

Read Exodus 1-2:10; Exodus 20:1-21; Matthew 5:1-12

The Law given to Moses is a wondrous thing. You remember the story: God's people, the Hebrews, descendants of Abraham, sons and daughters of Israel, were invited to Egypt by the Pharaoh through the love and provision of Joseph during the great worldwide famine. God elevated Joseph from prison to the throne for such a time as this.

In Egypt, the Hebrews prospered and multiplied. They were given the fertile lands of Goshen to pasture their sheep and flourished there. As time went by and they became more and more numerous, they did something different from all the other tribes who had found protection under Egyptian skies – they remained distinct and separate. They didn't blend in with the culture. They kept their uniquely Hebrew ways. They grew stronger and stronger, one people worshipping One God.

They became the bad example of a house guest staying too long. Eventually, to keep them under control, the Egyptian Pharaohs curtailed their freedom and lowered their status from welcome guest to slave. Their occupation changed from sheep herders to brick builders. Ironically, these worshippers of One God spent their days building temples for Egypt's many gods. They cried out in misery. The Pharaoh didn't hear them - but their God did.

It's a beautiful story of rescue. All the babies of the Hebrews were to be killed by the midwives as soon as they were born, but those Jewish women were a hardy bunch, giving birth to their babies before the midwives could arrive. The mother of one baby boy made a water-proof ark for her infant son, lined it with a blanket woven in the Hebrew style, and set it adrift on the waters of the Nile. Pharaoh's daughter found the basket and the baby and raised this child as her own. Because he was lifted from the waters, she named him Moses.

God spoke to this grownup Moses through a burning bush and prepared him to confront Pharaoh with one simple demand: *"Let my people go!"* Ten terrifying plagues later, the freed slaves filed across the Red Sea on dry land while their God closed it back up over the pursuing Egyptian chariots and horsemen. A vast wilderness spread out before them—the hope of a promised land awaited. But first, they would need to learn more about the God who called them his people.

Moses went up to the mountaintop to listen to this God who made bread fall from the sky and produced water from a rock. There were trumpet blasts, thunder, and lightning as a great cloud descended on the mountaintop. "You will be my people; I will be your God. You will be my treasured possession, a kingdom of priests, a holy nation" (Exodus 19:5-6). If they were to be transformed from slaves into messengers of freedom, they would need instructions. God carved his commandments and laws onto stone tablets with his own finger. These laws were drastically different from anything they had observed in their land of captivity. These laws were much more complex and detailed than anything their ancestor Abraham had given them. These laws formed a new nation. A new people. A people dedicated to following the One God.

These laws covered everything they needed to know for day-to-day living. There were instructions on what to eat and how to cook it. There were instructions on how to worship and when. There were instructions on how the community protected sexual relationships, on how to pay restitution if you caused harm to a neighbor, on the mistreatment of sojourners, and on how to care for widows and orphans. They addressed how to deal with mildew and how to cure diseases of the skin. There were over 600 laws! It would take a lifetime to learn God's laws, which would protect them as a people and instruct them on how to look more like him. "This is who I am; this is how to look like me. I am holy, and I require you to be holy, set apart for my purposes."

We know these laws by the top ten big ones. The ones that start, *"I am the Lord your God, who brought you out of the land of Egypt, out of the house of slavery. You shall have no other gods before me" (Exodus 20:2-3).* These beginning laws teach how to love and respect God. Then, the laws turn to respecting our parents, spouses, and neighbors. You should be in good shape if you follow those top ten laws. Obeying 600 laws was overwhelming; ten should be doable. But it turned out the people had a hard time sticking to just those top ten.

The people failed to follow even the first law as the generations came and went. God sent messengers to warn them they were headed for trouble of their own making. They didn't listen. They nodded, acting like they agreed, and headed to the hills to dance before the little gods. Judgment came, they were carted off into captivity, they repented and returned and tried again. My simplified explanation is that God told his people, "If you want to act like the Persians, I'll send you to live in their house for a while and see how you like it. If you want to act like the Babylonians, I'll send you to live in their house for a while and see how you like it."

A thousand years had come and gone, and a small remnant of these Hebrews was still holding on, once again living in a "captive land" – this time in their own land, yet under the rulership of the Romans. Rome had granted them permission to keep their Temple in Jerusalem up and running, and their priests bought their position of power and promised to keep the peace in this closely guarded land. A slender thread of hope was still attaching these Hebrews to the fire that once burned on Mount Sinai. Everyone was still going through the motions of obeying the law, hoping and praying that God would send someone like Moses to save them.

And then Jesus, the descendant of Abraham, the descendant of Israel's son Judah, the descendant of Israel's King David, ascended the mountain and spoke these words:

"Blessed are the poor in spirit, for theirs is the kingdom of heaven." He continued, *"Blessed are those who mourn..." "Blessed are those who are meek..." "Blessed are those who hunger and thirst for righteousness..."* And he had them. He had their undivided attention. He spoke to their broken spirits, their sorrow and suffering, and their great desire to experience the righteousness their God had promised. This man did not explain the law from a distance. This man looked into their eyes and knew their hearts. He knew them. He was one of them. Yet he seemed to know this God of theirs in a way they did not.

Jesus spoke of the kingdom of heaven as if he had been there. Jesus talked of comfort for those mourning with compassion and tenderness. Jesus saw the world as if he knew the wonders forfeited by Adam and Eve when they hid from their Creator. Jesus seemed to know the righteousness of their God and was convinced they, too, could experience His righteousness in their own lives.

As his words continued, they began to see their God in a new way. They had become worn out with God's Law – not because it brought freedom and life – but because in addition to the hundreds of laws God had sent down the mountain with Moses, God's priests and scribes and teachers had added even more laws, called the oral traditions, to help everyone keep the law. God's law had been changed from a good thing meant to unify God with his people to a heavy burden that separated God from his people – and each other. Only a very elite few had the time, the money, and the education to be *good enough* at "keeping the law." The law had become more important than the people. Or at least *the appearance of keeping the law.*

We modern folk seem to pay close attention to the miracles of Jesus and the supernatural Spirit of God – and find it more pleasant to ignore those pesky rules. We pat each other on the arm and say sweet things like, "God is love, and God forgives, and God is good and compassionate." We aren't too sure what he forgives since we have made everything under the sun acceptable in his eyes. And blessings? It is easy for us to look around at our freedoms and good fortunes and decide God has blessed us right down to the tips of our toes! But for right now, before we read these words introducing us to the teachings of Jesus, we need to get into the skin of these ancient Hebrews, living under the sword of Roman rule, burdened under the heavy weight of religious law, immensely aware of their daily sinfulness and their separation from a holy God. Their hands were aching from never-ending toil and trouble; their hearts were breaking from the sacrificial blood they offered at their Temple, which was never enough.

Remember way back in Exodus when the people were overwhelmed with the outward manifestations of the presence of God? The thunder, lightning, trumpet blasting, and smoking mountain were just too terrifying! "You speak to us, and we will listen," they pleaded with Moses. "Just don't let God speak to us or we will die of fear!" (Exodus 20:18-21).

Along comes Jesus with callouses on his hands, yet his face reflects a distant light. Like Moses, Jesus has been on the mountaintop with God. He has come down to share with the people not only the law but also the reality and the essence of life in God's kingdom. Unlike Moses, Jesus had not just drawn close to the thunder and lightning of God – he alone was the narrow door opening the way to God and his kingdom. They didn't realize that God himself had come down from the mountain dressed like them in skin and bones.

Jesus was about to shatter their little world. God was no longer staying safely at a distance.

36

When You Don't Feel Very Blessed

Read Matthew 5:1-12; Luke 6:17-26

"Blessed are the poor in spirit,
for theirs is the kingdom of heaven.
Blessed are those who mourn,
for they will be comforted.
Blessed are the meek,
for they will inherit the earth.
Blessed are those who hunger and thirst for righteousness,
for they will be filled.
Blessed are the merciful,
for they will be shown mercy.
Blessed are the pure in heart,
for they will see God.
Blessed are the peacemakers,
for they will be called children of God."
Matthew 5:3-9 NIV

So, let's try looking at these again. Sometimes, God has me circle around and around a passage of scripture. I read it in different translations. I look up word meanings. I read the commentaries of wise believers.[1] I get stuck. I take a break as days and sometimes weeks go by. I take a walk. I pray; I ask the Holy Spirit to teach me – to open my eyes and heart, and sometimes he leads me around through the back door. The last thing I want to do is shortchange God by making his Word seem dull – or just as terrifying, to water down his meaning or misrepresent his character. And then I ask myself, why am I doing this in the first place? But God will not let me go. I return. I erase. I rewrite. I continue. Because he has given me a word this year: finish. You know that word, don't you? I keep thinking I am to finish what I have started. But I am wrong. It goes like this:

And I am certain that God, who began the good
work within you, will continue his work until it is finally
finished on the day when Christ Jesus returns.
Philippians 1:6 NLT

Or

I am convinced and confident of this very thing, that He who has
begun a good work in you will [continue to] perfect and complete it
until the day of Christ Jesus [the time of His return].
Philippians 1:6 AMP

God will continue… God will perfect and complete. A good work. This is good work – to seek to understand who God is and why he sent his own Son to rescue us from death and deception. So, I continue. I read the scripture and ponder his words. And really, is there anything more important we could be thinking about?

In my little safe world, we often say, "I have been blessed!" (meaning with good things from God). Do we ever think of being blessed by God with difficult things? Is that what Jesus is teaching? As I read over these beatitudes – these blessings from God – I realize they are very much a cry and an answer. An unspoken cry of the people. Jesus answers their cries with what God is doing that is unseen.

Blessed are the poor in spirit…We are hard-pressed on every side. Our spirit within us is discouraged. I read the explanation of being "spiritually bankrupt." Empty. Lacking. Not having enough. Don't you think it would be the opposite? When we are full of spiritual hallelujahs, we will bust down the doors of the kingdom of heaven, right? Nope – that isn't what Jesus says. Consider yourself blessed when you are running on empty – for you will receive the fullness of the kingdom of heaven!

Blessed are those who mourn… Blessed are those who are meek… There are so many reasons in this world to mourn. If you are in deep sorrow over loss or grieved and heartbroken, Jesus tells you God will be your comfort. For those humbled by circumstances into a place of meekness and humbleness – not at all what our materialistic culture elevates – you are in the perfect position to inherit the whole world. "Impossible!" we silently think. Jesus tells us that the kingdom of heaven has a very different order of priorities. Perhaps things are not what they appear to be at first glance. Something unseen is going on that may be more real than what our nearsighted eyes can see. In his kingdom, there will be no mourning, no more tears, and we will stand in his strength to inherit the wonder and beauty of his perfect earth.

Is our hunger for self-righteousness or *God's righteousness*? We may be sorely disappointed if we are busy trying to bring about man's version of right and wrong. Have I received God's amazing grace and *mercy*, receiving forgiveness for my own ugly sin? If so, am I merciful to those around me? Then, I shall receive mercy to the fullest.

And what does my heart look like? Pure, like God's? I don't think so! I can't get through the hour without ugliness pouring out of my mouth… or at least filling my thoughts – and we know where all that comes from, right? Our hearts. The most inside thing there is! It is much easier to appear all squeaky clean on the outside – but no, Jesus is examining the state of my heart. Asking if it is pure. I must admit it is in a sorry, unclean state. I keep my pride and my resentment hidden safely there. I guess I am not going to get to see God after all. Shoot.

Peacemakers. Okay. I may have a shot there. My older sisters used to call me a *peacemaker* because I couldn't stand harsh words or arguments. A household with five females had a lot of that going on. My younger sister would probably disagree because I seem to stir up plenty of trouble for her. (I wrote this as we were selling our childhood home, downsizing, and packing all her worldly belongings to move into her new home. I had a *long* to-do list.) But I think we are talking about a different kind of peace here –between me and God – which only Jesus will bring. Only then will there be peace between me and others.

People love to say these words of the Beatitudes. They sound so lovely and poetic, and the story will undoubtedly find its way to happily ever after. But there is that additional blessing we may prefer to ignore. Consider it a blessing from God to be *persecuted for righteousness' sake* on account of Jesus. It is one thing to be insulted because of our actions or falsely accused because someone dislikes or disagrees with us. But that is not what Jesus is saying. Looking like Jesus and reflecting God's righteousness is the crime that will offend people enough that they will wish us dead. This is where the blessings from God get hard. *Rejoice and be glad, because great is your reward in heaven!*

Every blessing Jesus holds out to these followers hungry to see God is not meant to be a new commandment or a heavy requirement to lay on their backs. This is not another "to-do" list. It is a fountain of encouragement; it is Jesus looking at the people, seeing their emptiness, and filling the loss with God.

You are discouraged in your spirit –
Rejoice! God's kingdom is open for you!
You are mourning with great loss in this world –
Rejoice! God himself will comfort you!
You are humble and understand your broken state –
Rejoice! There will come a time when your
Father will give you this very earth!
You long for God's righteousness and his mercy
and to have a heart like his –
Rejoice! For as you draw close to him,
He will fill you with his righteousness, his mercy, his purity.

These truths of God were there in the words of his prophets and hidden in the foundation of his law, but here was Jesus looking into their faces, seeing their pain and their longings, and answering with the provision of God, introducing the righteousness of his kingdom. "This is temporary," Jesus was saying. "There is something more. It is real and eternal." Listening to these glory-filled proclamations of Jesus, they held their breath with hope.

Matthew painted Jesus high on the mountaintop, close to the sun breaking through the clouds with glowing shafts of light. Luke's version is on a plain: level ground, openness all around. Simple. Direct. There are four cries and the answers: You are poor – you will have the riches of the kingdom. You are hungry now – you will be filled and satisfied. You weep now – you will laugh again. People hate you for loving God. You will be excluded, reviled, spurned for your love of the Son of Man – but your reward will be great in heaven.

Then Luke includes four woes matching up with the blessings that may not be as welcoming to our ears. Woe to you who are rich – you have already received your wealth. Woe to you who are full now – you shall be hungry. Woe to you who laugh now – you shall mourn and weep. Woe to you who are praised now – the false prophets were spoken well of in their days. Are you offended? Is Jesus judging your superiority, success, and pride in your accomplishments? Are you feeling the sting of arrogance? Have you distanced yourself from the righteousness of God?

If you are living the glory days now, right here in this life, oblivious of those around you who suffer – perhaps Jesus is warning you that your future will not be as rewarding. I am betting the fine religious leaders in his midst were thinking, "What future? I have everything now. I know God's Word backward and forward. God has rewarded me with a good life because I am good. What makes this Jesus think things will change?" I must take note of this profoundly difficult teaching. Where will I find myself in this blessed kingdom of God? I may be the one who is feasting and laughing today. Maybe I need to look closer at my traveling companions on the other side of the road.

Jesus began his ministry with an invitation to draw closer, listen carefully, let go of all the noise and bother of the world, and see with our hearts the God who loves perfectly. The difficulties of this world would be temporary; the joy of God's kingdom would be perfect and eternal.

This story isn't quite over yet. There is another blessing hidden away in the words of Jesus. It is found behind another story that isn't what it seems to be at the time. Jesus had ridden into Jerusalem to the shouts of Hosannah and a king's welcome. Before the week was done, he had been executed on a Roman cross at the request of the Jewish religious leaders. Blessed are those who are poor in spirit, those who mourn, those who are meek… Could there have been anyone who felt the despair of those words more than his disciples after watching him die in agony?

Jesus, buried in a rich man's tomb, sealed and guarded, burst beyond the darkness of death to walk through locked doors to comfort his disciples and to breathe into them the breath of the Holy Spirit of God. Death defeated, he would enter his Father's kingdom and hold the door open for them. For us.

Thomas missed it all. When he was told what had happened, he was adamant in his disbelief: "Unless I see his nail-marked hands and place my fingertips into his wounds, I will never believe." Oh, how many have made this same statement of disbelief?

Jesus returned and invited Thomas to touch his wounds. Thomas's response was immediate. *"My Lord and my God!"*

Jesus asked him a question and predicted the future with the next beat, *"Have you believed because you have seen me? Blessed are those who have not seen and yet have believed" (John 20:29).*

That is the blessing I will claim. I have not placed my hands in his wounds – yet I have believed. John, who was there that day, concluded, *"...believe that Jesus is the Christ, the Son of God, and that by believing you may have life in his name" (v. 31).* Have you been blessed?

37

Pass the Salt and Turn on the Light

Read Matthew 5:13-16

"Let there be light," he said. And there was light. *"And God saw that the light was good."*

There it is—the beginning. Light entered the world. "Life began!" I want to proclaim. But that is not quite right. I jump too quickly and overlook the order of things. First, God separated the light from the darkness. There was brilliant, marvelous, glorious light before the sun, moon, and stars. God gave it a name: day. And the darkness he called night.

I think of my days. I like to rise from my bed while it is still dark out. A cup of coffee. My Bible. I ease into what will soon be the day. The light seeping into the darkness and through the windows is my first clue that morning is coming. Often, the glow of orange painting the clouds beckons me to come out and lift my eyes to the heavens. Long before the sun appears over the horizon, the skies are already singing their song of praise to God for his creation of light.

Jesus, Son of God, said, *"You are light."*

Are we really this precious, this beautiful, this valuable? Were we first in God's mind when he spoke all of creation into being? Can we illuminate the darkness? Can we reveal God's beauty around us? Are we necessary to make all of life thrive and grow? Are we able to bring warmth into what has been lifeless and cold? Do we have these same qualities as light?

"You are light," Jesus said. *"You are the light of the world...let your light shine before others..."* Why? *"That they may see..."* See what? *"Your good works and give glory to your Father who is in heaven."* Our light is for God's glory. Our works are meant to praise God just as the skies at dawn's first light praise him.

I have to sit with this idea for a little while. I grew up in the South. If you did, too, you may be familiar with this idea I am wrestling with. My mother was adamant about many things. (The first thing that pops into my mind is you never ever brushed your hair in the kitchen or in public, but I meant to say something else.) She never praised us. She certainly never bragged about us to others. And she taught us it was unseemly and unpleasing to "toot our own horn." In other words, to draw attention to ourselves, to elevate ourselves. It isn't easy to think of myself as something extraordinary like light! I grew up battling between being insecure, unsure of myself – my actions and words – and desiring to feel good about who I was.

Entering adulthood and into a male-dominated profession, I quickly realized I could not stand back and be shy about my abilities, strengths, or experiences – all of which prepared me to take on increasingly difficult roles. I had to be confident. I had to assure potential clients that I could not only do the job but would be able to do it better than anyone else I was competing against. I had to describe my process and relay my vision. I had to show them my zeal and enthusiasm.

There can be a fine line between what is necessary to succeed in a work situation and being perceived by friends or family as arrogant or prideful in the worst way. It crushes me to think of myself as bragging.

Or being bossy. Or prideful. But I also know God has gifted me with strength – and leadership abilities – and a vision of the big picture, enabling me to make decisions easily – sometimes big, sometimes a thousand small ones. And I don't mind admitting when I have made a wrong decision – we adjust, make a new decision, and keep moving forward. For over 20 years, I had two jobs simultaneously, and both had the title "Director" attached to them. You didn't take on those roles unless you were not afraid to let your little light shine!

As I read these precious words of Jesus, I see that our light shining has a purpose: we do not proclaim ourselves but Jesus Christ. It is his light, not ours, and that makes all the difference.

I am reminded of Paul's instructions to those new believers in the wordly city of Corinth.

For God, who said,
"Let light shine out of darkness,"
made his light shine in our hearts
to give us the light of the knowledge of God's glory
displayed in the face of Christ.
But we have this treasure in jars of clay
to show that this all-surpassing power
is from God
and not from us.
2 Corinthians 4:6-7 NIV

We are dusty clay jars made from the earth. God's glorious heavenly light within us shines through the cracks and the broken places out into the darkness. It is not us. It is an all-surpassing power that belongs to God. We have it purely because of Jesus. He came that we may have true knowledge of God and his glory. How can we be anything but humbled?

"You are salt," Jesus told us. And I think to myself, "Yes! Let me be salt! Let me be flavorful and yummy!"

The cabinet by my stove is filled with variations of salt; from "Everything But the Bagel" to "21 Spice Salute," salt is our favorite go-to for making the food we have prepared tasty. Salt not only enhances taste but also preserves. Before our modern day of refrigeration, salt was the answer to make bacon and ham last the winter. If I am like salt, I change the chemical structure of my surroundings – protecting and preserving something for good that will last into the future.

We never think of salt going bad or losing its saltiness. In Jesus's day, valuable salt gathered from the sea contained other compounds (magnesium, potassium, calcium sulfate). Salt was not only used as an additive for food but it was also used agriculturally as a fertilizer to improve the soil. During times of high moisture, sodium chloride (salt), the most soluble mineral, would dissolve and wash away, slowly leaching out of the soil, leaving behind a white substance that appeared to be salt but had none of its flavor or attributes![1] It lost all value and worth and was good for nothing. It was thrown out and trampled underfoot. Lord, don't throw me out! May I be used to flavor, preserve, and fertilize the ground!

I started exploring these stories of Jesus long ago. All I need to say is the year 2020. You know the time of darkness and isolation and separation. My husband Jeff and I led a small group of "just married" couples at our church. In January, we committed to meeting with them for a year to share ourselves and walk with them through this complicated relationship called marriage. March came with its mandated lockdowns. The church where we were members stopped meeting in person. It was a difficult time. Our small group continued to meet via video calls. We had started as five couples and gradually dropped down to two. We questioned why we continued. By the end of the summer, we began meeting outside on our Sunday nights together. Below is my story as we rolled into the shorter days of fall.

One of our guys shook his head as I voiced my concern about meeting outside as the darkness began to descend earlier and earlier each week. "No, this is so nice. The strings of lights and the candles give us plenty of light. This is perfect." I listened as Jeff closed us in prayer, thanking God for our hunger for relationships and giving us the desire for community. Our conversation had gone later into the night than usual. Everyone had something to say as we discussed how men process reason while women combine reason with emotion and action. Everyone had an opinion and enjoyed the freedom to express it! We have been conversation-starved, and last night, in the candlelight, we feasted on a banquet of words as spirit connected to spirit.

In our current world of silence and separation, sitting under the spreading branch roof of wisteria in my front yard, gathered with others, was salt. Each thought expressed, adding flavor and enjoyment. Here, each person's voice speaking into the darkness was light. Salt and light. We gathered in Jesus's name to remind each other how to look more like him.

This is my prayer for us, dear reader. Lord, let us be your salt and goodness in this hungry world. May our words be your words to elevate, protect, and preserve, to offer a life that steps into eternity. Lord, let us be your light and your clarity in this dark world. Reach into the darkness around us, shining your light into every relationship and conversation. Lord, make me into your salt. Lord, make me into your light. Amen.

38

The Law and Our Broken Hearts

Read Matthew 5:17-37

We all have friendships and relationships that go much deeper than others. There are women I have been friends with for many years, but our relationship seems to hover close to the surface. Our conversations are very polite, and we touch on all the basic things going on in our lives, but we never go deep enough to need a flashlight to see what is under the covers. We share our lives but don't feel quite connected enough to share our hearts. And then there are those few friendships where we spill everything out and know we are safe and understood despite our messy thoughts and jumbled emotions. We don't hesitate to pull the band-aid off and inspect the wound.

Forgive me, Jesus, but this is where I think you are headed with this whole conversation about the law, anger, lust, divorce, oaths, and revenge. If we can make it through all that, we may be ready to hear what you say about loving your enemy.

During these last days of Jerusalem and the Jewish Temple system and sacrifice and priests and keeping the Law, a whole lot of people were just going through the motions. You might say they had a "friendly acquaintance-type" relationship with God and his Law. Lots of talk, lots of business - the subject of God and what he required was always on their mind, but their hearts were missing. If you pause to think about it, you might realize something was sad and broken underneath it all. Jesus came in to rip the band-aid off.

He came in the door, exposing the heart of the matter.

There were already rumors afoot that he had come to tear things down, break the law given to Moses, and dismantle the prophets' admonitions. "Oh, you couldn't be more wrong," he begins – looking his accusers in the eye. *"I have come to fulfill them!"* He seems to know what God's kingdom looks like from firsthand experience. And the essence of God's commands seems to be very much in effect there. He is adamant they will remain very much in effect here. Not only that, but he also seriously warns anyone who teaches others to disregard God's Law. And then he shocks them all with this impossibility – unless you are more *righteous* than the most virtuous person you know – you will never enter God's kingdom. Well, that is discouraging. We may as well give up and have a fine time tearing up the town.

And then, one by one, he holds up a command to the light. It is like a soap bubble of truth in his hand. He raises it for all to see; he turns it this way and that, examining it until you can see past the shiny surface and look deeply into and through it.

"*You have heard it said...*" he begins. "Oh yeah, of course, everyone knows you shall not murder," we think dismissively. "I would never do that!" (Exodus 20:13, Deuteronomy 5:17. ESV Note: The Hebrew word also means causing human death through carelessness or negligence.) Jesus knows murder starts not in the hands but in the heart. He brings up the real beginning of the problem: anger. Anger progresses to name-calling, accusations, and refusal to be reconciled. What makes you think you can have a relationship with God (offering your gift, seeking communion before his altar) if you refuse to heal the broken relationship with his child? Murder is the final act of anger. If you are holding on to anger, you are already in the middle of that running death leap. Well, that got our attention.

We were friends for a short time with a very vivacious couple. They were at the mercy of a wrong done against the husband through a business deal that had gone wrong. Their prayer request was that the judge would rule in their favor; the wife was adamant that it would be a monumental case that would change business practices. We gradually started noticing that this couple seemed to always be in the position of being taken advantage of. Were they too kind? Were they naïve to the ways of the world? We started to wonder what was going on. It didn't take but a moment's research to discover that this wasn't their first court case. They had a long history of suing their neighbors. Hidden underneath their innocent appearance, they nurtured angry, unforgiving hearts. Behind them was a long wake of destruction.

"You have heard it said..." Jesus continues, picking up the next bubble of truth. He looks deep into the heart of adultery and finds the first glance of lust. Man, is this ever a problem! How do we walk through this world without seeing something so appealing that it sends our thoughts off, running into darkened rooms where we shouldn't go? The human body can be pretty alluring. And desire is a powerful thing – really an irresistible drug in a way. It gets tangled up with worth and power and all sorts of little pots of wants and needs. The phrase "lustful intent" is the key to controlling this looming overwhelming danger. That's the way the ESV translates it. Intent. "What are your intentions, young man?" The answer we are waiting for here is "honorable" or "dishonorable." Does my look honor this person – or dishonor them and their family?

Many years ago, a dear pastor of mine preached that he had discovered that if he felt attracted to an attractive woman, his most effective response was to pray for that woman... and her husband. He had found that it was difficult to be drawn to desire if you were praying for the woman and her marriage. There is also the rule that I think many church leaders adopt of never being alone with a person of the opposite sex. It may seem extreme – but what they are doing is protecting themselves from "looking with lust." They are guarding their intentions by putting up strong guardrails. Dangerous distractions and going off the road through lust don't usually end there – it often takes us right into the consequences of dishonorable intentions; we crash into someone's heart and body we have no right to, we wreck our marriage, we destroy long-term happiness and joy. Which naturally connects to the adjoining bubble, divorce.

Marriage is exceptionally slippery and hard to hold onto. Divorce is more common than not. Adultery is one of the quickest ways to get there. I have known a small handful of women who have held on tightly and refused to let go when their husbands desired to abandon the marriage. I admire them for their love and determination. We can easily declare adamantly that "she should leave him." Take a step back, my well-meaning friends. This is not yours to advise. God is in the business of healing what is broken. That includes marriages. That includes trust. That includes sexuality. God desires healthy and whole relationships for us. Let him repair what we have broken.

I swear. Good Lord, I do. Here is an interesting one: *"Do not take an oath at all, either by heaven, for it is the throne of God, or by the earth, for it is his footstool..."* Well, that dismantles the whole practice of the "place your hand on the Bible and solemnly swear" procedure before you give your testimony in a court of law! The reasoning here by Jesus is so logical that you can't help but agree. Let your words and actions be truthful so your honor is never questioned. Your yes means yes. Your no means no. Yet, I have met people who live their lives tangled up in lies. There is never just one. I have heard experts describe how they are often clued into the falseness of someone who is lying. The liar tends to do a lot of "explaining." To paraphrase Shakespeare's famous line from *Hamlet*, "Me thinks he doth protest too much." Be careful of how you use your words; they are incredibly valuable – to you and those you speak to!

If we circle back to where we started, laying these insights over the relationships of acquaintance and deep friendship, I think Jesus, who knew the face of God and the rooms of his kingdom, wanted us to understand the depths of God's heart that we had been missing. Jesus knew that the attitude of just obeying the law was shortchanging us. We saw what was on the surface, just enough to say we knew this big God. Jesus knew there was so much more. He wanted us, the created, to know the heart and spirit of the Creator. He wanted us to enjoy the freedom that comes from a secure and deep relationship with our great and mighty God. Face to face, heart to heart. What kind of relationship do you want with the Father? Look closely at the words of his Son – he can take you there.

39

The Law Only God Can Keep

Read Matthew 5:38-48; Luke 6:27-36

"Say you are sorry," I demand from the driver's seat as I glance into my rearview mirror, trying to catch my son's eye. The cars in front of me change lanes, slow down, and speed up, positioning themselves to exit the interstate and preparing to turn right or left. It is rush hour traffic, and everyone is anxious to get home after work and wherever else they have all been. I am tired. My two young ones in the back are tired. But I am sure I must teach them admission of wrongdoing, humility, and the path back to healing by apologizing. My son remains silent. Angry. Refusing to let those words come from his mouth. And his heart.

I am adamant. My voice becomes more demanding and more insistent. "Say you are sorry right now." This scenario is nothing new. These two siblings know exactly how to torment each other. Locked into seatbelts just an arm's length away from each other, she uses her words and facial expressions; he uses his longer arm to strike the first blow. She lets out a wail. He gets in trouble. I try to referee. We spent way too many years locked in this unproductive pattern.

I tried many solutions to help them deal with their frustration with each other. I once placed them in two chairs, facing each other – forbidding them to get up until they had worked things out. I had read of something similar in teaching warring siblings to resolve their anger. (I think in the magazine article, the kids had ended up giggling and making faces at each other, and everyone lived happily ever after from that moment on.) I stepped outside to the front yard to talk with a neighbor. You know this isn't going to end well, don't you? After about ten minutes, I could hear the two screaming at each other on the other side of the glass and brick wall. They did not work things out. Faces red, their anger had escalated off the charts. My mistake. Left to their own devices, they could only see their point of view. I don't think they liked each other very much until high school – maybe college!

It is common popular thinking to "Just go with your heart…" You hear it spoken differently, from "Trust your feelings" to "Make yourself happy." God knows this is terrible advice. Listen to what he taught through the prophet Jeremiah.

The heart is deceitful above all things
and beyond cure.
Who can understand it?
"I the Lord search the heart
and examine the mind,
to reward each person according to their conduct,
according to what their deeds deserve."
Jeremiah 17:9-10 NIV

The heart desires what the heart desires. It has no concern for anything else. If you live your life only listening to the desires of your heart, you will leave hurt, pain, and destruction in your path. And you won't be too happy either. Oh, baby, I have been there. The heart is very good at lying to you. God knows this. He tells you – don't trust it – your own heart will deceive you.

If your sister has just whispered something mean and hurtful into your ear, your first response is to hurt her back. It is instantaneous—a knee-jerk reaction. If a stranger has hurt you, it is easy to retaliate without thinking too much about it beforehand. After all, doesn't God instruct an eye for an eye and a tooth for a tooth? Go ahead and hit them back. Hold on a minute! This is where it is good to go back and look at these instructions in context.

Exodus (21:23-25) and Leviticus (24:19-21) were guidelines for the Jewish court system not to allow the punishment for a crime to exceed the original crime. If you read only the familiar part of the scripture in Leviticus, you get this: *"Anyone who injures their neighbor is to be injured in the same manner: fracture for fracture, eye for eye, tooth for tooth. The one who has inflicted the injury must suffer the same injury (NIV)."* This applies equally to foreigners and native-born people. If you look at the context in Exodus, it is referencing a pregnant woman who is hit when people are fighting, goes into labor prematurely, and there is serious injury! Her husband and the court work together to decide the punishment for the offender. If you read through the laws of the ancient Hebrews, you realize these were laws of protection and limitations to help a society determine what was just and unjust. They were the bare minimums of establishing morality for a large group of immoral people - people discovering what the One God they were following required. His justice was extreme. Go ahead and read through the laws of Leviticus. I am pretty sure you don't want to go back there.

Our laws are based on those Mosaic laws. Yet we who follow Jesus know how the focus shifted when Jesus showed up. "Yes," he said. "You have heard it said, an eye for an eye – but I say, if anyone slaps your right cheek, give him the other cheek to slap also." This is extreme submission. I don't know how many can respond to a slap this way unless Jesus is in the mix. Unless our submission is first to God and his righteousness, his justice.

Dr. Martin Luther King, who was primarily a man of God's Word, followed this teaching to dismantle the racial discrimination of the twentieth century. He insisted that everyone walking with him in protest turn and offer the other cheek. They did not fight back when they were slapped and beaten, water-hosed, and attacked by dogs. Their ability to receive attack willingly was so powerful that it was televised into America's living rooms, changing the course of history. I am sure God walked with them to expose evil as evil.

Jesus spoke to people who were living under Roman military rule. He was talking to people who their own religious leaders were often abusing. They were in a position of powerlessness; to fight back was a death wish or banishment. Oddly, to refuse to fight back physically against evil gave them power over wrong. Again, look at what the reaction to prejudice did in the 1960s in Selma, Alabama. "You are hitting me, and I am receiving it; my grace exposes and overshadows your evil." It was a reaction that was entirely against human nature. It turned the world upside down. It pointed to something supernatural. To someone supernatural. Then and now.

The reaction to the action here is to *give* instead of to take. If they demand one cheek to slap, offer your other cheek too. If they require your inner garment, give them your outer one as well! (In the ancient world, this would leave you naked and cold, my friends!). If they demand you carry their load for one mile, insist on going two with them. (This referenced the practice of a soldier temporarily conscripting a commoner to carry equipment). If they ask, insist, demand, force, sue, or beg, the recommended response is to give. I think Jesus is warming up to the idea that will become revolutionary in his message: lay down your life for another.

Okay, I know what you are thinking. Well, maybe if I love that person, I could do that. Or the more philosophical among us are thinking – maybe if it was for a "just cause," I could react that way. Ha! Jesus is not going to let us off so quickly. And here it comes, the showstopper statement: *"But I say to you, Love your enemies and pray for those who persecute you...*" That is where most of us draw the line, walk away, and ignore that our ears have ever heard such a thing. Because let's be honest here – it is so much easier to hate our enemies and savor speaking against them - to daydream of revenge. Love them? "That is pretty impossible," we think if we are being honest.

And then Jesus explains why. If we love the unlovable, the evil ones who are our enemy – if we are praying for good for the ones we hate – the ones who are hating us and persecuting us, then we begin looking like our all-powerful, all-loving Father. We must – not optional – we must be *perfect*, as our Father in heaven is perfect. Shoot. How in the world are we supposed to do this?

The simple answer is we can't. We can't be perfect like God. We can't love like God. We can't forgive like God. We can't forget like God. We can't turn the other cheek, give all we have, walk the extra mile carrying the additional burden, give to everyone who asks, and loan to everyone who borrows. There would be nothing left of us. Exactly. I think that is precisely his point. Give yourself away. In doing so, you become more like your Father.

We will see it soon enough. Jesus will show us how it is done. He will turn his cheek to receive the kiss of his friend and betrayer, Judas. He will turn his other cheek to his enemies in Roman uniforms as he is slapped and mocked and spit upon. He will be stripped naked to receive the cuts of the whip. He will carry the heavy weight of the cross up the hill to the place of death. He will give his life to beggars who can never repay him. He will loan his innocence of guilt to the guilty. He will love his enemies and pray for those who persecute him. He will be tortured and bleed and die, a prisoner of his enemy, a criminal against his people.

Why did he do it? How did he do it? I don't know.

Maybe Jesus looked so much like his Father that he was. That's what he seemed to say, anyway: "If you have seen me, you have seen my Father." (John 14:9). What is really scary is that he tells us to do the same things he is doing. I don't know how to do that. Do you? I don't know that I want to. Is it time to turn around before the going gets rough? But then again, I don't know that demanding an eye for an eye is the way to go, either. I see the people shouting that in the streets these days, which doesn't end well either.

I am to love those who hate me? I will need a lot of practice to pull off this admonition to look more like my Father. This command to refuse to seek revenge or demand earthly justice is just too difficult. I will need to keep my eyes on this teacher Jesus. I think he is telling me to stop holding on so tightly. To let go, to turn, to give.

Loving those you love is hard. Loving those you hate is revolutionary. Redirecting defeated people to let go of the fairness of the law and choose to love beyond the law was the teaching of a madman. It is a complete wonder we ever heard this here on the other side of the world two thousand years later.

Our gospel writer, Luke, ties this all up neatly with a beautiful bow. Looking more like your God requires you to *look closely at your God.* And this is what you will observe: He gives, expecting nothing in return. He is kind to the ungrateful. He is merciful to the wicked. Yes, I want to look more like this God Most High. This may require me to look less at myself and less at my neighbors. I remember again the mess I made when I forced my kids to sit facing each other. It was impossible to reach that place of love, kindness, and mercy on their own. There must be a better way; I guess I better be careful to keep my eyes focused on Jesus – because his eyes are on God.

"But to you who are listening I say:
Love your enemies,
do good to those who hate you,
bless those who curse you,
pray for those who mistreat you.

But love your enemies,
do good to them,
and lend to them without expecting to get anything back.

Then your reward will be great,
and you will be children of the Most High,
because he is kind to the ungrateful and wicked."
Luke 6:27-28, 35 NIV

40

Talking to the Secret God

Read Matthew 6:1-18

Well, here we are at this prayer of Jesus. How many of us were taught the Lord's Prayer as a child? Why did Jesus think it was necessary to model prayer for us? If I slow down and concentrate on these words beat by beat, maybe it will help me see the heart of the relationship between Father God and temporarily earth-bound Son.

Jesus started with the warning to be careful of your motives for righteousness, be aware of how you give, and be aware of how you pray. He will bookend this upcoming prayer with the same warnings concerning fasting. Are you doing these things to look righteous before your neighbor? Is one eye on your fellow man in need and your other eye on that person you would like to impress? Do I elevate myself with pride in my generosity and the lovely sound of my poetic prayers that have a subtle undercurrent of self-righteousness? Is fasting a burden? Or is it a virtue signal that I am holy? These warnings give me pause.

Within these warnings, Jesus brings up the idea of the secret God. The one who is there in the quiet of the sunrise and the still of the day. The one who is there with you alone. What do conversations with this God who sees you in secret look like? I first discovered this secret God as a teenager and needed to pour my newly broken heart out. Teenage girls discover love, hurt, hope, and disappointment in such raw doses that they dare not speak of their pain to another human. For me, the prayers of a shepherd boy, defeated warrior, rejected friend named David were salve for my soul. My first Bible readings on my own were the Psalms of David. He poured out his heart with sorrow and frustration – yet he praised the power and righteousness of his God. I learned from his written prayers the sweet presence of this secret God.

Jesus starts his prayer with a warning and a promise: Do not heap up empty phrases (as the Gentiles do!) because your Father *knows* what you need before you ask him. So why bother praying if God already knows our needs? It is because we need to know what we need. Often, I am unaware of my heart's longings until I spend time talking it out with my Father. It is a conversation that deepens a relationship. I talk. He listens. He guides my thoughts, and I listen. His Spirit moves within me, opening my eyes to the unseen truth, challenging my complaints, righting my wrong thinking, clarifying my confusion, telling me to act, and silencing me to wait. And sometimes insisting that I act on something I did not intend to do.

Jesus begins his prayer with the most intimate opening connection: father to child. I am reminded of a fall night a few years ago. I had walked out under the dark sky of the Blue Ridge Mountains, stars piercing through the black, a fire illuminating the circle of chairs waiting for us there. In one chair, my nephew sat, his daughter leaning against him, stretching out her long legs, his arms wrapped around her as they talked. This is father. This is child. Is this what Jesus thought of as he remembered times with his heavenly Father, stretched out, surrounded by the stars of the universe, embraced in his arms?

In one little pronoun, Jesus included us in this intimate relationship. He didn't say "my"—he said "our"—our Father. We are invited into this sweet, welcoming relationship. Unbelievable. But to balance the familiarity, there is the majesty—in heaven, above all the unknown universe—his name, his essence, is to be respected, revered, and kept holy above all other names. We are never to use his name carelessly. We are never to take his presence for granted.

He is King above all creation. His will is always accomplished in his kingdom, his home, his heaven. We are reminded to ask that the same may be accomplished here.

This is the problem, isn't it? On that first day, he gave us freedom and choice. We took that freedom and ran with it—straight into the dangers of another's arms. His will is often undone on our earth; it is a good first request that his will be accomplished instead of our own.

Then we have the reminder that our sustenance – the most basic need, food to nourish us – requires more than the work of our hands; it requires the grace and mercy of our God. The Israelites first learned this hard lesson in the wilderness on the other side of the river of captivity. They looked at the vast land with the far horizon and realized for the first time what it was to be alone. And empty-handed. Everything they needed would need to be provided by… well, to complete that thought, they had to open their hands and let go of any illusion of self-provision. Everything they needed would come from God. Guidance from the cloud. Water flowing from the rock. Manna falling from the heavens.

Manna. It would fall from the sky. It would taste sweet. It would last for one day unless needed to carry over to their non-working day of the Sabbath. Give us this day – just one day at a time – our bread for the day.

Jesus reminded them and God of their utter dependency on him. The following request is equally life-giving: forgiveness. It is food for the soul. Again, it is something only God can provide.

I grew up in a Baptist church. I went to first grade at Our Savior Lutheran Church school, where we recited this prayer every morning in chapel, so I have never known which noun to use to describe this vast chasm of separation; is it *sin, debts,* or *transgressions*? I am reading the ESV translation this rainy morning, and I will use their word from Matthew, *debts*. Our debts are something we owe one another. No doubt it needs to be paid, but we are beggars, penniless, destitute, empty-handed, and cannot make amends.

I think of a time when a friend hurt me. Our relationship was damaged. I held that hurt close and her distant. I wanted to forgive her and return to the sweet fellowship we once had, but I sat frozen, refusing to offer up my heart again. I wanted her to acknowledge the destruction she had caused. It festered in my thoughts like an unhealed wound. I walked around limping with a skinned knee, the blood still fresh.

Why did I hold so tightly to this hurt? Pride—stinking, filthy pride. It is easier to mourn a hemorrhaging broken relationship than to do what Jesus reminds me is the healing antiseptic: to forgive. First, I will offer my broken heart to God, asking for forgiveness from him. And I must forgive her even if she doesn't ask, even if she never acknowledges the loss of the sand emptying out of the hourglass. *"Forgive us our debts, as we also have forgiven our debtors."* Oh no. I seem to be the one who needs forgiveness!

I am reminded that our debts, sins, and trespasses are not against our family, friends, neighbors, or acquaintances, but against our One and Only God. We answer to him for all separations and offenses. Our trespass is against God when we refuse to forgive.

I am reminded of the fine women and men in Charleston who forgave the troubled boy who sat in their midst and then murdered their mothers and fathers, their sisters and brothers. They cried and mourned and forgave. I am reminded of a man who would hang on a cross, stripped of all worth, naked and bleeding and struggling with great effort to speak as he took his last breaths, saying to his Father, *"Forgive them… for they know not what they do."* This needs to be my prayer with every resentful, debt-counting breath: "Forgive them, forgive me… for we know not what we do."

Next in this prayer comes the big request that we say so quickly by rote that we dare not consider it for long: *"And lead us not into temp-*

tation..." My goodness, does God do that - lead us into temptation? It appears he allows it. I think of the conversation between Satan and God about Job (Job 1:6-12). It also appears God gives his permission for his own Spirit to lead us there; Jesus experienced this firsthand. He had sought out his cousin John for baptism, and immediately after God proclaimed his approval of Jesus's obedience, Jesus journeyed into the wilderness. Satan met him there. He tempted him with all manner of gilded opportunities. Promises and lies all wrapped up together. Jesus knew about being led into temptation. Jesus knew about being delivered from the almost irresistible power of evil.

We need to see this enormous need for ourselves. Note to self: pray daily to recognize if God is allowing me to be led into the heart of darkness. If so, he does it with great purpose: to test, strengthen, guide, and direct me. I will need his power to resist the devil. I remember his warnings to us through Cain's story: "Sin is crouching at your door. It desires to have you. You must rule over it" (Genesis 4:7).

Some translations of Matthew do not include the prayer sign-off (the doxology) that most of us know by heart: *"For Yours is the kingdom and the power and the glory forever. Amen (NKJV)."* The earliest texts from the fourth century do not include it... and do include it! This doxology was believed to be used in worship as early as the first century – although it may not have been part of the original text.[1] The use of it varies among the Catholic Church and Protestant denominations. You can spend hours researching it, with valid points in every opinion. For me, it is the final reminder of Who we are talking to. We are leaving our hopes, desires, and requests with the King of the kingdom, who is sovereign overall. We are laying down everything at the feet of the Powerful One who spoke the universe into being – from the granite mountains to the down feathers of the most delicate bird. We are looking for fulfillment from the glorious God who fills the heavens with his light and creates angel song. And not just for the day – like the temporary portion of bread – but forever like forgiveness, which only God can provide. *"For Yours is the kingdom and the power and the glory forever. Amen."*

Amen. Our grandson, at two, was learning to say the blessing before we ate. He would reach out to hold our hands, listening intently with eyes closed, waiting until we reached the end to shout out, affirming his agreement with a long, drawn-out "A-men!" Let it be so! May it be true. May it stand as a covenant between us and our Father!

This, my friends, is prayer. This is what talking to your Father looks like. What a beautiful gift. What a glorious adventure. It is simple. It is powerful. It is yours. And all the children said, "Amen!"

David's Prayer as They Made Offerings for the Temple

Therefore David blessed the Lord in the presence of all the assembly.
And David said:
"Blessed are you, O Lord, the God of Israel our father,
forever and ever.
Yours, O Lord, is the greatness and the power and the glory
and the victory and the majesty,
for all that is in the heavens and in the earth is yours.
Yours is the kingdom, O Lord, and you are exalted as head above all.
Both riches and honor come from you, and you rule over all.
In your hand are power and might,
and in your hand it is to make great and to give strength to all.
And now we thank you, our God, and praise your glorious name.

"But who am I, and what is my people,
that we should be able thus to offer willingly?
For all things come from you, and of your own have we given you.
For we are strangers before you and sojourners,
as all our fathers were.
Our days on the earth are like a shadow, and there is no abiding.

O Lord our God,
all this abundance that we have provided for building
you a house for your holy name
comes from your hand and is all your own.
I know, my God, that you test the heart
and have pleasure in uprightness.
In the uprightness of my heart I have freely offered all these things,
and now I have seen your people, who are present here,
offering freely and joyously to you.

O Lord, the God of Abraham, Isaac, and Israel, our fathers,
keep forever such purposes and thoughts in the hearts of your people,
and direct their hearts toward you."
1 Chronicles 29:10-18

41

Treasure Search

Read Matthew 6:19-34

I am really at a loss with numbers. I just can't remember them. They are slippery things that slide around, refusing to gain purchase in my brain. Point of fact: neither Jeff nor I can remember how long we have been married. I just can't get that very important date to memory! Isn't that ridiculous? But there is one date I remember as a touchstone. It really isn't a day - it is a whole year: 2009. I remember that year as if it is burned into my soul; it was a year filled with day after day of loss.

It started in January. I had built a career in a business that is based on temporary contract work. I had one client through one production company that had sustained me financially for several years. It was a comfortable relationship, and we did good work together. I had sensed that the tide was changing – and it did. They had hired a new producer who had decided that the most talented people lived in New York. I did not. Work would no longer be coming my way. Okay. Open my hands and let the sand slip through.

February, my husband lost his job, along with 2,000 other employees, as his company restructured and closed its southern division. He had worked there since he was 17, climbing from the loading dock to

Vice President. It was a stunning event. My husband had always been our stability and constant. The world he had worked in for so many years was getting much smaller, and finding a way to start over would be very difficult.

March brought challenging situations for our children, who were on the verge of graduating from high school and wading through college. Out of respect for their privacy, I won't begin to list the heartbreaks there, but we found ourselves in all sorts of meetings with mentors, principals, coaches, psychiatrists, and lawyers. It was not good. I cried a lot.

There were four car accidents. They had a common thread: either we rear-ended someone, or they rear-ended us. One was a hit-and-run. And, oh yeah, we had to put our dog to sleep—Sweetie, who had shown up when our daughter was four.

The last week of May, a windstorm tore through my mother's yard in Greenville, South Carolina, while she was visiting me in Atlanta, Georgia. Seven trees came down, pines and oaks all tangled together in such a destructive dance that the local news came to film the aftermath. With the power down, cousins showed up to clean out my mother's freezer and refrigerator, to negotiate with the power company, to schedule the tree guy to begin removing the trees – all of this without her asking – or even knowing at the time.

When we discovered all that had happened, we decided my mother should stay with me until things got sorted out. We prayed a prayer of gratitude that she had not been in her house when the trees came crashing down. She asked innocently, "I wonder what will happen next?" We didn't have to wait long. That evening at 7:20 in my backyard, she suffered a stroke, fell and cut her head on a terracotta planter on her way down, and died at Emory Hospital 40 hours later. I think I was in shock. It was June 1. We had not even made it through half the year, and I was over my head, drowning in loss.

That was a year of having everything I held onto tightly ripped from my hands. God's Word spoke to me through texts from my best friends and passages I had taped to the inside of my laundry room door. I learned what praying without ceasing looked like. With my sword raised high, I strapped on the armor of God and went into battle, swinging with all my might. I was humbled, I was strengthened, I was oddly comforted and at peace amid the attacks that continued to batter our home and our hearts.

This is where I go when I think of my treasure: the year 2009. It was a year of losing so very much, yet through it all—the fear and heartbreak—I knew my God was with me. As the song goes, "You never let go of me." My eyes were on him, and he held onto me.

If I read this passage about laying up treasures, I can start condemning myself for my preoccupation with earthly "wealth." Yes, sometimes I feel anxiety over the physical, tangible things like where we live, what we eat, or how we clothe ourselves. And when I read this admonition to consider God's provision for the birds of the air and his glory on loan to the lilies of the field, I wonder if we are being too worldly when we save and invest our money to provide for the future. I don't think that is the meaning here.

Here is the big question: "… and which of you, by all your worry, add a single hour to your life?" (Matthew 6:27). When I found my mother unconscious and bleeding on the ground, my immediate thought I could not let go of was: "If I can just go back in time three minutes… I could stop this from happening." It was a thought that continued to haunt me until my wise older sister forced me three days later to revisit where my mother had fallen. "You did not do this. You could not change this," she lovingly insisted. And I knew it was true. We small humans work so hard to hold onto this world. Jesus was telling us – this world is not your treasure – your treasure is hidden somewhere else.

Your treasure is with God in his heavenly Kingdom. It is held in safekeeping for you there.

Everything we hold on to so tightly here is already moth-eaten and rusting. It is already in the hands of the thieves. It is already withering and ready for the fire. Our eyes search for treasure here in these temporary things. Jesus tells us to look to the Creator of light; let him fill our whole lives with the health and wealth of what is eternal. And an incredible promise is here: Your heavenly Father already knows what you need. He already knows about the temporary things you need while you are here in this temporary place.

God was showing me in my year of loss that my treasure was not in the work of our hands, or mental health, or educational success, or physical safety, or any of the things that I thought I depended on. No one was under my control; I could not preserve the well-being of my husband, children, or mother. Like Job, I learned that God remained when the things I held tightly were being turned upside down. Seek God and his righteousness, Jesus advises us. What I was seeing on this physical earth did not seem right. But I knew with absolute certainty my God was righteous – so that is where I stood.

I did not need to ask what would befall me the next day – I knew there would be enough trouble waiting behind door number three. Best to stay standing on the firm foundation where I was and let God work out the details of tomorrow. Best to keep my eyes on him and his light. Best to trust him to know what I *really* needed. I learned my treasures would never be safe here in this world. It would be best to store my true treasures in his House in his kingdom - along with my heart.

42

The Hardest Teachings

Read Matthew 7:1-6; Luke 6:37-42

I am picking up these challenging words of Jesus after laying them aside for a long while. Reading stories of healings and miracles is easy and pleasant, but these teachings on the mountain hit hard against my soul. And here it is again today—something I don't want to hear because I know too well that he is speaking directly to me. *"Judge not."*

Do not judge. This is my struggle. It is the self-righteous clothing I slip into over and over again, casually judging others—strangers who walk by me, my dear ones who sit next to me. What is Jesus's meaning when he tells us not to judge? I roll it over in my mind. My version of judging is measuring, holding something up to examine it closely to compare it with possible perfection. More likely than not, it will not be perfect.

What did Jesus have in mind with this warning? Was he talking about judging according to the Law of Moses? Was he talking about judging another's unseen morals, like looking for the dark sin staining their souls? Or was he addressing what was visible on the outside - their actions? Their appearance? Just what should we be careful not to judge?

Our friend Luke elaborates: Do not judge or condemn - and he instructs us on what we should do: forgive. Do not judge *others*, do not condemn *others*, forgive *others*. Can I add that specific noun, *others*, to help me? And that leads to the rest of the thought: Do not judge others, and God will not judge me. Do not condemn others, and God will not condemn me. Forgive others, and God will forgive me.

God alone is our judge. We take what is his when we step into his place and sit on his throne of judgment.

This is the sin that seeks me out personally every single day—measuring myself against the others around me. The problem is that someone ends up rising above, and someone ends up falling below. It could be me or them. Either way, it is a problem.

Luke continues the words of Jesus: "Give and it will be given to you." With the measure you use, it will be measured back to you. The question here is, "Am I generous, or am I stingy?" I love the illustration here of a good measure, pressed down, running over, poured into your lap. It is a description of generosity. Abundance.

There is a locally owned ice cream stand in our neighborhood. We went there quite often when the kids were young. High school teenagers worked there. Occasionally, you would have a young kid distractedly talking to her co-worker as she dipped your ice cream. She would balance the scoop loosely on the top of the cone without pushing any into the funnel, meaning you ended up with very little ice cream. But most of the time, you were greeted by a cheerful teen who pressed the ice cream deep into the funnel of the cone, scooped again, pushed the cold cream hard until it filled the mouth of the cone, and then scooped again, pressing it all together into a glorious, almost overflowing, rounded mountain of mint chocolate chip, before looking you joyfully in the eye and handing it carefully through the window. I have never had too much ice cream. "That will be two dollars, please."

This is God's version of our relationships with others: overflowing, yummy ice cream. Giving, forgiving, not judging, not condemning.

His illustration of our self-righteous judgment is our attempt to get a teeny tiny splinter out of our friend's eye while we are blind with a fat stick stuck in our own. We need to attend to our own blindness first. Often, it is hard to see our faults. We grow numb to the pain in our eyes. "Slow down," Jesus tells us. Take a good look at yourself before attempting surgery on someone else. And I must remind myself – I probably don't know the whole story of how my friend ended up with that splinter in their eye in the first place. Perhaps I need to ask more questions. Maybe I need to hear their voice before voicing my own.

And thrown smack up against this is a cautionary warning: "Do not cast your pearls before swine." I like that old-fashioned-sounding King James version. "Do not throw your pearls to the pigs" is a more contemporary version. "Lest they turn to trample you." We are told not to judge, but we are called to be discerning. We are wise to read a situation, to be aware of someone's character, and to keep precious things protected from those who only seek to harm and destroy.

I would not trust my pearls, my precious innocent children, to the care of a neighbor with a questionable reputation. Or a family member who made me uncomfortable for some intuitive reason. I would not disclose my heart concerns with a woman I have noticed to delight in gossip or who speaks with an undercurrent of superiority. I would not share precious truths the Holy Spirit was teaching my raw heart with a co-worker who thinks God is a delusion and a crutch for the ignorant.

My limited experience with swine was watching my nephew's two hogs devour the turkey carcasses one evening after Thanksgiving dinner. It was very violent and very loud. They continued stomping the mud and rooting for remnants with their snouts. I was thankful for the strong fence that separated us as they threw their full weight against each other, looking for that last morsel.

Be wise with what is rare and precious. The hogs will be unaware of the difference between a priceless pearl and a turkey bone.

These teachings are difficult to hold on to and follow, so I will pause here. I will think about my judging nature and try to return that heavy responsibility to God. I will think about forgiveness without measure. Who am I holding myself back from after feeling the prick of their words and the sting of their slap? I have difficulty forgetting the hurt, so I will take it to my Father, who can forgive me so that I may forgive others. I will look with generosity into the faces of others. I will open my arms in abundance the same way my Father does. I will slow down and replace criticism with compassion. But I will be wise and discerning, placing my precious pearls in willing hands and careful hearts. That should be enough for this day.

43

Knocking on the Door, The Golden Rule, The Narrow Gate, Smiling Wolves, Rotten Fruit, and Sinking Sand

Read Matthew 7:7-29; Luke 6:43-49

I grew up in the country. It wasn't deep country – in 10 minutes, we could walk the downtown streets of Greenville – but in my community, houses sat on large stretches of property surrounded by pastureland, peach orchards, cotton fields, and woods. Our neighbors across the street had big barns and chickens, and they got a gentle old horse named Lucy. That started it. Soon every kid around was begging their parents for a horse or pony.

Of course, I asked. I dreamed of having one. I would canter to the mailbox when my mother asked me to get the mail. But I didn't believe that in a million years, my parents would get me one. A horse was an expensive ask, and my parents were not extravagant people.

I was amazed when Daddy delighted in searching out and buying a high-spirited, beautiful pinto pony. I named him Apache and spent summer days riding him through pastures and across fields, trailing behind my cousins on their horses. I honestly did not deserve such a fine gift.

Jesus tells us our Father's generosity may surprise us. Go ahead and ask. He delights in giving.

Seek him and his will, and you will find a sweet relationship, divine direction, and godly guidance. Knock on his door, and don't stop knocking until that door opens. I need to learn this. I need to live here with my arms stretched wide, expecting to receive. Why am I so afraid I will be disappointed, discouraged, defeated?

I think of the three-year-olds in my life. They ask for a lot! And they get most of it – because they ask for what I desire to give them: good things. Now, if they take off out the door without me, grab a handful of cookies out of the package, or stomp their little feet as their voice escalates into a high-pitched wail, it is a different story. Jesus tells us God is much the same, only better. Do not be afraid to ask, to seek, to knock on God's door with our requests – we may find it is open – and he has been waiting there for us all along.

Whenever I think of the Golden Rule, I think of a fire station on the corner of East North Street and Stone Avenue. I don't know if my memory is correct, but I think we took a field trip there in the first grade at Our Savior Lutheran Church. I remember enormous red firetrucks and firemen dressed in navy blue handing out little wooden rulers with "Do Unto Others As You Would Have Them Do Unto You" printed in bold gold letters along the 12-inch straight edge.

That idea was ingrained in me from school to church to family life. It has always been part of my understanding of how life should look. It was unquestioned. It was an unchanging given. Always treat others well. Care about them as much as you care about yourself. If everyone were taught this simple and pure rule in early childhood, most of our problems would be solved. And Jesus thought the same thing. At the end of this statement, he included, as if it was the exclamation point that concluded the matter, *"This sums up the Law and the Prophets (NIV)."*

He will say it another way at another time,

"'Love the Lord your God with all your heart and with all your soul and with all your mind.' This is the first and greatest commandment. And the second is like it:
'Love your neighbor as yourself.'
All the Law and the Prophets hang on these two commandments."
Matthew 22:37-40 NIV

In other words, love with your whole being – and let your actions reflect that love. When you do this, you satisfy the requirements of every law of God.

And then comes the warning: this gate built with love is narrow. To walk through it is difficult. It is much easier to take the wide, well-traveled road. Looking out for yourself and pushing others aside is much easier. And keep your eyes averted from the ones fallen into the ditch.

I know that road. I have been there. It is the yellow brick road heading to the Emerald City. Success is just around the corner. Emotions are your guide, and it is easy to justify your actions. Concentrate on what is right for you. Because you deserve to be happy. You only have one chance at this game called life, right?

If this is the road you are on, I hope you stub your toe, sit down long enough to nurse your wounds, and realize you are heading in the wrong direction. You are on the wrong path. It is never too late to turn around. There is even an excellent word for it: repentance. It will get you going in the right direction to the right destination.

Jesus tells you something else about that wide pathway: there are ravenous wolves there, dressed in sheep's clothing. They look good, speak well, appeal to your heart, and ask for your trust. It is incredibly difficult to see the dark intentions behind their smooth appearance. They will deceive many. Jesus did not wish for us to be fooled. He gave us a clear illustration from nature: look for the fruit.

My uncles shared a large cow pasture down the road from our house. It was where my pony Apache grazed, along with my cousin Jill's pony and herds of cows. It was a wonderful playground for the kids in the neighborhood. We would climb over the wooden gate and take off running across the rolling hills. There were springs to the left where the cows found water, and we caught tadpoles. A long line of trees was at the top of the hill near the far end, where we could find shade on a hot summer day. We made hiding places among the tall red grasses and knew to avoid the beautiful purple thistles with their spikey thorns. We were always barefoot.

Jesus warned that grapes do not grow on thornbushes; thistles do not produce sweet figs. I think of people who show up in the public realm who appear to wear the robes of a religious teacher, yet their words mock the teaching of God's Word. They smile and have a loyal following, yet their fruit is sharp with the death of the innocent, and their flower is formed by self-righteous arrogance. Their scent is the rotting fruit of destruction, overtaking anyone who disagrees with them. Oddly, those who agree with them are rotting and don't even know it. These are the wolves. Do not be deceived. Look at their fruit. Does it look like God's good fruit?

Following on the heels of the deceptive wolf are the most terrifying words I can imagine, *"I never knew you; depart from me."* I never knew you. This should strike terror in your heart. Does Jesus recognize you? Does he know your name? Do you spend time seeking him? Do you sit with him, sharing your thoughts, concerns, joys, and sorrows? Do you listen to him? Have you said "yes" to his invitation, *"Come, follow me"*? Or is your knowledge of Jesus second-hand?

There are deceiving substitutions some have made for a genuine relationship with Jesus. We think it is good enough that "our momma knows him." We went to church while growing up. We are busy doing good work that he would approve of. If asked, we may identify ourselves as Christian. But do we know him personally? Does he know us? If you have said yes to his invitation to follow him and have a relationship with him, he has changed you. There is a "before" and an "after." It is as evident as the man who once was blind and now can see. He has opened your eyes. He has opened your ears. He has opened your hands. He has opened your heart. He has changed your mind. You cannot know Jesus and remain unchanged.

Jesus was very clear about who he was. *"I am the way and the truth and the life. No one comes to the Father except through me. If you really know me, you will know my Father as well" (John 14:6,7a NIV).* That is the key to doing the will of God the Father; it is by walking through the door of his Son, Jesus. The most significant change from before to after is that we no longer seek to do our own will – to find our own path. We seek the will of our Father - and we walk his path. And that way can only be found through the gate of the Son.

Through that gate, there is solid ground—a firm foundation. Walking there, our actions will begin to find footing on the words of Jesus. His teaching can be trusted; it is unchanging truth. Jesus would be the cornerstone the prophets had foretold. He would be the perfect stone that all the other stones would line up against to form a solid and trustworthy foundation. Without Jesus to build on, the house is weak, the foundation crumbling.

Have you ever had a time when your world seemed to be falling apart? Things and people you rested on, depended on, were suddenly gone or too weak to stand? In the dark night, I have found that Jesus is still there. He is whispering wisdom and assurance. He is our rock, our sure foundation. Build on his truth, his righteousness alone. The house you build on his foundation will stand against the most terrible storm. The house built on the foundation of your own strength will crumble like sand when the rains begin to fall.

When Jesus said his amens and rose to leave for the day, the great crowds of people were astonished. They were speechless. No one – even their most educated scholars and devout leaders – had ever taught like this. Something was profoundly different about Jesus.

He spoke with knowledge. He also spoke with authority. Every word had power.

His teaching was something new. Something revolutionary. Who could possibly do the things he was teaching? Who could have known these things? This is more than following the Law. This is, I don't know - dare we say it - *better*?

44

Surprising Faith, Generous Mercy

Read Matthew 8:5-13; Luke 7:1-17

It is difficult to understand the separation between the Jewish people and the Romans. It is difficult to understand the separation between these Hebrews and everyone else. We need to understand the absolute line of separation placed around God's Chosen People, or we will miss much of their story. What separated them was their Law – God's commandments for them. Every moment of every day was defined by it.

The Law given to Moses was established so the Hebrew people would know their God was a holy and perfect God. These new commandments were given to them as they came out of captivity in Egypt to teach them how to be his people; God knew it would be all too enticing to enter Canaan and blend in with the native people there. Their natural desire would be to embrace that culture, marry their beautiful daughters, and bow down to their pagan gods. If they did, within a generation, they would no longer be a chosen people with a chosen purpose, worshipping the one true God. So, God placed a hedge around them with his Law.

His Law taught them what to eat and how to prepare their food. It taught them about disease and cleanliness. It addressed what clothing they wore and forbade ornate hair ornaments and tattoos – in other words, looking like their neighbors. It taught them how to gauge morality, raise their children, treat their neighbor, care for their parents, and honor their business associates. Above all, the Law set apart the Jewish people to be specifically dedicated to God and an exclusive community. Anything possibly assimilating them into those who did not keep the Law was considered "unclean." Their never-ending goal was to stay "clean" and holy, as their God was "clean" and holy.

To worship God and enter his presence, one must be clean by perfectly obeying his law. Every person who had broken the law was deemed unclean and could not be part of worship or part of the Jewish community until they had made the necessary sacrifices to become clean again. Every person outside the law was unclean. Every Roman was definitely unclean! If a Jewish person touched or was touched by a non-Jewish person, then they became unclean. They would have to go through very elaborate procedures and make a specific sacrifice at the Temple to be declared clean again by the priests. It was a timely and costly offense.

So here we are with this little situation with the centurion. In the eyes of the ancient Jews, it is more complicated than we Gentiles of modern times understand. A Roman, non-Jewish centurion has requested a Jewish rabbi to heal his servant. We need to pause for a moment to understand who a centurion is.

Centurion meant "captain of 100," responsible for over 100 foot soldiers. Working their way up the ranks, these highly respected men were promoted because of their skill and courage in battle and loyalty to Rome. They had a reputation for bravery, deliberation, constancy, and strength of mind.[1] During the time of Jesus, the Roman army was charged with keeping the peace in Judea. These set-apart Jews couldn't avoid contact with these unclean foreign Romans in their land.

Luke acknowledges in his writing what the audience of Matthew would have already known; the Roman centurion would probably not approach Jesus himself but would send a representative. Interestingly, these representatives were elders within the Jewish community who thought so highly of the integrity and generosity of this specific Roman military leader that they approached Jesus for him. There must have been a strong relationship of respect in place – and I think this servant must have been very valued and very ill (lying paralyzed, suffering terribly and at the point of death) to merit this much unusual effort. And it is equally interesting that the Jewish leaders were admitting they were powerless to help – and they believed Jesus could. They *pleaded earnestly.*

Emotions are running high. Relationships are deeply intertwined. Jesus, the healing Jewish rabbi, changes directions and goes with them to the centurion's "unclean" house.

But he doesn't arrive. Before anyone else has grasped this, the centurion understands that power is not physically constrained. Jesus does not need to come physically. He only needs to say the word. *"Say the word, and my servant will be healed."* Ah, how often we forget the power of words!

This Roman centurion understood that words harnessed authority. He saw it in his own life and the authority entrusted to him by the Roman government. He spoke, and the men under his command responded. He saw the same thing in this rabbi Jesus. Jesus spoke with the authority entrusted to him by the God who governed all things. He knew the words spoken by Jesus would be perfectly carried out. All things seemed to be under his authority. *"Say the word, and my servant will be healed."*

This was an unusual surety of faith from a surprising person – an outsider, a Gentile, a Roman. And Jesus marveled!

Our Jewish disciple Matthew cannot help but marvel with Jesus. He, of Jewish descent, waiting for the arrival of the Jewish Messiah, can hardly believe that throughout Israel, the Jewish people are failing to see and understand what this outsider has so quickly grasped. This man of authority is worth trusting. This Jesus speaks, and lepers dance, and the sick are healed. Jesus tells his Jewish followers, "Many will come from distant lands – from the east and the west – outsiders that are quickly called unclean – yet they will be welcomed to recline at the table and eat from the banquet of life with your fathers Abraham, Isaac, and Jacob in the kingdom of heaven. Yet you, their blood descendants, will be locked out, crying into the darkness" (Matthew 8:11-12). Unspoken is, "He who has no reason to believe in me believes. You, who have been prepared for my arrival all your life, are slow to believe."

Jesus speaks the word of authority: *"Go; let it be done for you as you have believed."* And the servant was healed at that very moment. Oh! To have the sure, undoubting faith of the centurion! Can you imagine surprising Jesus with your faith in him?

Our doctor, Luke, follows this miracle with another. Jesus journeys 20 miles from Capernaum to the town called Nain, followed by his disciples and a great crowd. His reputation is growing. Where is this town of Nain, and has it had any historical significance? It is located on the northern slope of the Hill of Moreh. On the southern slope, the great prophet Elisha raised the dead son of the Shunammite woman back to life (2 Kings 4:18-37).[2] Keep this little miracle of life and death in mind.

A funeral procession emerges as Jesus and his followers draw near the town gate. There is great mourning, of course, but even more significant because this was the only son of a woman who is widowed. She has not only lost her son - but she has also lost her future. With no male to provide for her, she will soon lose her home and become destitute. Jesus looked at her and felt great compassion for her.

He speaks to her. He reaches out and touches the bier – the young man's body is wrapped in a cloth shroud and is carried on a litter to the place of burial. Oh, no. The compassion Jesus feels is so great that he has reached out to touch a dead body, making him ceremonially unclean for seven days. According to the Law, Jesus will need to cleanse himself with the water for impurity combined with ashes from a burnt heifer sacrificed by the priest on the third day and again on the seventh day to be declared clean again (Numbers 19:1-12). But right now, we aren't thinking of this because Jesus is speaking a command to a dead man. *"Young man, I say to you, arise!"*

The dead cannot hear. As his beating heart stopped and the breath of life left his body, this dead man lost the ability to see, smell, feel, speak, and hear. Every organ in his body ceased to function. Decay began immediately. Have you ever been with a loved one when they died? It is disturbing how quickly that person ceases to be your beloved one. Their spirit is gone. Their physical body remains - almost a stranger. I have held the hand of my sister and my mother as they passed beyond this world. As I walked out of the room, looking back at them, I knew they were no longer there. The remaining body had no life. Their soul had separated and departed. They were gone.

"Young man, I say to you, arise!" With these words of Jesus, everything within the young man returned to life. He heard. He breathed. His heart began to beat. He sat up. He spoke. And Jesus gave him to his mother. Ah. There is a familiar phrase. These Jewish mourners have heard this story before. The prophet Elijah had done the same; the Lord listened to Elijah's voice, and he too had raised a widow's son to life and "given him to his mother." Her grateful response had been, *"Now I know you are a man of God, and that the word of the Lord in your mouth is truth" (1 Kings 17:23-24).*

As the crowd with Jesus sees life replace death, they perhaps think of the stories of Elisha and Elijah, the great prophets sent to their people by God. Could this man Jesus be such a prophet as this? Could this man Jesus be the prophet, Elijah, returning for the great and awesome day of the Lord? (Malachi 4:5). The people are seized with fear and trembling as they praise the glory of God.

The dead come back to life. Ashes of mourning are replaced with the oil of gladness. The Lord is glorified. Was this the promised One who would come clothed in garments of salvation and the robe of righteousness? (Isaiah 61:3, 10). Could it be true? The good news will spread fast - beyond Judea and into the surrounding county. And each one who hears will ask, "Can this be the One we have been waiting for?"

45

Doubt

Read Matthew 11:1-19; Luke 7:18-35

Doubt. How could he doubt? Cousin John, filled with the Spirit of God before his birth, was the one who proclaimed, *"Behold the Lamb of God..."* John baptized Jesus with water in expectation of him baptizing with fire. John saw the dove descend and heard the voice of God say, *"This is my Son..."* yet he is questioning, doubting, asking, *"Are you the one who is to come, or shall we look for another?"* How could John doubt?

How often do you doubt? When we are alone, standing behind our locked doors, experiencing the hard things of life, knowing life is fleeting and temporary, it is easy to ask, "Jesus, are you who you say you are? Or should I look for the answers somewhere else?"

I must ask myself, "What are my expectations of a Savior?" Is it to remove all my problems, relieve my financial burdens, and heal my physical illnesses? Am I looking for companionship and compassion? Freedom from self-condemnation and reversal of my past mistakes? To make all my dreams come true? Perhaps yes. Perhaps this and more!

Maybe John expected the long-awaited Messiah to have an iron fist that would shatter the yoke of bondage. Perhaps he longed for immediate freedom from the Romans and expected righteous judgment. Maybe he was longing for a tidal wave to topple the fortress of tyranny, and Jesus seemed only a gentle ripple rolling onto shore. What were John's expectations? What are ours?

Jesus was not offended by John's doubt. I don't think he is offended by ours. He tells John to judge by what is plainly seen and heard. "Look at what I do, listen to what I say. Didn't God tell you this would happen? Don't you see God reflected in me? Look at *me*." And there is the evidence that stacks up line by line:

The blind see.
The lame walk.
The lepers are healed.
The deaf hear.
The dead are raised back to life.
The poor hear the good news.

Jesus is fulfilling scripture. He is doing what God foretold that his Messiah, his Anointed One, would do. I am sure John was well acquainted with these prophesies of Isaiah:

In that day the deaf will hear the words of the scroll,
and out of gloom and darkness
the eyes of the blind will see.
Once more the humble will rejoice in the Lord;
the needy will rejoice in the Holy One of Israel.
Isaiah 29:18-19 NIV

Then will the eyes of the blind be opened
and the ears of the deaf unstopped.
Then will the lame leap like a deer,
and the mute tongue shout for joy.

Water will gush forth in the wilderness
and streams in the desert.
Isaiah 35:5-6 NIV

"I, the Lord, have called you in righteousness;
I will take hold of your hand.
I will keep you and will make you
to be a covenant for the people
and a light for the Gentiles,
to open eyes that are blind,
to free captives from prison
and to release from the dungeon those who sit in darkness.
Isaiah 42:6-7 NIV

The Spirit of the Sovereign Lord is on me,
because the Lord has anointed me
to proclaim good news to the poor.
He has sent me to bind up the brokenhearted,
to proclaim freedom for the captives
and release from darkness for the prisoners.
Isaiah 61:1 NIV

Jesus was reminding John, remember what God has told you all along? Don't take my word for it – take God's!

Jesus ends this bold affirmation of his works, which point to who he is, with this promise of blessing: *"Blessed is the one who is not offended by me."* This, too, is a reference back to the words of Isaiah concerning the One who would come in the name of the Lord.

The Lord Almighty is the one you are to regard as holy,
he is the one you are to fear,
he is the one you are to dread.
He will be a holy place;
for both Israel and Judah he will be

a stone that causes people to stumble
and a rock that makes them fall.
And for the people of Jerusalem
he will be a trap and a snare.
Isaiah 8:13-14 NIV

A stone, a rock, a trap, a snare. An offense. Yet a holy place! Read his words again; *"Blessed is the one who is not offended by me."* Because Jesus is offensive. If we straighten our backs and raise our chins with pride, we will stumble on the stone placed firmly on solid ground as the cornerstone. With blind eyes, we will trip and fall, offended. We didn't see; we didn't hear the words of life because we were busy comparing ourselves to others. And we think we are pretty darned good at measuring up against them. We don't need to be healed. We are not broken. We are righteous. We are good. Good enough.

John wanted to make sure he knew who Jesus was. Jesus knew exactly who John was. He was not a swaying reed easily blown this way and that way by the changing winds of public opinion or political favor. He was not seeking comfort, or riches, or vanity. He was a prophet sent by God to speak his warnings; he was an alarm to point in the right direction. He would stand firm and strong to the end. Soon, Salome would be dancing before Herod Antipas her erotic enticement and ask for John's bloody head on a platter for payment.

"Yes," Jesus acknowledges before the crowds. "John is God's prophet and more; he is the messenger sent to you to prepare the way for me." In Matthew's telling of this, Jesus bluntly explains that John is the messenger *"Elijah who is to come."*

In both Matthew and Luke, Jesus points again to prophecy, this time from Malachi:

"I will send my messenger, who will prepare the way before me.
Then suddenly the Lord you are seeking will come to his temple;
the messenger of the covenant, whom you desire, will come,"

says the Lord Almighty.
Malachi 3:1 NIV

This bold claim must have taken their breath away! If Jesus is saying what they suspect he is saying, then John is the Messenger Prophet Elijah, and he – Jesus - is the Lord of the Covenant they have been waiting for! Could this be possible? This flesh-and-blood man wearing the robes of a teacher?

He presses harder into John's identity: "He is greater than any man born of woman…" Jesus elevates John above Father Abraham, Moses of the Law, and prophets Isaiah, Elijah, and Elisha! But he isn't finished. "*Yet the one who is least in the kingdom of God is greater than he.*"

Well, let that sink in for a minute.

You. With all your junk and failures and mess in your wake. Your brokenness. Your selfishness, mean words, and ugly thoughts. Can you not only be welcomed into the kingdom of God but also be considered greater than the best of the best, the holiest of the holy? How could that be? The folks hearing these words could not understand yet – but we know that God has plans to clothe us with the righteousness of his own Son. We will become holy in the healing baptism of his Living Water; we will be washed clean in the blood of the perfect Lamb. Again, we are reminded of the words of Isaiah (53:5, 11 NIV).

But he was pierced for our transgressions,
he was crushed for our iniquities;
the punishment that brought us peace was on him,
and by his wounds we are healed.

After he has suffered,
he will see the light of life and be satisfied;
by his knowledge my righteous servant will justify many,
and he will bear their iniquities.

We will walk in the kingdom of God in the righteousness of God's Son, our scarlet stains washed away by the blood of the Lamb. We will be clothed in white linen bought at a great price. John had taught that he would wash with the baptism of water, but One was coming who would wash with the baptism of the fire of God's own Spirit—fire that would purify and refine. Had that baptism arrived? Almost. Hold on. It would be coming.

At the moment, this was too much to take in. We see it in the responses. Those who could see the darkness of their sin marveled that God's justice could open a door for them. Those who only had eyes for their own righteousness rejected Jesus's words and were offended. They closed the door to a God who was bigger than their own ideas of who God should be.

Jesus, without missing a beat, compared them to the children amusing themselves in the marketplace. "March to our tune!" they call out. "John was too righteous and too judgmental for you. I am too celebratory and too quick to forgive for your liking. You hypocrites! You want to have it neither way. You want God to march to your tune. Yet God's wisdom is found in both John and me; our living testimony points to the justice of God."

John wouldn't dance for them. Jesus would not weep for them. John offered repentance. Jesus offered forgiveness and the joy of life to the fullest. This was something very different from their idea of what obeying God was like. And it certainly didn't align with their idea of what a Messiah would look like.

Jesus's words and actions were becoming like a two-edged sword, cutting deep and exposing the thoughts and intentions of the heart. The people who were well aware of their sins were being embraced into this new idea of God's kingdom. The people with the highest recommendations and the cleanest clothes started feeling like outsiders.

John must have gotten it wrong. This rebellious Rabbi couldn't be the One they were waiting for. His sharp tongue cut too deep. If he didn't fall into line soon, it would be time to silence the messenger. And the message.

46

An Easy Yoke

Read Matthew 11:20-30

Both writers, Luke and Matthew, tell the story of John's doubt and Jesus's reassurance. Almost word for word, they repeat each other. But from here, Luke tells the story of the weeping woman, and Matthew tells of the coming condemnation of unrepentant cities. Both are stories of hardened hearts. Luke, a kind and compassionate doctor, tells of the repentant sorrow of an outcast woman compared with the unrepentant pride-filled religious leader. Matthew, our factual accountant, tells of unrepentant cities filled with Jewish men and women who should recognize their miracle-working Messiah yet remain aloof and prideful. Jesus makes a blind man see, and their only response is, "Do it again!" Entertain us. Tell us a story. Perform a magic trick. Make us wonder and marvel and say, "Ah!"

What is the point of Jesus's mighty works? They are a signpost planted in the ground, directing the people to a mighty God. These miracles elevate our eyes to see a wonderous God and should humble us and take us to our knees in repentance.

There are harsh words here from our Jesus. Where is the meek and mild man with the outstretched hand of mercy? This is someone we have not seen. He "denounced" the people of the cities where he had performed amazing miracles. To denounce is to "publicly blame or pronounce as evil, to accuse."[1] He would pronounce "Woe to you," meaning grief and distress, deep suffering over coming ruinous trouble.[2] Doom. This sounds like the voice of a judge and a coming judgment.

Korazin stood about two miles northwest of Capernaum. Bethsaida was located on the northeast coast of the Sea of Galilee, on the east side of the Jordan River. This area was the Galilean base of Jesus's early ministry, and many of Jesus's miracles were experienced here.[3] Yet these people did not hear, they refused to see, they were not humbled and repentant, and they refused to allow the generous Spirit of God to produce a miraculous change in their lives.

They are compared with the cities historically associated with the evil of idol worship: Tyre and Sidon. How would those evil cities have reacted to the privilege of hearing the words of Jesus? He declares they would have repented quickly, dressing in ashes and sackcloth to express their deep mourning over their sin outwardly. But not Capernaum. Jesus predicts its coming destruction.

With this denouncement, Jesus brings up the destination we are all hurtling toward. The one they – and we – ignore entirely. The Day of Judgment. It is easy to ignore because it has not come yet. We think it will never come. We count on it to be a fairy tale, a superstition, an ancient device to invoke fear and gain control. Thinking we all die and ease into some "other better place" is more soothing. If you are a Bible reader, you know this idea of judgment isn't ignored so easily. Let's look at this pretty terrifying, deeply detailed story of the sin and the destruction of the city of Sodom.

God told Abraham that he had heard the cries of the people. He would stand for the wickedness in Sodom no longer. His angels arrived at the city's gates with one last offer of salvation before the fire began to fall. The city's men justified their desires and thought they could take by force what God had sent in grace and freedom. Even

Lot, Abraham's nephew, was reluctant to be rescued. "Let us stay here just a little longer." Nothing could delay the judgment, which was beginning to rain down on the outskirts of town. All who did not accept the hand of rescue were destroyed in the rain of sulfur and fire (Genesis 18:20-21,19:1-26).

Jesus tells those who know the story well, "It will be worse for Capernaum – yes, you and your beloved hometown – than it was for those within the walls of Sodom!" They won't believe it.

Ignore his words. Be true to yourself. Do what pleases you; whatever brings you pleasure. Seek your passion. Oh, how easily we listen to the lies of the world! And ignore the truth of God. They closed their ears; they closed their hearts.

Many who should have recognized him turned away in apathy and arrogance because they saw no need for a Messiah, a Savior. Yet he offered profound mercy to those who would come to him in humility and dependence.

Almost within mid-sentence, Jesus turns to God his Father in gratitude. Even Jesus sounds humbled to me! He is amazed that the Lord of Heaven and Earth would reveal profound wisdom and understanding of heavenly things to the children, the innocents, those seemingly unimportant ones of low worth, while the elevated, educated, important, influential ones would lack understanding.

Yes, Jesus knew – without doubt – his connection to the Father and the Father to him. He speaks of "knowing." This intimate knowing of each other – the Father of the Son and the Son of the Father is extended to *"anyone to whom the Son chooses to reveal (the Father)"* (Matthew 11:27). His words continue to express the exclusiveness of Jesus; he alone is the way to the Father. It is an invitation. "Come to me!" he invites us. It is an invitation to all who labor and are heavy-laden and is fulfilled with a promise of something good - rest.

The Jews of that day were weary from the weight of the Law of Moses, which had become a burden with the additional oral laws meant to clarify it created by the religious leaders. Add to that the weight of Roman law. And the heaviest weight of all – the weight of the sorrows of this world. And our sin. Oh my, how can anyone stand under the crushing, overpowering weight?

Jesus offers to share the burden, placing the weight on his own shoulders. He describes himself as gentle and humble of heart. He provides rest for your soul. Placing yourself in his hands, under his yoke, will ease the labor and lighten the burden. What does that look like? I have seen that little invitation change a life. This is my sister's story. Go back with me to August of 2007.

I am walking on the beach at Tybee Island with my husband, teenage son, and daughter. We are waiting for sunset this late Saturday afternoon. I am listening intently on the phone as my sister's best friend Carol quotes this scripture passage; *"Come to me, all who labor and are heavy laden, and I will give you rest."* She is telling me that my sister, who has been throwing up for three days as her body rejects the nutrients she has been receiving through a catheter during the last-ditch effort to prolong her life for just a few more months, has claimed this scripture as her comfort.

First, let me tell you that I am not a person who talks on the phone when I am with other people. I pour all my attention into the people I am with. But this was a significant exception. My sister was Jewish. She had very sincerely converted to Judaism early in her twenties and had no interest in the Christian faith we had been brought up in. My sister was dying. And now, within the space of four days, my mother and Kathy's best friend both were telling me that Kathy had accepted Jesus as her Savior.

Carol, Kathy's comedic sidekick from their days in college, had spent Friday night with Kathy at her house. Her body could no longer fight the cancer that had left her emaciated, connected to tubes, in a hospital bed, under the care of hospice with no hope in sight. Carol, in desperation, asked Kathy if there was anything that could bring her comfort.

Kathy directed her to a glass cabinet in the dining room. On a shelf, in the back, was a Bible. Surprise number one. It was a Christian Bible with the New Testament. A friend had given it to Kathy eight years before when Kathy's husband had left her. A card was tucked inside from our Aunt Olive (who since had passed away), sent with biblical passages of comfort around the same time. Throughout the Bible, those passages were underlined. Kathy directed Carol to Matthew 11:28. Carol read it to her. And then, looking at her to make sure she understood what they were reading, Carol said gently, "Kathy, those are the words of Jesus." Kathy said, "I know. I have accepted him as my Savior." Surprise number two.

I would receive the call to come to Tampa as quickly as possible on Sunday afternoon. On Monday, I would make the long drive to arrive by my sister's side, who was now in a hospice facility, heavily medicated against the constant pain. It was a long three weeks as we waited for death. That seems like a ridiculous statement unless you have been there, waiting.

In those last days, I heard for myself Kathy's new thoughts about this Jewish Son named Jesus. Those are stories for another time. But let me tell you this: every single time I hear or read or say these words, *"Come to me, all who labor and are heavy laden, and I will give you rest,"* I feel the tears, I bite my lip, I choke back the sob.

"Come." It is a simple invitation. It is not complicated; it is not heavy. But it is most certainly personal. The word invites us to a person, the very Son of God. "Come to *me*…" "…and I will give you *rest*." Rest. What a holy and precious word. It is so sacred and valuable that God set aside an entire day for his own rest - and then surrounded it with laws to protect it for those who came to him.

Rest. My Lord and Kathy's Savior called her to step out from underneath the pain and strife – because he had something much better.

I am betting that whatever hard and heavy load you carry, Jesus offers you the same. Come, lay down your heavy burdens. Take on the yoke of Jesus. Learn from him. And rest.

47

The Anointing

Read Luke 7:36-50

If you walk in the circles of Bible study, you know this story: the story of the sinful woman who anointed the feet of Jesus. Luke's story here is different from the stories told by Matthew (26:6-13), Mark (14:3-9), and John (12:1-8). Those three tell us their story takes place at Bethany six days (or two days) before Passover in the house of Simon the leper. John even names names: Lazarus, recently raised from the dead, is there. His sister Martha serves (of course!), and his sister Mary is the only one who has listened closely enough to know Jesus is bound for death and anoints his body for burial. Judas complains about the waste of the expensive ointment. Jesus defends her beautiful offering.

Here in Luke, we have a different story of a different anointing for a different purpose. This story takes place in the home of a Pharisee named Simon. Okay, so the name is the same... so it is easy to think they are the same event – but this dinner takes place a year before the death of Jesus, and the reasons for the anointing are very different.

Once the Pharisee's invitation to dinner is accepted and Jesus is comfortably reclining at his table, the story concentrates on this unknown, unnamed woman. But perhaps she is not unknown and unnamed to Jesus. One thing we all know very clearly in black and white is that she is a woman of the city, a sinner. She doesn't sound like a respectable woman with her own home, dinner waiting on the table, and children lined up with clean hands and combed hair. She sounds like that woman you don't want to talk to, you don't want to be seen with. One of those other women. The ones who had the rough childhoods. The ones who made the wrong decisions in high school. The ones who were attracted to the wild boys and the fast life. One of those women. Unclean, for sure. Not included, not invited. A woman of the city. A sinner. Just so we are clear here.

And what is she up to? Every word, line by line, spells it out. She has brought an alabaster flask of perfumed ointment. I have read that it was probably a small pottery flask hung from a cord around her neck. I imagine it is usually tucked within her clothing for safe keeping, resting close to her heart, warmed by her skin, its fragrance waiting to be released. Standing *behind him*, at his *feet, weeping*... This was not the stance of a proud woman, a respectable woman, a woman who felt equal to or entitled. This was the posture of a woman begging. This was a woman with no pride and no expectations.

And it gets worse. Her tears are plentiful - flowing enough to wet the dirty, dust-covered feet of a man who has walked many miles to get there. And her hair is undone. In this culture, she might as well have been naked. Women did not uncover their hair, much less loosen their waist-length tresses for all to see. A woman's hair was uniquely precious and associated with intimacy. To wipe his feet with her hair was a whispered caress to accompany the kisses of her lips. Oh my!

Can you imagine this happening at your dinner party? I doubt you could have remained silent. I think you would have been out of your chair in a minute, escorting this "woman" out the door. Interestingly, we know, just as Jesus did, what Simon, the dinner host, was thinking. In his small mind, he condemns Jesus. In silent judgment, he arrives at an arrogant conclusion. Obviously, Jesus can be nothing more than a charlatan - someone who is less than he claims. Obviously, if this were a man of God, he would not allow this woman – unclean, condemned, untouchable - *this sinner* to touch him. Obviously, he is nothing more than a man with a knack for inventive teaching. If he were anything more, he would have already rebuked her. He would have already kicked her away.

Jesus does not speak to the woman at his feet. He asks to tell Simon a story. He tells of a money lender canceling the debts of two of his debtors. One owes ten times as much as the other. Jesus asks Simon which of the two would have more gratitude. But he asks this way, "Who would *love him* more?"

As Simon dismissively answers, "The one with the larger debt," Jesus turns to look upon this greater sinner with the most to be forgiven, this woman with the more significant debt. I imagine his eyes are filled with tenderness, and his voice is soft and kind - yet his words are directed at Simon.

"I entered your house, but you withheld the common courtesy of offering water to wash the dust from my feet. She washed my feet with her tears.

"I came in fellowship; you offered no welcoming embrace or a kiss of greeting. She has lovingly bent low to kiss my feet with humility and gratitude.

"You neglected to anoint my head with the blessing oil; she has poured out her precious fragrance of healing upon my feet.

"Therefore…"

The spoken words of Jesus are very different from the unspoken harsh words of judgment of Simon, the religious leader. These are words of judgment, spoken clear and true. These are not the words of a teacher, a prophet, or a miracle worker; these are the sentencing words of the Son of the Most-High Judge:

"Therefore, I tell you,
her debts, which are much larger than you know,
her sins, which are much greater than you can imagine,
are forgiven.

Because she has been forgiven much, she can love much."

Simon has the opportunity to learn this: if he can only acknowledge his own debt and sin, then he, too, can be forgiven. Then he, too, can love like that.

Did Jesus come to judge? Or to forgive?

If you are wondering about that, slip back with me to a different evening and a different conversation with another Pharisee - this one named Nicodemus. The disciple John told us this conversation as if he had been in the room. John declared that Jesus had not come into the world to condemn the world since the world was already condemned - but that the world might be *saved through him.*

For God did not send his Son into the world to condemn the world,
but to save the world through him.
Whoever believes in him is not condemned,
but whoever does not believe stands condemned already
because they have not believed in the name of God's one and only Son.
John 3:17-18 NIV

The woman at the feet of Jesus knew she was already condemned. She was crushed under the weight of her sins. But somewhere along the way, she had encountered God's one and only Son, and she believed he was who he said he was. She believed her sins, though many and egregious and publicly, disgracefully committed, were forgiven. Gone. Her scarlet stains had been washed white as the snow.

Her heart was humbled. She cried in repentance. She received the gracious, glorious gift of forgiveness. The curtain separating her from a holy God was torn; she looked into the face of God's Son and was free. Forgiven much, she was filled with much love.

"Your faith has saved you; go in peace." Your faith. Is that really all it takes? This faith is not a vague feeling or a self-affirming subject-less faith. It is faith—convinced and committed—in a Person. It is faith that this flesh-and-blood man was more than a healer, a teacher, or

a prophet of God; he was the Son of God who had come to forgive much and offer God's peace.

I wonder how Simon responded to that generous offer.

48

And the Women Who Followed

Read Luke 8:1-3

The church where I belong has a very active Women's Ministry. It has been exciting for me to be embraced by all these women, the circle growing each time I attend a new event or show up for weekly prayer together. One week, I encountered a whole new thing. These women not only reach out to wrap their arms around one another, they reach out to other women. The ones outside the circle.

At a retreat they offered, I heard some of their stories. The woman just out of jail since last week. The woman who declared she was told her whole life that she was unlovable - only to experience now being loved deeply by God. The woman who shared the photograph taken on her wedding day after coming out of a ten-year spiral of heroin and homelessness. The woman who begged another to sing for her, sobbing with her head down as she sang the loving words of a Savior.

This started two thousand years ago when women began leaving the lives they were living to follow this teacher and healer named Jesus. Some women had lived a life of good things - a fine husband, successful children, and a beautiful home. Some women had experienced the harder things - destructive relationships, lost children, and forfeited responsibility. These women found common ground. They walked a new road behind Jesus. They broke with what their society expected of them. They reached out to place an arm in support of one another. And they grew in strength and wisdom. And love.

This was Jesus. This is Jesus. This was revolutionary. It still is. I am reminded of the closing prayer of Jesus – it will be a while before we get there – but it is worth hearing a bit of it today:

"The glory that you have given me I have given to them,
that they may be one even as we are one,
I in them and you in me,
that they may become perfectly one,
so that the world may know that you sent me and loved them even as you loved me."
John 17:22-23

Jesus gave his glory away! The glory given to him by the good Father was given to those who would believe. In the act of believing, they would become perfectly one with each other; this unity was made possible because of the great love living within them of the Father and the Son! They became one—perfectly one—sharing the glory and love of Jesus. Let me leave this thought for just a moment—we will return.

Culture and context are crucial in understanding – well, just about anything. I grew up in a time of women's "liberation"; women already had the right to vote and were found in the workplace as often as finding their fulfillment in managing the home. But the availability of "The Pill" had changed a woman's ability to have more control over when she conceived a child. Enter the "Sexual Revolution" and the opportunity to have sexual encounters outside the safety of marriage – if a woman chooses to. There were marches for women's rights, bra-burnings, and all sorts of liberations. It was the 1960s, heading fast and furious into the 1970s. Women were demanding equality with men in every area of society.

I had grown up in the home of a woman from a different generation. Some call it the "greatest generation": those who became adults in the 1940s. She was not what you would expect. She was the oldest daughter of a dairy farmer, loud enough to make her voice heard in a family of four older brothers, two sisters, and another brother trailing behind her. She was the only one of the eight to go beyond high school. After graduating as a Registered Nurse, she enlisted as an Army Nurse serving in WWII, married a handsome Air Force officer, and left her country life for a place as distant as California, where they bought a house and had two daughters of their own. The communists were invading Korea, and her reenlisted husband's plane went down over the ocean there. My mother moved back to her hometown, sold her house in Los Angeles, built a new one in Greenville, and bought a new car and a gun to protect herself and her girls. After her second marriage to the man who would become father to my younger sister and me (Yes! Four daughters!), she continued to run her household with confidence, strength, and great respect for her husband. This was the woman I grew up with. I didn't need any lessons in women being as capable as men. I was living with one.

Today in our culture of women's rights, I am afraid we think we need to hit men over the head with a hammer – or at least in the knees to cripple them so we can stand over them and roar about how strong and important we are. I just don't think that is necessary. I really like men. I love being married to one; I love being the mother of one. I have loved working with them. I love the differences between a man and a woman. I birthed one of each, and I can tell you from experience there are certainly differences – good differences. I celebrate them. But I will acknowledge that in these days of division, churches are getting very tangled up with too many discussions about how and where to stand with men and women ministering together. So, let's go back to the world of Jesus and look again at what was happening there.

First, we must acknowledge that in the ancient Jewish culture, women were not considered equal to men. No way. Women were utterly dependent on the men in their lives for provision and protection. We must acknowledge this ancient land of Israel (like every ancient land!) was very, very different from the culture we are experiencing in modern America. That is why the Word of God has been fascinating from the beginning in how it includes stories of women's hurts, sorrows, hopes, and joys. And it became even more so when Jesus showed up on planet Earth. Women played out prominently in story after story, miracle after miracle. And here – out of seemingly nowhere, we get this listing, by name, of specific women who were not only there in the life and story of Jesus– they were actively affecting the ministry of Jesus. In a really good way.

In Dr. Luke's telling of the good news of Jesus, we have recently left the house of Simon, the respected Jewish leader, where Jesus has lovingly praised the actions of a sin-filled woman whose gratitude of being forgiven has caused her to "love much." With a skip and a hop, we are traveling with Jesus and his entourage through cities and villages, proclaiming the good news of the kingdom of God. Remember, this is good news. They are on a mission to show and tell what this kingdom of God looks like. And among the odd assortment of disciples from very different walks of life, there are also *"some women who had been healed of evil spirits and infirmities."* This is not just a boy's club. Let the girls come in, also.

Women important enough to be called by name. Luke starts with *"Mary, called Magdalene, from whom seven demons had gone out."* We are not told she was a prostitute. I wonder if this assumption occurred because people connected her with the woman in the previous story. Regardless, she had been a troubled woman, living with more than one demon condemning her. She had lived a difficult life that had separated her from the respectable folks and had taken her to dark places alone. Broken and hopeless, somewhere along the way she had met Jesus, and everything, everything had changed. I am betting she still had the scars of a battered life. Wounds deep and painful. I wonder if she was still raw from the shame of her life as an outsider. But she had been forgiven much, so now she could love much. This was Mary called Magdalene.

Then there was Joanna, the wife of Chuza, Herod's household manager. She would be quite different from Mary of Magdalene. Joanna's husband was a high-ranking official in Herod's court. She was part of the aristocracy. Highly respected. I am guessing she was a woman with great responsibility and deep connections. Can't you imagine her carrying the role of administration and planning? She would have been a leader, capable of opening closed doors and influencing situations. And here she was, listed with the likes of Mary. She will show up again at an empty tomb. And again, in the early church. She would be found trustworthy and loyal.

We don't know a thing about Susanna. But I am guessing those early readers of Luke's story did since she is named. And then there were the others. Many others. Who *"provided for (the ministry of Jesus) out of their means."* Probably financial gifts – but perhaps in other ways as well. You know us women.

So put this important piece of information into your brain: It wasn't just the men who were there with Jesus. Women—important enough to be called out by name—were there, traveling from village to village with Jesus. Women who "provided" were thought valuable in sharing this precious and profound good news of the kingdom of God.

We women can easily think our efforts to serve the living Jesus are small or unimportant. We sometimes ask ourselves why we continue. Does it make a difference in the big scheme of God's world? It does. It continues to do now what it did two thousand years ago. It continues to take Jesus farther down the road. What we do paves the path into the next village, the next neighborhood, the next house, the next heart.

Whether you are Mary Magdalene, Joanna, or the unknown Susanna, Jesus has a place for you in his world. He has rescued you from darkness, released you from your demons, cured you of your weaknesses, and you, too, can follow behind him, telling his story.

49

The Unforgivable Insult

Read Matthew 12:22-50; Mark 3:20-35; Luke 8:19-21

Sometimes, I wish our three gospel writers, Matthew, Mark, and Luke, had gotten together to align their stories in a more orderly fashion. John gets a pass since he was writing in a different style; these other three appear to be writing sequentially but are not exactly. Instead, their stories are grouped by theme to show the character of Jesus – which was brilliant – but it keeps me up in the air as I try to follow along an orderly timeline. Here we go again. All three tell the story of Jesus's biological family, who are worried about him. They show up outside, unable to get inside the inner circle because of the great crowds spilling into the streets surrounding Jesus. Why are they worried? What has just happened to cause them enough concern to call him home like a disobedient child late for supper?

Matthew sets the stage by telling us what started all this: Jesus healed a demon-oppressed blind and mute man. The people were amazed (of course!) and asked one another, "Can this be the Son of David?" In other words, "This healer Jesus performing miraculous signs that point to God, is he the One we have been waiting for—the anointed descendant of King David?"

The Pharisees, teachers of God's Word, cannot deny the miracle, so they deny the source of the miracle worker's power. (And they only have to think such a thing because, once again, Jesus discerns their thoughts!) They deny God's power and substitute it with the most odious insult they can think of—"This Jesus is not empowered by God but by Beelzebul!"

First, I must tell you, when I hear the word Beelzebub (easily interchanged with Beelzebul), it comes to me in my daddy's voice. He was the only person I have known to use that phrase – he called the devil "Old Beelzebub." I imagine it coming from hellfire-and-damnation preachers and revival tent meetings. But my daddy said it with a lilt to his voice and a light in his eyes that hinted at the shenanigans of pranksters. When I taught the stories of the kings of ancient Israel, I found out who this devil Beelzebub was.

The worship of Baal-zebub, the god of Ekron, was first mentioned in the Hebrew scriptures in the first chapter of 2 Kings. The King of Judah, Ahaziah, fell out of a window. Instead of inquiring of the Lord God of Israel, he sent messengers to inquire of the enemy Philistine god Baal-zebub if he would live or die. God was not happy about this. He sent his prophet Elijah to warn the king, "Is it because there is no God in Israel that you are going to inquire of Baal-zebub, the god of Ekron?" Burning fire came down from heaven to consume a hundred soldiers and prove God's point. King Ahaziah died, as God had told him he surely would. We get the point here that exalting Baal-zebub above the God of Israel is playing with fire.

The name Baal-zebub comes to us in two parts. Baal was the name for the Canaanite fertility god, and Zebub means "exalted dwelling." This pagan god was apparently "the lord of flies." This idea of flies is odd, but it may have something to do with flies that gather on the blood of the sacrifice. Beelzebub is the Greek form. After the time of the Philistines, the Jews changed the name to "Beel-boul," meaning "lord of dung," or the "god of filth," which later became a name of bitter scorn in the mouth of the Pharisees. The Jews used Beelzebul as an epithet for Satan, the prince of demons.[1]

Aha. This begins to explain a lot. Especially if you connect the dots between what happened to King Ahaziah disregarding God's power in favor of the power of a pagan little 'g' god named Baalzebub. And now, God's teachers, who know better, are claiming Jesus receives power and is a follower of this same pagan god Baalzebub – who is of Satan, prince of the demons.

God will not be mocked. His power will not be stolen or maligned. What is done by the Spirit of God must be honored. To attribute these mighty works of God's Spirit to the works of Satan is unforgivable. It is denying the power and mighty work of God. It is abhorrent. I think it is stated most clearly by Mark 3:29. The verse before reassures us that all sins will be forgiven,

> *"but whoever blasphemes against the Holy Spirit never has forgiveness, but is guilty of an eternal sin."*

Oh, here is that other confusing word: blaspheme. Again, we picture those tent preachers with a raised fist shouting eternal damnation in a loud cinematic voice. Blaspheme means "the act of insulting or showing contempt or lack of reverence for God" or "the act of claiming the attributes of a deity."[2] Merriam-Webster shares this quote from John Bright in 1889, "for a mere man to suggest that he was ... divine could only be viewed ... as *blasphemy*." Well, exactly – there you go.

The Pharisees, self-appointed keepers of God's laws, are preparing to accuse Jesus of blasphemy – claiming to be divine, like God. Jesus is saying, "Beware of insulting God by denying his works, refusing to show reverence for the power of God. God's Holy Spirit is evident in these miracles!"

He asks them questions: "How can Satan cast out Satan?" "How can a kingdom stand if it is divided?" "How can a house be strong if it is divided against itself?" Perhaps he is saying, "Look at what I am doing. Is it for good? Does it look like what God does? Does it line up with what God values? Am I restoring life? Am I healing what is broken? Am I unified with God?"

In Matthew 12:33-37 he uses the easy-to-understand parable of discerning a tree by its fruit. A good tree produces good fruit. Apparently, he is looking at rotten fruit from these accusers who pretend to be speaking for God. Our patient Jesus loses his patience and slips into John the Baptist mode. "You brood of vipers! Your words reflect your heart. You speak evil because you nurture evil in your heart! There is a judgment day – and you will be condemned by your own words reflecting your own heart. You will be accountable for every careless word!"

They can't leave it alone, these scribes and teachers. How confident they are! They are sure they can have the last word. "Teacher (insert the tone "condescending" here), we wish to see a sign from you." They don't have a clue what they are asking. And Jesus gives them an answer they cannot comprehend. It is one of my favorites!

"I will give you a sign. The sign of Jonah."

Three days, three nights in the belly of the great fish. Jesus will spend three days and three nights in the belly of the earth. Buried and dead to this world, he would preach the word of repentance to the dead, just as Jonah had been sent to the condemned of Nineveh. (This incredible story can be found in Jonah 1-3). The people (and cows!) of Nineveh fasted, repented, and will be there to rise again at judgment. Will these "teachers" of God's Word? Even Gentiles – like the Queen of Sheba – will be there to "rise up at the judgment with this generation and condemn it." Even a foreigner recognized the wisdom of King Solomon – and traveled far to behold his greatness. Someone much greater than Solomon was in their midst – would they fail to see it?

Jesus likened them to people who think they have gotten rid of evil – or an unclean spirit living in their "house." They sweep and mop and clean and get things physically in order – not realizing they have prepared a space for evil to return. And so, the evil returns with a vengeance, more powerful and tenacious than before. They are carefully going through the motions of following every letter of the law but don't fill their house or their heart with God. If their house were filled and overflowing with God's Spirit, there would be no room for the devil.

Do you understand yet that Jesus is not just "teaching" little children who have gathered around his pastel hand-tinted robes as birds flutter in the trees overhead? There is no orchestral soundtrack playing behind his words. His words – seen through the authority of the religious intellectuals - are dangerous. The Pharisees have come from Jerusalem. The scribes are taking notes for evidence. The crowds have grown, continuing to gather relentlessly, pushing in closer, insistently so that *"they could not even eat."* His family is concerned. Probably a little scared for his safety. And his state of mind. What in the world is he thinking – challenging the religious leaders from Jerusalem, for goodness' sake? He must be out of his mind!

It is a family intervention. Mary, his mother, has gathered her troops – her other children – her sons, her daughters. Perhaps they can reason with him. When Jesus hears they are calling him to come out to them, he redefines relationships. In Judaism, there was nothing – other than God – more important than family. Remember? Honor your father and your mother. "My family? Who are my mother and my brothers? Whoever does the will of my Father – he is my brother and my sister and my mother." I don't think Jesus was disrespecting his family. Like his 12-year-old self at the Temple, he was doing his Father's work. He was widening his circle of family. He was including others who were doing the work of his Father.

There he was. Jesus. He had healed a man possessed by demons. And so, he was accused of being one of them. The people crowded around him, hoping he was the one who would release them from their suffering. The religious leaders had come all the way from their Holy City, hoping he was not. He offends them. They offend God.

His family is worried and wants him to come home and close the door. Maybe all this will just go away. But word is spreading. And the crowds are growing. And Jesus doesn't seem to be in a hurry.

50

Forgiven, Not Forgiven

Read Matthew 12:31

Sometimes, we need to pay close attention to Jesus's precious words. Much of our understanding of God comes to us secondhand. Someone tells us what God said. A preacher, a teacher, a friend, the church. All of that is good – but if we do not read his Word for ourselves, we can easily get tangled up in wrong ideas. It continues to amaze me that we can read God's very words! And we are promised that his own holy and precious Spirit will teach us! How is that for firsthand knowledge? I wrote this as a blog post shortly after studying this passage we read now. I hope it will clarify this verse, which I believe is often misunderstood.

"So I tell you, people can be forgiven for every sinful thing they do and for every bad thing they say against God. But anyone who speaks against the Holy Spirit will not be forgiven."
Matthew 12:31 ERV

Michael is insistent. He will not be denied. His phone calls usually come in at the most inopportune time, and I ignore them. I become as stubborn as he becomes determined.

"I am not answering," I say aloud, resenting the ringing that finally is silenced as it goes to voicemail. "This is a free call from an inmate at Augusta State Medical Prison. This call will be recorded…" drones on as the mechanical voice clogs my mailbox. I delete the voice messages, but it will fill up again before the day is done.

These phone calls are only three or four minutes long but require my complete attention, so I choose when to accept them. Oddly, I talk to Michael more frequently than family or close friends.

Often, he is obsessed with getting me to order him a food or clothing package—especially coffee or a digital watch. I have given up trying to convince him to learn to tell time with a clock with something as complicated as hands. But just as often, he calls because something traumatic is happening that needs to be told.

A brown recluse spider has bitten him. He has had a convulsion, fallen down the stairs, broken his jaw, and is on a liquid diet. A fellow inmate hid under his bed during the night, and everyone was on lockdown until they discovered him. He needs money for his in-debt friend because the loan sharks will kill both of them if they aren't paid back double by Thursday. You never know what the newest emergency will be. And you never know if they are real or not.

Michael has schizophrenia and has brain damage from smoke inhalation and a long history of dramatic life experiences that started in early childhood.

I occasionally ask God why he has me involved with this incarcerated child-man whose constant attempts at suicide often have had the potential to harm others in the process. God reminds me that Michael has no one else. He is the abandoned orphan, the unloved one. The human being made in God's image who fell through the cracks and into the abyss of nothingness. It is hard to love the Michaels of this world.

This week, when I finally answered his call, it was the story of his friend killing himself. He was a good friend. One who would share coffee with him. He was addicted to meth and cut himself, and they sewed him back up and strip-searched him and put him back in his cell; he cut himself again last night, and he bled out, and Michael had to insist they go into his cell and check on him, but he was already dead. Now his friend was going to hell because he killed himself.

Me: "Whoa. Michael, that's just not true."

I slow him down to explain there is nowhere in scripture where suicide is unforgivable. Suicide is a result of mental brokenness – an illness – when someone believes there is no hope. When a person is overwhelmed with too much unbearable pain. The unforgivable sin talked about in the scriptures has nothing to do with suicide.

I choose my words carefully to explain this idea many struggle with. Especially since Michael wrestles with demons who tell him to "hurt" himself.

He has the pink scars on his wrists. He has an indention on his throat from the tracheotomy that opened his breathing passages when he tried to kill himself by setting his apartment on fire. He lives behind bars because he went into an elementary school with a borrowed high-powered gun and a backpack of bullets and told the woman in the front office they were all going to die that day. They did not. God intervened. The woman told him to lay his gun down and that she loved him as helicopters circled above, the law officers returned Michael's fire, the media reported, and the children escaped. That attempt was suicide by cop. I have told you the story before. I just want you to understand this is a very real problem that has been a constant in Michael's life.

Michael's voices in his head tell him to harm himself in the most insidious ways. So, Michael is safely tucked away behind locked doors, metal bars, and razor wire. But the suicide attempts continue whenever his medication is slightly off. He attempts to hang himself, he hoards pills to overdose, or he finds enough metal to cut his wrists.

We need to get this idea of committing suicide sending you forever to hell put to rest.

Jesus warned the religious leaders of his day they were heading in the direction of sin that couldn't be forgiven. And it was not because they were contemplating suicide.

"Therefore I tell you, every sin and blasphemy will be forgiven people, but the blasphemy against the Spirit will not be forgiven."
Matthew 12:31

The Pharisees - the people who should have recognized the works of God's Spirit - saw Jesus healing physically and mentally sick people (specifically a demon-possessed man who was blind and mute) and adamantly denied this power came from their own God. The people asked each other, "Can this be the promised son of David? The Messiah sent by God?" The religious leaders saw their authority slipping away and declared that Jesus was healing by the power and might of Satan.

Think of the insult to God! Instead of praising God for the miracle, they accused Jesus of using the power of God's adversary, the devil, to do good. They gave the glory meant for God to the accuser, the deceiver, the lying serpent.

This story is so important that it is told by three gospel writers: Matthew, Mark, and Luke. Don't get tripped up by confusing words like Beelzebul and blasphemy. I am reaching for the more straightforward translation of Jesus's response to these accusatory religious leaders' thinking. It can be found in the Easy-to-Read Version.

"I want you to know that people can be
forgiven for all the sinful things they do.
They can even be forgiven for the bad things they say against God.
But anyone who speaks against the
Holy Spirit will never be forgiven.
They will always be guilty of that sin."

Jesus said this because the teachers of the law
had accused him of having an evil spirit inside him.
Mark 3:28-30 ERV

A miracle is a sign pointing us to God. Attributing that power to Satan instead is unforgivable. To look in the face of God, to experience his Spirit urging repentance, and to continue to deny him repeatedly is the problem. Our hearts become hard, and our attitude becomes defiant. Arrogantly refusing him places us on the outside of his forgiveness. Please think about that. If we deny him and reject God's Spirit calling to us, how can we accept the forgiveness he offers? We are the ones who shut that door and lock it.

Suicide. I don't believe our loving God, who offers compassion to the ones weakened, tormented, and destroyed by physical or mental anguish, condemns the sufferer.

I think of a sweet friend of mine who carries that burden of self-harm in her head. I found a psalm that I pray often for her – and I have penned her name above it. The words of the psalm writer first thank the Lord for hearing his voice and his pleas for mercy. And he remembers the anguish of the snares of death surrounding him. "Return, my soul, to your rest," he reassures himself.

"Lord, you saved my soul from death.
You stopped my tears.
You kept me from falling.
I will continue to serve the Lord
in the land of the living.

I continued believing even when I said,
"I am completely ruined!"
Yes, even when I was upset and said,
"There is no one I can trust!"
What can I give the Lord
for all that he has done for me?"

Psalm 116:8-12 ERV

How do I end this story? Perhaps it doesn't end. There may not be a nice, neat bow here. I just want to lift the burden of condemnation off this desperate, heartbreaking act of suicide.

Jesus tells us the power of forgiveness is deeper, wider, and more powerful than we can grasp. "People can be forgiven for all the sinful things they do." Hold on to that, my friends. Don't let go. And hold on to the ones you love. Give them the truth of God's Spirit—in it is love and forgiveness.

51

How Does Your Garden Grow?

Read Matthew 13:1-23; Mark 4:1-20; Luke 8:4-15

I grew up in the country on the edge of the city. There were peach orchards right down the road, butting up to the pastureland of my grandfather. There were cotton fields on the other side of those pastures where my uncles' cows grazed. I remember seeing it harvested by the folks who lived on the Hudson place. I remember riding in the back of a pickup truck with my cousins as hay bales were gathered from the field next door to their house. Peaches, cotton, hay. By the time I was out of elementary school, all those trees and fields were bulldozed, and streets cut across the hills like ribbons. One new neighborhood after another permanently changed the landscape.

I know nothing about planting. I know nothing about tending crops. I know nothing about harvesting. Especially a harvest that my life depends upon.

Jesus talked to people who were well acquainted with the source of their daily bread. Their roads wound through fields ripe with grain: wheat and barley. Agriculture was so important to these people that their religious calendar closely aligned with the growing and harvest seasons. The barley harvest was lined up with Passover, and the wheat harvest was lined with Pentecost. The harvest of grapes, figs, olives, and pomegranates concluded with the Feast of Tabernacles.[1]

The men, women, and children were intimately connected with the land they lived on. Their hands were calloused from laboring in the fields, and their skin was bronzed from the sun. They broke the soil with an ox-drawn plow or a stone hoe, preparing it to receive the seed. The ground was worked to remove the weeds as the tender plants grew. They watched the sun, prayed for rain, and counted the moon's seasons until harvest. They knew the importance of fertile ground and abundant crops.

Not only was the preparation of the ground important – the seeds were precious. Folks didn't just go to the store and buy some more. What they had was limited. Important. Their very lives depended on the bounty of the harvest. It is too easy for us to miss this in our modern world.

They understood the story Jesus told of seeds being sown. Much better than we do. It made it very easy to hear the words and move on without thinking too much about it. All three of our writers tell the parable in two parts: the public telling and the private explanation. The disciples ask Jesus point blank, "Why do you do this? Why don't you speak more clearly?" And the answer Jesus gives sounds so harsh! I quote Mark 4:12,

> *But for those outside everything is in parables, so that*
> *"'they may indeed see but not perceive,*
> *and may indeed hear but not understand,*
> *lest they should turn and be forgiven.'"*

"Really?" you may ask. Didn't Jesus come to save his people? Doesn't he want them to *"turn and be forgiven"*? Matthew, our Jewish tax collector writing to his own Jewish people, goes into more detail about this speaking in confusing parables business. These are not the words of Jesus alone; these are the words of God! Jesus is quoting these words from the prophet Isaiah (6:9-10).

This is where we modern-day Christians have a disadvantage. We are not as familiar with God's long history with his chosen people. We are busy thinking about Jesus seeking the lost sheep and bidding the little children to come to him. We forget about God's people turning against him and each other: rebellious, corrupt, oppressive, thieving, bribing, adulterous, unashamed.

Let's go back to Isaiah. Just start right there at the beginning of chapter 6. Read it. Isaiah sees God. And it does him in. This is our problem; we have made God tame and docile to do our bidding. We forget he is holy and can shake the foundations of the earth. Isaiah was terrified at what he saw:

"Woe is me! For I am lost; for I am a man of unclean lips,
and I dwell in the midst of a people of unclean lips;
for my eyes have seen the King, the Lord of hosts!"
Isaiah 6:5

After a burning coal from the altar touched his lips, took away his guilt, and atoned for his sin, they could proceed! This tells you how unaware we are of our unworthiness. God is not unaware. He knows. The problem is we don't know - even when we are told.

When Isaiah agrees to God's plan to go and speak for him (Oh, notice, "Who will speak for us?") God's message to *"this people"* is this:

"'Keep on hearing, but do not understand;
keep on seeing, but do not perceive.'
Make the heart of this people dull,
and their ears heavy,
and blind their eyes;
lest they see with their eyes,
and hear with their ears,
and understand with their hearts,

and turn and be healed."

Isaiah 6:9-10

What have we just learned? These harsh words from Jesus came from the mouth of God! God, who created us, knows us so very well. He has seen, up close and personal, how quickly we choose the "other choice." Remember that first little conversation in the original Garden when the choice was to trust God or believe the serpent's lies? It was pretty easy to say yes to a lie. It was - and it still is!

This is a hard thing to admit. God gives us *what we choose*. We don't like that about him. We want him to remove all the difficult decisions and experiences. He gave us ears – so he should make us hear only what is good. He gave us eyes to see – so he should make us only see beauty. But oh… what is that *over there*? That looks interesting! Well, yes, it is a little offensive… but I think I could get used to it if I keep looking…

We are toddlers wanting cookies now. We are teenagers wishing to stay out late with our wild and crazy friends. They are certainly more fun than our parents. God teaches us what is good. He warns us we are crossing a line from which we will have trouble returning. But we hum louder so we drown out his voice. If we refuse to choose him because we have chosen something else, he gives us what we desire.

Jesus, like God, was not unaware of our very human nature. Read again the answer Jesus gives to his disciples' question in Matthew 13:11-13. The disciples – who were interested enough to ask the questions – had been given the knowledge of the secrets of heaven. Their knowledge would increase to an abundance. Others, who did not care to hear, or care to see or care to understand - what little they had would be taken away.

You know this, don't you? Think about the people you are close to. Do they spend time with you? Do they listen to your stories? Do they ask questions about what you think? Do they care about how you feel?

These are the ones you draw closer to. You give them more of yourself. They get you in abundance. It is the same in a relationship with God.

Are we ready to hear the meaning of the parable?

The seed is the Word of God (Luke 8:11). The soil is the hearts of those who hear the Word (v. 12). But there is a conflict. Satan does not want the heart to receive God's Word. He puts obstacles in play to prevent hearts from receiving, believing, and being saved.

If the seed (God's Word) falls on the path (a hard heart), the soil is packed solid by much traffic, and the seed is easily kicked away. The evil one insidiously snatches away what is sown in the heart before it is understood.

If the seed (God's Word) falls on rocky soil (a willing but weak heart), the heart receives it gladly and joyfully, but the soil lacks nourishment. The plant grows quickly above ground, but the roots that anchor it are small and shallow. It needs water and sun to grow and flourish – but it also requires the nutrients of the soil. A strong wind can easily uproot it. Under testing, tribulation, or persecution, the once hopeful plant shrivels, falls away, and dies.

If the seed (God's Word) falls among the thorns (a heart longing for the things of the world), the heart is divided. It is soil deceived by riches, pleasure, and the world's cares. Life is choked out, it never matures, and it never produces fruit.

If the seed (God's Word) falls on good soil (a heart that is soft and receiving), the heart will accept it, nourish it, and produce a large harvest of good fruit. I love the way Luke describes it: *"They are those who, hearing the word, hold it fast in an honest and good heart, and bear fruit with patience" (Luke 8:15).*

Let us have ears that really hear and eyes that really see. Hold on to the words of Jesus with an honest and good heart. He is preparing to produce an abundant harvest in you.

52

Little Similes of Lamps and Seeds

Read Matthew 13:31-32; Mark 4:21-34; Luke 8:16-18

Sometimes, the simple thoughts are the hardest. How often have you heard this passage: *"No one lights a lamp and hides it in a clay jar or puts it under a bed. Instead, they put it on a stand, so that those who come in can see the light" (Luke 8:16 NIV).*

You have the picture in your mind, don't you? Simple enough. Yet I am thinking… there must be more… Especially since this warning immediately follows: *"Take care then how you hear, for to the one who has, more will be given, and from the one who has not, even what he thinks that he has will be taken away" (v. 18).*

We just read this same warning sandwiched in the explanation of seed and soil. "Oh, dear Lord, I want to hear well!" I say aloud. I am reminded immediately of an open card sitting on my desk down the hall. I retrieve it, thinking the answer will be there. It was sent to me two months earlier by my church's director of the Women's Ministry. This passage of Luke 8:16 is penned on the left side of the card, and on the right side, she begins her message to me, "Thank you for putting the light of Christ on display for all the world to see through the beauty of the written and spoken word."

Aha. There it is. The light is not just any light. It is most certainly not my light. It is the light of Christ! Well, of course it is! We are not to hide the light of Jesus but lift it up to fill the room, to light the darkest corners, to expose what is hidden in darkness, to make known secrets that harm and destroy.

Have I put the light of Jesus on display, on a stand to be fully seen? Not always, I have to admit. I have tried to keep it concealed under my bed as if that would dim it! I laugh at myself. For many years, I wanted to keep it hidden away, only bringing it out when the coast was clear to show others who already had the light. That fearful tactic didn't usually work very well. God had other plans. He would out me. Someone would see that light slip out when I wasn't watching.

I am thinking of the years I spent directing television commercials, traveling to cities like Los Angeles, Chicago, or Toronto. I often worked with clients or crews I had never worked with before. I would slip up with a careless word about Jesus or prayer or an unusual action, and someone I was working with would suddenly have *that look* come across their face. And they would ask a question quietly. Or they would bring up something I had said that had struck a chord in them. And I would know that the reason I was there was not really for that job but to have that conversation with that person at that time. I was there to put the light of Jesus on a stand to fill their room. Jesus would not stay quietly hidden under the bed. He insisted on his proper place, lifted high.

If we follow Mark's passage, as is typical of his writing, he barely takes a breath before he is on to two additional similes explaining the kingdom of God. I must remind myself that this was what Jesus was all about – trying to help us understand what the very real, very permanent, very other-worldly kingdom of God was like. He had shown up in our world flying a banner of his Father's kingdom. Remember his message: *"The kingdom of God is at hand!"* Jesus didn't have a hidden agenda, although the religious leaders of the time wanted it hidden because they were just fine with how things were there in their little corner of the world, thank you. But Jesus had launched a full-out revival with magic tricks and miracles, teaching old truths with new authority and captivating the crowds of commoners and intellectuals who flocked around him. And he wasn't afraid to touch the lepers or talk to the women or dine with the sinners. If this was what this kingdom of God looked like, it was much more interesting than following rules and making the next sacrifice. People came to hear more.

"And he said, the kingdom of God is as if a man should scatter seed on the ground" (Mark 4:26). This seed has found receptive soil. It is hidden away from the farmer's eyes. Yet, night and day, something is going on underground—beyond the farmer's reach. There is growth! *"The earth produces by itself, first the blade, then the ear, then the full grain in the ear" (v. 28).*

I remember so clearly the wonder I felt when I was pregnant with my son and then my daughter. An egg, unseen within me, was fertilized. From that fertilized egg, cells divided and multiplied, forming a heart and lungs, eyes and ears, fingers and toes. I had absolutely nothing to do with it. It was amazing to me! And my goodness, when those babies were born! I had no authority to choose whether one was male or female. I had not designed their very individual characteristics. I had not created their very distinct personalities. They were each a unique miracle! I really don't understand how someone who has experienced the wonder of birth can deny the existence of God. The creation of life brought me to my knees.

The seed is planted, and the harvest has come. We may tend the crop as it grows, but we most certainly do not create it. Only God can do that.

When I look at this parable explaining the kingdom of God – whether through the mystery of a growing grain of wheat buried in the earth or a growing child buried within the womb, I think of my own mysterious growing faith in God's kingdom. We who profess that we call ourselves Christians believe that at the moment we say yes to the offer of salvation, our life is held in safekeeping for eternity. Jesus has become our advocate, paying the price for our sinful life, sitting at the right hand of our Father and Judge. They wait for our return. The Spirit of God has placed his seal (his unbreakable promise) of protection over us until that Day when we are safely within the gates of his kingdom. He has been given the responsibility to walk alongside us until we arrive Home.

Until then, here we are on planet Earth, a fertile seed sprouting and growing. First, we are a fragile blade peeking above the soil's surface, stretching up toward the warmth of the sun, developing and growing. We may encounter drought or torrential rain. The winter may be too cold; the summer may be too hot. Violent winds will blow. Wild animals may break through to trample us under their hooves or nibble at our budding fruit. This time to grow is precious and limited. The season is short. Soon, the grain will be harvested.

This isn't sad. It is good. There is a purpose in the growing. The abundance of the harvest is measured and celebrated. Maybe here. But more probably there. In the kingdom of God. What makes me think that? Jesus taught us that our treasures are not here on this earth – where moths and rust destroy them – but can be safely held for us "in heaven" (Matthew 6:19-21). There will be crowns and a new name (Revelation 3:11-12). And fine white linen clothing made from righteous deeds (Revelation 19:8). We don't know all the details, but Jesus was sure that what awaits us in God's kingdom is much better than anything we hold tightly here. Jesus spoke of a bountiful harvest. And with it comes celebration.

And then there is the story of the mustard seed. The teeny, tiny mustard seed grows from the darkness of the ground to become the largest garden plant, with branches stretching out into the sky for birds to find shelter and build their nests in its shade. This tiny mustard seed is comparable to the kingdom of God. Held in our hand, it is minor, minuscule, and challenging to see in its smallness. How could it become anything more than what it is? God will bury it deep and infuse it with life to grow and gain strength, beauty, and power until it reaches above our heads, bearing fruit with limbs spreading high and wide as protection and shelter. A home nurturing life. This is what the kingdom of God is like.

As a child, my favorite thing to do was climb trees. I loved being higher and seeing farther. In my grown-up neighborhood, a few streets behind us are connected, ending in a cul-de-sac. The children there roam freely, fighting imaginary battles from cardboard boxes with plastic swords and helmets. The house on one corner has a huge magnolia tree with spreading limbs that reach to the ground all the way around. On summer evenings, if you walk by, there are often various bikes and scooters, maybe a ball or a random toy scattered around on the grass at the base of the tree. And if you listen closely, you can hear child-talk and sometimes laughter as six or eight children perched high on the great limbs are hidden from sight by the dense, glossy leaves. I want to leave my dog on the leash with my husband and climb in there with them. I imagine it is cool in their dark, leafy treehouse. And I imagine it has the lemony fragrance of magnolia blooms. Could this be heaven? Is this what the kingdom of God is like?

Jesus wanted us *to know.* He used many such parables to tell us about his Father's kingdom. Why should he care to tell us about this place unless there was a very real possibility of us going there? I daresay, if there wasn't that possibility, wouldn't his words just be cruel? No, I think he wanted us to understand so we would look beyond this hard world to a better one *there*. He told stories of the goodness of the kingdom of God. Listen carefully – can you hear it?

53

Holding On to the Hand of Matthew

Read Matthew 13:1-52

When my daughter, Gray, was in the eighth grade, she became fast and furious friends with a young girl whose parents owned a beach house in Florida. They invited Gray and several other girls to spend spring break with them. You can imagine how unpopular I was when I said no. For years, we had been following the wise counsel of our youth pastor, who taught us to plan our family vacation during spring break to help avoid the "spring break in Florida craziness" that high schoolers usually cook up.

I tried to explain to my daughter how wonderful our long-planned trip out west would be. We would see enormous trees, towering red cliffs, and deep snow. She wanted sun, water, and her girlfriends. "I don't want to go to California and Nevada. That doesn't sound like any fun at all," was her unhappy response.

"Oh, it will be wonderful," I tried to explain. We will walk among trees that are a thousand years old. It will be like you are an ant among giants. And you will see land you have never seen; it will glow red in the sun, and you can climb up and sit inside dark caves within the face of the rock." Nothing I could say could make her enthusiastic about our destination. But since we were the parents and had more wisdom and vision than a 12-year-old girl, she found herself in this land that she couldn't imagine. And she loved it.

She stood inside hollow trees that soared into the heavens above her. She climbed red rocks to look out on vast vistas and sat in the cool of hidden caves. She flew across mountaintops on a snowmobile. She went horseback riding at the strangest little ranch in the middle of the desert, where peacocks roosted in the trees and rodeo riders waited tables at breakfast. And she wandered for a day or two in Egypt…oh, wait a minute…that must have been Las Vegas with its crazy larger-than-life amusement park architecture.

No matter how many words I had carefully chosen to help her see where she was going, there was just no way she could imagine the wonders she was about to experience. How can you imagine something you have never seen, never experienced? That is where we fall with the whole idea of heaven since we have no photos to look at, and the descriptions fall a little short of what we think will be exciting and fun. And I must admit, the description in the current travel guide of floaty clouds and angel music just doesn't sound that enticing – especially since we are supposed to spend eternity there.

"The kingdom of heaven is like…" Jesus told those who sat at his feet. He has been there. He and his Father have been preparing it for us, and they are pretty sure we will love it. They did a pretty good job designing and creating the universe and our planet Earth, so it seems like we could trust them a little bit with this new place – God's kingdom – but it's just so hard to imagine. Our desires are as limited as a child's previous experiences.

Reading through the descriptions Jesus shared about his kingdom, spoken in parables and similes, I decided I needed to pause for a day or two. I needed to back up in my reading. Were there little details I had omitted? Did I miss something by grouping the parables together instead of reading them in the context of Jesus telling them? I decided to go back to the beginning with Matthew the disciple, Matthew the eyewitness, Matthew the tax collector who was accustomed to lining up accounts in an orderly system. I decided to take hold of his hand and let him lead me through the day.

The first thing I had missed was the first line of Matthew's telling. *"That same day Jesus went out of the house and sat beside the sea" (13:1).* "That same day..." What was that day? It had already been a busy one. It had started with a lot of healing. Especially notable was the demon-oppressed man who was blind and mute. Untangling what the devil has tangled must be exhausting. And if that wasn't enough, those interfering religious elites had shown up to accuse Jesus of being filled with the power of the devil to undo the devil's work.

Smacking down their hypocrisy was no small thing. Let us be sure we understand no one else in all Judea was challenging the powerful Pharisees on their theology. No one else would dare to spin them around and shut them down as if they were misguided schoolboys. Jesus did not tiptoe the tightrope with them. He called them a *brood of vipers* (12:34). He called them evil! He warned them their careless words would condemn them on the day of judgment (v. 36). He called their generation evil and adulterous when they demanded a sign of his authority (ignoring the miraculous healings!). Jesus claimed to be greater than Jonah the Prophet and greater than Solomon the King in all his wisdom (vv. 41-42). Those were some pretty big claims. They were outrageous claims!

He had refused his family's intervention to return quietly home, and then, Matthew tells us, that same day, Jesus went out of the house and down to the sea. Great crowds gathered around him, so he got into a boat, where his voice would be amplified on the water as he sat down to teach.

I want to think about his tone of voice for a moment. I tend to soften his voice in my mind, making it gentle and soothing as if speaking to a sleepy child. I think I am very wrong in this thinking. I must remember he has just silenced the voices of both demons and Pharisees. The crowds were growing large enough to spill out of Peter's house and down the street and overflow the neighborhood so that a change of venue was in order. With all that in mind, I am betting his voice was filled with power and authority. It was a voice that rose to reach out and touch the weary farmer and the windburned fisherman in the back, carrying above the cries of babies and the rambunctious play of little boys.

There are stories of the great evangelist George Whitefield. He was a charismatic, dynamic preacher who helped spark the revival known as the Great Awakening throughout Britain, Scotland, Ireland, Wales, and especially the North American colonies in the mid-1700s. He preached outdoors in what was called "open-air gatherings" - very unusual at the time - because churches could not hold the enormous crowds. He also did not shy away from being critical of the established churches, so he wasn't always exactly welcome in their buildings!

He preached several times a day and drew crowds in the thousands. There were estimates of over 30,000 people in London and over 23,000 people in Boston. Benjamin Franklin calculated the number of people who could hear Whitefield's booming voice by methodically recording how far he walked away block by block until he could no longer hear his voice clearly.[1] All of this was before any modern means of amplification. Whitefield was not traveling with sound equipment. Neither was Jesus.

One other thing to think about: if he only had a handful of listeners, why would the religious elite of Jerusalem make the long trip to the outskirts of the Judean world to investigate and challenge him? The Sea of Galilee was a long, long way from the important religious capital of Judaism. Was Jesus causing such a stir that these leaders decided it was necessary to make such an arduous journey? Just how big were these crowds following Jesus? In the hundreds? In the thousands?

And the use of parables... If you have come to make an announcement and change the world, why speak in little stories that entertain but with meaning not so easily ascertained? Our very Jewish friend Matthew reaches back to prophecy to explain. From Isaiah 6:9-10, he referenced people's dull and hardened hearts. From Psalm 78:2, he pointed to the fulfillment of the predictions of the coming prophet whose teaching would be in parables, *"sayings from of old"* and things that have been *"hidden since the foundation of the world (Matthew 13:35)"* so that the future generations might know of the wonders and glories of the Lord (Psalm 78:4).

I think of a classroom of students. There are those who are just passing the time, hoping to be entertained until the next event, say, the games that begin at recess. Then, there are those who are taking notes and plan on staying after class to ask questions. And then, there are others from the faculty auditing the class who are hoping to find fault in the teaching so they will have grounds for the teacher's dismissal. Parables were a brilliant way to teach a lesson that would only be absorbed by the students who longed to learn. Parables can do two things at the same time - conceal the truth and reveal the truth. It depends on what you are looking for.

And there they are—eight little stories lined up here about what the kingdom of heaven will be like. Some are so vague that we scratch our heads and say, "What? What in the world does that mean?" Some are simple one-line comparatives. Let's look at them a little more closely because Jesus really wants us to understand what God has planned for us. He doesn't want us to miss the chance to experience great wonders.

Here is the big picture when we walk along with Matthew; he is the only gospel writer to use the phrase "kingdom of heaven," and he uses it approximately 50 times! Matthew clearly states that Jesus is the great king they had been expecting. Jesus is the son of David, who would rule over Israel. These parables were stories of encouragement, stories telling of the righteousness of this kingdom, the peace that would come through submission to the Father's will, and the ultimate purpose of this kingdom: joy! Matthew believes Jesus fulfills every role described in the scriptures; he will reveal truth like a prophet, have the ability to forgive sin like a priest, and have the authority of a king.[2] These are the glasses we need to wear as we watch Matthew unspool the stories of Jesus.

The first parable of the sower and the seeds answers the question we aren't even aware we should be asking: "How do you enter into this kingdom of God?" We have already discussed this parable, and hopefully, our hearts are honest and good, and we have embraced the seeds God has planted in our hearts. The second parable is also a story of a planter sowing seeds into his field. His enemy came in the night to sow bad seeds – weeds – which looked very much like the good wheat as it grew. Side by side, their roots intertwined. Pull up the bad, and the good will be destroyed with it. "Wait," the master of the field instructs his workers. "I am very aware of what has happened. We will allow them to grow up together, and I will sort them on the day of harvest."

The explanation Jesus gives is clear. The one sowing the good seeds is Jesus, the Son of Man – his description for himself. The field where the good seeds are sewn is the world… pause here just a moment! He didn't say Israel. His vision of how far-reaching his field extends goes beyond their little neighborhood. *The field is the world. The good seed is the sons of the kingdom (of heaven, of God)* (v. 38). The weeds are not. They are the sons of the enemy, the evil one, the devil. Yet they are all growing up together. In the field, in the world, intertwined.

This obviously occurs here on earth, before Judgment, before the harvest, and before the end of the age. In the wisdom of Jesus, the Master of the field, are we to grow together, these children of the kingdom along with the children of the evil one? We are not in a world separated out and surrounded only by God's children. The children of Satan are mixed in with us. And sometimes it is hard to tell us apart from one another. So, what are we to do? Grow strong. Let the swaying against the enemy strengthen you instead of tearing you down. Be aware that those standing in the field with you may not share the same father's love; some are children of righteousness, and some are children intent on evil.

The Master will sort it out at the end! His reapers, the angels, *"will gather out of his kingdom all causes of sin and all law-breakers, and throw them into the fiery furnace."* So much for the counterfeit believers who think they closely mimic the children of the kingdom. Satan is very good at imitation and confusion. God is not confused. He is protecting his own who will be gathered into his kingdom, shining like the sun.

These are not new words. God revealed them to his prophet Daniel, who lived in a foreign and evil land. He told him of the angel Michael, the great prince in charge of the good seed. Read Daniel 12:1-3. *"And those who are wise shall shine like the brightness of the sky above; and those who turn many to righteousness, like the stars forever and ever (v. 3)."*

Do not be disturbed or discouraged by the weeds entangling your roots, sharing your soil, and threatening to overpower you. God is aware. His angels are keeping watch. There will be a time of sorting at harvest. Hold tightly to what is righteous. Your light will shine in the heavens.

Jesus told a similar parable, which made sense to the fishermen in the crowd. I think of a late afternoon on a tiny wooden pier in a little village in the Yucatan in the 1980s. Jeff and I were in our early 30s, with no children yet, and we were staying in a thatched-roof inn right on the beach. There were only eight or nine rooms available for rent. One telephone in town was "open for business" three hours a day. There was only one television in the village, located in a house operating as a restaurant where the locals hung out. If anything happened in that little neighborhood, everyone knew about it. Apparently, a small fishing boat pulling up to that tiny pier was a big event. We had noticed adults and children suddenly appearing on the beach, gathering around the boat, which had just tied up.

The nets were spread out, spanning the small distance between the boat and the pier. Adults and children reached out to help the fishermen pull the fish out of the net. I watched as children expertly stretched the net, opening the holes, sometimes stretching it apart with their feet and hands as they dipped their heads down to extract a fish between their teeth. The sun was low and warm on their brown skin. There was good-natured laughter and chatter in their Mayan language. The good fish were tossed into buckets, and when the nets were empty, each helper received pay for their efforts with a few fish. They were happy and grateful.

Jesus told the story of one net lowered into the sea. It pulls up in its catch fish of every kind, both good fish for eating and fish that leave a bad taste in your mouth and have no value. All are gathered together. The angels will sort them out with judgment. The wicked will be separated from the righteous, and the wicked will be thrown out. They will be thrown into the fire where there is weeping and that old-fashioned description of *gnashing of teeth.* It is a harsh and sobering truth about what life will be like inside and outside the kingdom of God.

Please listen closely. If you are of the thinking that God is all love and all of us are his children and all will find their home in his kingdom, you need to look very carefully at these stories. Everyone will not find a happy ending here. Even many who look very much like you. Or if you are just trying to blend in – stop. Look closely at yourself. Are you carefully imitating the ones around you? Are you trying very hard just to fit in, slipping nicely into your pretty garment of good morals? Do not think you can slip in unnoticed. You will need to acknowledge you are wrong and unrighteous. You are the invasive weed, the foul-tasting fish, the liar who deceives. Admit who you are. Ask God for his perfect mercy. Accept the forgiveness of Jesus. He alone can make you new and welcome you into his kingdom.

There are two little similes of the value of this kingdom. The kingdom of heaven is a great treasure hidden and unseen by others in a field. Before banks and the stock market, when wars could erupt suddenly or an enemy could capture you, carrying all your wealth around was dangerous. So, you buried it. And perhaps you were never able to return for it. Years passed, and ownership of the field went from one person to another. It was not uncommon for someone's great treasure to be accidentally unearthed, with no one there to claim it. The kingdom of heaven is as valuable as an unexpected great treasure. Sell all that you have to obtain it.

The kingdom of God is like a precious, beautiful, priceless pearl you have spent your whole life searching for. Forfeit all you hold as valuable, for this one beautiful pearl is worth more than all the rest. These two stories tell us it is worth great effort to reach for this kingdom. Do not glance at it and walk away. Do not become discouraged and decide it is too much effort. Sacrifice all you have for this one great thing of great worth.

We have already looked at the humble mustard seed growing into a mighty tree. The kingdom that Jesus was bringing would start tiny, consisting of a handful of scared and mismatched disciples, but within their lifetime, it would grow into thousands of disciples and reach the edges of their known world. And it just wouldn't be for the Jews; the Gentile birds would also nest in its branches.

This talk of a mighty seed may bring to mind the promise God made Abraham. The Lord has just sent an angel to hold back Abraham's arm from sacrificing Isaac, pointing out the ram caught in the bush instead. But he isn't done with this little episode. God calls down from heaven a second time:

"By Myself I have sworn, declares the Lord, because you have done this thing and have not withheld your son, your only son, indeed I will greatly bless you,
and I will greatly multiply your seed as the stars of the heavens
and as the sand, which is on the seashore;
and your seed shall possess the gate of their enemies.
And in your seed all the nations of the earth shall be blessed,

because you have obeyed My voice."
Genesis 22:16-18 NASB

Now I know seed is another way to say descendant or offspring. But it is pretty interesting, isn't it? In other words, "What is the kingdom of God like? One small seed will grow to bless all the earth."

On the heels of this comes the comparison of the kingdom of heaven to a small amount of leaven mixed into flour to become dough. You cannot see what it is doing, but it will spread invisibly to change the flour chemically, causing it to rise, become softer and lighter, and make the baked bread more easily chewed.

Some versions of this passage list the amount of flour Jesus listed in his recipe: 60 pounds. That's a lot of flour. Our baker used a small amount of yeast, but it significantly affected the dough. This refers to the world and how the kingdom of heaven will spread. But it also refers to a person's life. What starts small and hidden in their hearts will change and grow that person, making them softer, lighter, and much tastier!

It seems we are done, but then you notice this last little question from Jesus, our teacher, "Do you understand these things?" He looks us directly in the eye, waiting for our answer.

If we understand the kingdom of heaven, then we have a responsibility as owners of God's home. This is the exciting part. We are not simply guests in God's kingdom. We take on the role of owner and host to others who wish to enter the door.

God revealed truth about his kingdom to his prophets of old. He continued to explain his kingdom through his Son, Jesus. We have been entrusted with keys to the storeroom, where we can bring out the older truths God has revealed from the beginning of time, as well as the new truths Jesus brought with him when he came to earth. Old treasures and new treasures. Bring them out and share their beauty with the world!

54

Rebuking the Wind and the Demons

Read Matthew 8:23-34; Mark 4:35-41; 5:1-20; Luke 8:22-39

A film producer I used to work with in LA, Carol, hired one of her good friends, Amy, who usually didn't do production work, to help out for the day as they were making all the arrangements for a commercial shoot. The director they were working with thought very highly of himself. He prided himself on having great taste and being very sophisticated and he treated most people around him as inferiors. Carol asked Amy to order lunch for everyone, and the director insisted on sushi and made a big deal of them ordering from what he thought was the best sushi restaurant in town. He went into great detail with Amy about exactly how he wanted his sushi prepared and made her repeat his order word by word so she would order it correctly. And he wanted to sit beside her as she ordered it so he could ensure she placed his order to his precise specifications.

Amy, this lovely, very Jewish woman, called the sushi restaurant and placed everyone's order, including his, in fluent Japanese. She paused to look at the director and, in English, asked him, "Was there anything else you wanted?" before closing out the order in perfect Japanese. I am sure, as he sat there, one thought was going through his mind: "Who is this woman? She certainly isn't who I assumed she was!"

What he didn't know was that Amy, the daughter of a military man, had grown up in Japan. She had not just been to the land of sushi; she had lived there. She ate the food. She spoke the language. She understood the culture and knew the people. This is sort of what we get with Jesus. *He has been to the kingdom.* He has eaten the food. He speaks the language. When we watch what he does, the way he talks, the way he touches, the way he responds to people individually in such a way that he appears to know their every thought, we walk away saying to ourselves, "Who is this Jesus? What kind of man is this? He certainly isn't who I assumed he was!"

Mark, who gets much of his information about Jesus from the fisherman Peter, tells us, *"On that day, when evening had come..."* Jesus suggests they set sail and head to the other side of the lake. This has been a long day. It is little surprise that Jesus would immediately fall asleep on a cushion in the stern of the boat. It is night; the boat rises and falls with the waves and the wind blowing. The men who pilot this boat are not novices. They are experienced sailors. Like the back of their hand, they know this lake with its potential for sudden storms and high waves. It must be an incredibly terrifying storm for them to fear for their lives. The rain stings their face as the waves break over the boat's side; water fills the hull.

Have you been there? Your little boat is in the process of capsizing in the night, and Jesus is asleep as if nothing is happening. We may find ourselves screaming to make our voice heard above the howl of the wind, "Jesus! Don't you care what is going on here? Wake up! How can you be sleeping at a time like this?"

He awoke, rebuked the wind, and spoke to the sea, *"Peace! Be still!"* And there was a great calm.

Who, then, is this, that even the wind and the waves obey him? The disciples in the boat were afraid of the wrong thing. Isn't this us? We are looking at the fearsomeness of the world around us, terrified of how easily it can destroy us, unaware that the man sleeping in our boat is more powerful and potentially more dangerous than we ever imagined. He is not an imposter, a poser, a pretender doing magic tricks with secondhand knowledge of sushi. We best pause a minute and figure out who we are dealing with. A teacher of things undisclosed. A healer of illness and disease and deformity. But he seems to have authority over even the forces of nature. Who, then, is this?

Before they had a good answer, the boat bumped up against the distant shore of the Gentiles. They find pigs grazing on the hills, a crazy man (or two), and a graveyard. It doesn't take but a moment for everyone to figure out they aren't in Kansas anymore. They aren't even close. The storm must have taken them quite off-course. The country of the Gerasenes, or Gadarenes (the name of the larger region), is on the very eastern side of the Sea of Galilee and was not part of Israel. It was a center of worship for the Hellenistic god Zeus and the Roman god Jupiter, and pigs were the required sacrifice on their altars. Like I said, Jesus and his seagoing friends are on the wrong side of town in a foreign land.

And they have a greeting party.

He is a mess. Completely insane, living among the dead and sleeping in the rain. He has broken every fine law of society and every shackle placed on his arms and legs. Blood scabs on his skin from his own marks of self-hatred, and he cries out with pain and rage. There is no containing him. He is dangerous to himself and others.

And he knows Jesus's name. And his identity. *"What have you to do with me, Jesus, Son of the Most High God?"*

I think in our heart of hearts, we all cry this out into our dark nights. Why in the world would the Son of the Most High God come across the sea for us? Can't he see we are bleeding and broken? The chains meant to keep us in line are broken and dangling useless. The good, fine folks of the town make sure they don't come too close.

"What have you to do with me?"

There is conversation while Jesus ignores this objection and goes to the heart of the matter. Jesus is already talking to the demons, bossing them around like they are wind and waves. He demands they leave and negotiates where they may go - after he finds out their name. Interesting, this little detail. *"My name is Legion, for we are many."* This is a mighty force there to do battle. Against the power of Jesus, they cower and beg.

This is Jesus. He looks for what is rotten and cleans house, sending the demons into grazing pigs who race for the bottom of the sea. That isn't the end of the story. It never is. The good people of the countryside come to see what in the world is going on. And it terrifies them. For good reason.

Two thousand pigs dashed against the rocks and drowned in the sea is no small occurrence. These were the pigs needed for sacrifice to their god. How ironic that they were now demon-possessed and dead. What did that say about their god? And another thing – those pigs were very valuable – and now they were destroyed. Who was going to pay for such damage and loss? These storm-tossed fishermen needed to leave.

Never mind the crazy man sitting there like he was in his right mind again. Never mind that he was speaking coherent sentences and wearing clothes. Legion had begged Jesus not to send them out of the region but into the pigs instead. Now, it is the townspeople's turn to beg Jesus to do something for them: get into his boat, depart from their country, and return to where he came from.

Is this the way you see Jesus? Does he show up uninvited, threatening to wreck your world? The changes he brings are too extreme and too costly. His power is too out of your control. No, it is much better for everyone if we just let things stay the way they already are—the way they have always been. We can deal with the little bit of crazy on the outskirts of town.

Jesus made a trip through the waves of a storm to land on one man's rocky shore. He found him bleeding and naked. And Jesus didn't sail away until he was clothed and "in his right mind." If you think you are too much of a mess for God, be encouraged by this story. You cannot scare Jesus off with your out-of-control life. He isn't afraid to deal with your demons. He doesn't flee from your upraised fist and anger.

I know a woman with a heart for our city's hungry. Once a week, she shows up in a poor section of town and unloads a hot meal from her van that she has prepared from donated discarded food from grocery stores. She has baked chickens in a local church's industrial ovens and spent hours preparing vegetables and dividing bread. It is enough to feed over 200 people who otherwise wouldn't have a meal that day. One day, an angry young man showed up to bully the crowd that gathered, shouting obscenities at them and threatening violence to anyone who looked at him. The police had been called to no avail.

Kathy felt the Holy Spirit prompt her to go to him. She laid down her serving spoon. She walked over to the ranting young man, put her motherly arm around him, and said knowingly into his ear, "Baby, this is not who you are. This is not who you are." He stopped his pacing immediately. He looked into her face. And burst into tears. "I know," he said, "I know. I am small, and if I don't act tough, they will beat me up. I have to be tough."

When Kathy told me this story, it reminded me of Jesus and the crazy, dangerous man on the shore of the Gerasenes. Jesus saw him. Jesus saw the demons twisting him inside out. He knew that man was not the demons who were tormenting him. They had their own identity. Their own name. And Jesus had the authority to make them leave.

Who, then, is this? Who is this that even the wind and the sea obey him? Who is this that unclean spirits tremble at his command? If you are suspicious that this man, Jesus, may be closer to the Son of the Most High God than mere man, what is your response? The unclean spirits begged him not to condemn them into the great abyss before their day of judgment. The townspeople begged him to go away and leave them be. The man once possessed by demons begged to go with Jesus – that he might be with him. There seemed to be a whole lot of begging going on – and everyone had their own reason.

Interestingly, Jesus seemed to give everyone what they wanted... except the man who started everything. Look carefully at how Jesus responded to him. Maybe this is the best response of all:

"Go home to your friends and tell them how much the Lord has done for you, and how he has had mercy on you" (Mark 5:19).

Could this be his advice to us? If we have found ourselves released from our demons, healed, and clothed, should we be telling our story?

You may need to ask yourself a few other questions as you sail away from this story of insanity on the shore. Who is in your boat? Who has landed on your shore? Who has rebuked the wind and cast out the demons? Who, then, is this Jesus? Are we still afraid? Is our faith still small? Did the fishermen traveling with Jesus end up in the bottom of the sea? Or did the demons?

55

A Sword and A Cross

Read Matthew 10:1-42; 13:53-58; Mark 6:1-13; Luke 9:1-6

Jesus heads back to his hometown, his disciples trailing behind him. Matthew says it is after he taught the parables about the kingdom of heaven. Mark says it is after he has healed the anonymous bleeding woman in the crowd and raised the daughter of Jairus from the dead. Either way, Jesus is no longer simply the son of the carpenter. It is the Sabbath. He teaches in the synagogue where he grew up.

They have lots of questions. They question his wisdom about the Scriptures. They question his authority to heal. They think they know him so well. They know who he is and where he came from. They know his mother, Mary. They know his brothers and sisters, lining them up with familiarity: James, Joseph, Simon, and Judas. He is one of them. He has arrived home in Nazareth only to find that the familiar faces still have the familiar expectations. They have heard about all the profound teachings, the miraculous healings, and the crowds that hang on every word. All they see is the little boy who once lived down the street. Nothing special to see here.

"Who does he think he is?" they ask, offended. Their pride blinds them. They are blinded by jealousy. Jesus could only be the son of the carpenter in his hometown. He could never be the Son of God. Not in Nazareth. Jesus says this is an old story. The prophets God sent to their people before him also were rejected. And that chapter is closed with the sad judgment that he did not do mighty works there because of their unbelief. Unbelief. It is a terrible loss not to believe.

This is a reality to consider before starting our next adventure with Jesus. He is sending out his disciples alone. They will need to be prepared for rejection. For unbelief. For the sorrow of closed eyes, closed minds, closed hearts, closed doors. Matthew goes into great detail about this event and the instructions of their teacher, Jesus. He is sending his inner circle out, two together to do what they will one day need to do alone.

He is not sending them out to Disneyland. This is not a vacation by the sea. He is very clear here that he is not bringing peace to the earth but a sword. These words of Jesus are all in red. These are not words of a love song. These are glorious yet terrifying words. These are the warnings of a brewing storm and preparations for battle. Read this chapter carefully. It is unsettling that Jesus did not candy-coat what an adventure with him would look like. It is good that we pay attention.

Jesus starts by seeing the need; so many long to hear what he has to say – they long for healing and the comfort of God's words. Jesus compares them to a field that is ripe and ready to be harvested. So, Jesus delegates. He trains his disciples and sends them out. Going out on their own, they will begin to understand more about who Jesus is - and they will be better able to stand when Jesus is suddenly taken away from them.

Jesus didn't send out everyone in the crowd. He handpicked twelve. As we discussed earlier on this journey, I have always had difficulty remembering the names of the Twelve. Different people called them different names. And I get this. Jeff's nephew is one of those guys; he grew up as Brent. When he entered the Marines, he started going by his first name, Thomas. But when our kids were young, he thought it would be amusing to have them call him Flannigan, which they did for years. It is just as likely for us to call him Thomas as it is to call him Flannigan, which isn't even his real name, and half the time, I forget he goes by Thomas, and I call him Brent.

Okay, let's look at the inner circle of the twelve disciples. We have Simon, whom Jesus renamed Peter. His brother Andrew and two other brothers, James and John, the sons of Zebedee, were nicknamed the Sons of Thunder, which tells you a good bit about their personalities. Then we have Philip and Bartholomew, who was called Nathanael by John. There was Thomas, whom we know as "doubting Thomas," but he was also called Didymus. And, of course, we know Matthew, the tax collector, but he was also called Levi. He could have possibly been the brother of James the Lesser, the son of Alphaeus (not to be confused with James, the son of Zebedee and brother of John). Then there is Thaddaeus, also called Jude or Judas, the son of James. We are almost to the end… And then there is Simon the Zealot, who may not have been a Zealot at all but just from Canaan, and then finally there is Judas Iscariot, whom Matthias later replaced. And I must admit, I no longer feel too bad that I can't keep them all straight. These guys were Jesus's inner circle. These were the guys he was closest to, and he concentrated on teaching them what he was all about.

Jesus begins by first giving them his authority. Authority is such a powerful word. I love the way Merriam-Webster defines *authority*. It is the power to give orders or make decisions, the power or right to direct or control someone or something, the confident quality of someone who knows a lot about something or who is respected or obeyed by other people, and in my opinion, this is the best: a quality that makes something seem true or real.[1] It was the most crucial tool his disciples would need. Jesus was literally saying, "I will give you my authority to do what I do. I will empower you with the authority God the Father has empowered me. When the people see you, they will see the power and authority of God."

Do you remember that movie from long ago, *Crocodile Dundee,* about the Australian crocodile hunter from the outback who ended up in New York City with the city girl? The two of them are walking along the city streets at night when three robbers show up, pull out a switchblade, and demand his wallet. His girlfriend advises him to give them his wallet because they have a knife. He softly laughs and replies, "That's not a knife," as he reaches into his pant leg, pulls out a huge hunting knife, and holds it up. "That's a knife." He reaches over to slit our hoodlum's leather jacket to demonstrate the sharpness and the reach of his knife. The three immediately hightail it out of there. Authority. It is carrying a big knife and having the skill to use it when your adversary is looking for easy money with little effort and a switchblade. The disciples would have a big knife of authority.

What follows are precise instructions that read like a crash course in Ministry 101. Their message and purpose are simple: God's kingdom is near. It is at hand. It is close in time or place… or may already be happening! Heads up, listen, pay attention. You are standing on the track, and a train is coming. Do you hear the engine and feel the vibration of the wheels along the rails? Look with your eyes, listen with your ears, and open your hearts to understand that God has sent his Messiah into the world. And this Messiah seems to be bringing the realness of God and his kingdom.

Where do they go, and who do they minister to? They only go to the lost sheep of Israel. He starts with those who are the closest first—those who should already know our God, those who share family blood, and a history of walking with the Lord. I think this is often where he desires us to start: with those closest to us—with the ones he conveniently brings along our path, right to our own door.

How are they to tell this message? With powerful words backed up by God's authority. That authority becomes very visible through miraculous signs: heal the sick, raise the dead, cleanse those who have leprosy, and drive out demons. That would certainly get their attention. The ability to heal such extreme problems would bring the people to the disciples. Don't dismiss this too quickly by thinking, "Well, sure… if I had the power to 'heal the sick, raise the dead, cleanse those who have leprosy, and drive out demons,' it would certainly be much easier to tell people about Jesus."

You may not have a ministry doing those miraculous works, but I am betting someone is doing those things not too far from you. This past year, I met two different women who said yes to God when he chose to send them out to perform miracles. One has a passion for women on the other side of the world in desperately poor communities where young girls are considered a curse and a financial burden to their families. Food is often withheld from them, and they are sold into sexual slavery before they are out of childhood. I support this ministry financially.

The other woman has a passion for women under the bondage of drug and alcohol addiction here in our backyard. These women end up losing everything – their families, their homes, their children – and if they keep going, they lose their lives. I support this ministry by showing up with a smile and a helping hand.

Both ministries reach out to touch these girls and women who are physically dying and spiritually dead. They are as untouchable as lepers, unclean and incurable, outcast from the rest of the world around them. The demons of evil and hopelessness torment them. But God comes into their lives with the authority to heal through the two women who started these ministries. On both sides of the world, lives are changed. What has been dead is brought back to life. Maybe we do have the power to heal the sick, cleanse those who have leprosy, and drive out demons. Look around you for those who believe God is still performing miracles.

Jesus instructed those who go out to labor in the harvest fields not to worry about what they need, for God will supply their needs. What does God want me to provide for the laborers? Am I being stingy with what God has given me? I am reminded that everything I have comes by the grace and fullness of God's abundance. This is certainly not the way our culture thinks. But it is the way God thinks. It is the way

Jesus taught. You can almost miss this instruction as it slides right by: *"Freely you have received, freely give" (NIV)*. I can do that.

Jesus continues with specific instructions: As you enter a place, find out "who is worthy." This makes so much sense: seek others who value what you value. Look for people who offer you fellowship and hospitality because they are concerned about the same things you are concerned about.

Give your blessing going into the house from the very beginning. Bring your peace as you enter. But if they do not receive your message and the peace you offer, move on without looking back, shaking the very dust from them off your feet. It sounds so harsh, but you have gone in with an open heart and an open hand. If they reject God and you, move on without looking back. There are many more waiting for you ahead. Do not tarry.

And with this, the words of Jesus change drastically. Suddenly, we are in enemy territory. *"Behold, I am sending you out as sheep in the midst of wolves, so be as wise as serpents and innocent as doves" (Matthew 10:16)*. Beware. There is great danger waiting for you.

Jesus wanted to equip his disciples to succeed in their mission. He did not want to set them up for easy failure. He did not wish them to be naïve. He wanted them to be street-smart and wise to the ways of the world. Like our buckskin-wearing crocodile-hunting Australian in the middle of the asphalt jungle, they needed to be strong and fearlessly bold. They needed to be wise or, even better, shrewd – aware of who they were talking to and where they were. Yet they were to remain blameless, above reproach; their ways and manners were to hold no threat or ill intent. It is a powerful combination to be both wise and innocent when you are walking among wolves.

With the very real warning, "Be on your guard against men," Jesus opens the door to see behind the dark curtain of the future and to spell out the dangers of the mission. This was not going to be for the faint of heart. If you long for adventure, the high stakes, and the adrenaline rush of cliff diving, this may be the job for you. The rest of us wonder how we went so quickly, from blessings going in the door to watching for the knife plunging into our back.

Jesus spells it out very clearly. Arrested and brought to trial before governors and kings. Flogged - even in your synagogues – where men come to worship God! A brother will betray his brother, a father will betray his child, and children will testify against their parents. You will be persecuted, tortured, and accused of serving the devil. You will be hated – all because of Jesus!

Jesus wants us to understand our words about him will cost us significantly. You may have thought you could float over the top of everything Jesus is saying, but you will have to make a pretty big jump when you hear his warning that your most dangerous enemies will be within your own family. The ones you love and trust. They will despise you. They will betray you. And if you love them more than you love Jesus, then you are not worthy of his love. Ouch. Who can do this? Here is where I want to take a step back. I am sorry, Jesus, but I am not so sure anymore about following you.

There is a tiny encouragement hidden away here: "Do not be anxious how you are to speak or what you are to say - for what you are to say will be given to you in that hour – the Spirit of your Father will speak through you" (10:19-20). I am wondering how much consolation this is. And then I remember. Things that are happening now. As recently as yesterday.

Another ministry I support reaches out to persecuted Christians in dangerous places. They share stories about areas like modern-day Iraq. A young man raised in a Muslim home accepted the salvation of Jesus. He told his cousin, who did the same. Both young men were tortured by their own families. They were starved and beaten. One man was hung from the ceiling by the neck by his brothers, demanding he refuse this Jesus and pray the Islamic prayers. All the fingers on both hands of one man were broken. Miraculously rescued by fellow Christians, their passports recovered, both men have been spirited out of the country and into a safer house.

"Flee!" Jesus told them. "Go to the next town! Have no fear of those who can kill the body but not the soul. Nothing is covered that will not be revealed; what I tell you in the dark, say in the light, what I whisper in your ear, shout from the rooftops. Everyone who acknowledges me before men, I will acknowledge before my Father who is in heaven. You are of great value!"

But it gets worse – this difficult picture Jesus paints. Because he makes the impossible demand – you must pick up your cross and follow him. I really hate that he said that. Quite frankly, I do not want to embrace the idea of anything to do with the Roman cross. And I have never seen it except on my television screen from the comfort of my sofa. It is easy to look away when it gets too gruesome. The men hearing these words knew what that horrific execution looked like, sounded like, smelled like.

It is a hard offer that Jesus extends. Follow me. Leave everything else behind. Give up the life you want for the life I want for you. You may be accused of being the pawn of evil. You may be hauled into court. Your family may turn against you. Your most trusted friend may betray you. You may be tortured. You may die for my name. If you lose your life for my life, that is where you will find true life.

Who would possibly accept that offer? Why didn't this whole crazy invitation to follow a dying man into death die out with Jesus? Why are we still having this conversation 2,000 years later? Because something about it rang true. And something about it became more real and more appealing than anything else.

Even the very hairs on your head are numbered. So don't be afraid. You are valuable to the Father. You are worth more than many sparrows – and the Father knows about the life and death of every single one. "Acknowledge me – Jesus, his Son, before men, and I will acknowledge you before my Father in heaven." Jesus promises us something that we can find nowhere else; Jesus tells us with absolute certainty *we are known.*

God knows us in a way that no one else does. God has something much bigger going on than the little we can see here on this earth. This is nothing in comparison to God and his kingdom. This is a short moment compared to eternity. "Life with me," Jesus tells us, "is worth so much more than the little life you have envisioned for yourself." And when we grasp that – even dimly, even for just a moment, our heart sings with hope, and we know it is true.

I have had things in my life that I was terrified of. I was filled with fear that I would never fall in love and stay in love long enough to get married – much less have a successful marriage. I was terrified of the pain of giving birth to a baby. And then to do it again. I went down a career path that was so overwhelming I would fight to not throw up from the anxiety I felt as I was driving to work. I fought God with every logical reason I could imagine when he relentlessly called me to lead a women's Bible study. I was convinced it would be a painful failure. I did not want to watch my daddy slowly die from a brain tumor. I did not want to hold my mother's hand as she quickly died from a stroke. I did not want to become responsible for my sister Kathy's estate, and I did not want to plan my sister Ann's funeral and burial. I am betting there will be other things I do not want to do that I will find myself doing. What is my point here?

In our small lives, we go through huge life-changing events; some are mental, some are emotional, and some are physical. Beforehand, what is on the horizon seems impossible, overwhelming, terrifying. We think there is no way we can get through it. But when it arrives, one day at a time, we put one foot in front of the other and walk through what appeared to be downright impossible from a distance. God will not take us to a mountain that he will not help us climb. It may be a mountain that is incredibly steep and overwhelmingly difficult. We will need him to guide us every step of the way.

We hear Jesus's voice whispering in our ears. "It will be worth it," he tells us. "Take up your cross and follow me. It will be worth it."

"How small a thing death really is! Looked at from beside the Lord of life and death, 'great death' dwindles to a very little thing. We need to revise our notions if we would understand how trivial it really is. To us, it frowns like a black cliff blocking the upper end of our valley, but there is a path around its base, and though the throat of the pass is narrow, it has room for us to get through and up to the sunny uplands beyond. From a mountain top, the country below seems level plain, and what looked like an impassable precipice has dwindled to be indistinguishable. (It is a small and trivial thing), to those who look upon it from the heights of eternity."[2]

The Acts — Alexander Maclaren

Did these twelve men do it? Did they go out as sheep among wolves? Did they take up their cross to follow him? It appears they did. There was one exception. His name was Judas. He followed for a short while. When he turned back, with betrayal in his heart and silver in his hand, he could not live with himself. He hung himself before he could watch Jesus hang on his cross.

The others went out as sheep among the wolves. They would not be the only ones to do so. Many more would do the same long after Jesus was supposedly silenced. They continue to come, and they continue to follow, knowing that saying yes is a dangerous thing. Look carefully at these warnings. To follow Jesus is not an easy thing. It will be difficult – more than you know. But looking at Judas, I am reminded that to refuse to follow is suicide. Jesus is still making the offer. "Take up your cross and follow me. It will be worth it."

56

A Tale of Two Banquets

Read Matthew 14:1-21; Mark 6:14-44; Luke 9:7-17; John 6:1-15

We start with the rumors. The stories of the wonderous works of Jesus have found their way into the house of Herod the Tetrarch. There is much speculation about this man, this possible prophet named Jesus of Nazareth. Some think he is the long-awaited appearance of Elijah. Others remember Jesus had said John the Baptist was the Elijah who would herald in the Messiah (Matthew 11:13-14). Others claim John has been raised from the dead. Herod scoffs at this since he was the one to give the order for John's execution. Should he believe in ghosts? He made a note to have Jesus put in an appearance there in his courts. It should be entertaining.

Wait a minute—what has happened to John? Our writers almost mention it in passing. The last thing we knew, John was in prison downstairs in Herod's dungeon for pointing out the religious sin of Herod marrying his sister-in-law, Herodias.

Suddenly, we gain admission into King Herod's royal palace, where his birthday party is in full swing. He has invited all the movers and shakers from miles around. Tables are laden with food, and the drinks flow freely. High officials, military commanders, and all the leading men of Galilee and beyond are in attendance. Anyone who wanted to be someone was there.

Gifts are presented, including a show-stopping dance by Salome, the daughter of Herod's brother Philip and sister-in-law Herodias. Salome, unnamed in the Bible, but recorded by the historian Josephus, is Herod's niece (and currently his stepdaughter!). Now, I think Herodias calculated this very well. She knew the seductive charms of her daughter. She knew the weakness of her husband. And though that nasty Nazarite prophet called John was off the streets, and the crowds could no longer hear his accusations of her wrongdoing, his very presence in the dungeon made her skin crawl. She was ready to be done with him and his loud mouth, and this may be the time to do it.

And so, Salome dances. It is not a pretty and lighthearted dance of joy and laughter. It is something much more. Something calculated to make a man lose his senses and offer half his kingdom. And the price for the dance is way too high. And grotesque. We have this strange and uncomfortable glimpse into the world of the wealthy, empowered rulers and what they can destroy with a careless word. They slaughter for amusement the precious ones of God. The executioner is summoned. John's head is brought to the celebration on a golden platter.

This is not what we expect for God's chosen ones. I know, I know, we just heard what Jesus warned his disciples would happen – but still… It makes us want to close the book and say, "No, God." We don't understand how God can allow such horror and hurt to the ones he loves. "You sent them, God, with your message! And this is the outcome? Can't you devise a better way to get your Word to us, other than sending your message in the form of mere men? Men who so easily can be torn and destroyed?"

And this is where we see the humanness of God's prophets and his Son. Though God sends them, though they speak for God, they still hurt and bleed and die. Can you imagine the heartbreak of John's disciples? Can you imagine Jesus's sorrow as he held them in his arms, and they wept? There are no words of comfort that can ease the pain of death. We humans are fragile. We are born, and we die. And Jesus came as one of us.

This is the mystery we can never wrap our minds around. God placed his very own Son in human skin. And with that skin came all the human limitations. Human hunger. Human fatigue. Human hurt. Human sorrow. In this man's skin, God experienced his fallen world. He had created paradise, Eden. Stars singing, Adam naming the animals, the cool of the evening. All things good and beautiful.

But we humans chose something else instead. We opted for making our own choices, making our own decisions. We wanted to be in control of all that happened. We turned away from God, deciding he couldn't be trusted. We thought it would be better if we just looked out for ourselves. You see the problem there, don't you? It wasn't long before blood was on the ground.

So, God sent prophets to call us back. We killed them because we didn't like what they had to say. No one was going to tell us what to do. So, he sent his Son down to talk with us. The problem was that he had to put on our skin, and he had to experience our cuts and bruises and bloody knees from falling down.

I wonder what it was like to feel human emotions. I imagine his conversations with his Father went something like this:

"Dad, you just can't understand how much they hurt. How lonely they are, how sad they are, how hopeless they feel. They hunger, they thirst, they feel too much heat and too much cold. Their bodies break and bleed and get worn out. They love, but they lose, and they suffer, and when that love is gone, it is an ache that knows no relief.

"Maybe we made a mistake; these sensations we intended for good are used to torture them now. Love became dangerous in their hands. And this thing called death is too much for them to hold."

And so, Jesus wants to be alone. He gathers his disciples like a momma hen and withdraws quietly, heading to a solitary place. A place where he can spend time in the warm embrace of his Father.

A place where he can find the peace and comfort that can only come from him. But before his boat reaches shore, the crowds have already found him, their feet running fast, their expectations high. They have no idea that he is mourning the death of his cousin. The one who knew him while still in his momma's womb. They have no idea of the pain in his heart and the questions in his head. They only see a healer, a teacher, one who seems more like God to them than man.

Because of their hope and their belief, we see what God the Father must look like through the response of Jesus the Son. His heart is filled with compassion; he doesn't turn them away; he reaches out to them. Compassion is something much more than having empathy - feeling another's distress.[1] Compassion desires to lift suffering off the weary shoulders. Compassion walks alongside carrying the burden.[2]

Jesus looks at the people as sheep without a shepherd. Where is their good shepherd to find sweet grass and lead them to still waters? Who is anointing their head with oil to ward off each day's distress? Who is protecting them from the wolves and finding those who have wandered off and become lost? I am reminded of God telling the prophet that he would shepherd his sheep. *"I will seek the lost, and I will bring back the strayed, and I will bind up the injured, and I will strengthen the weak..." (Ezekiel 34:16).*

He saw them. He taught them. He cared for them. And then, because he could, he fed them.

A young woman told me a story of being very hurt by an old family friend, a woman she had grown up with and thought of as being an intimate part of their family. The young woman had flown into town with her boyfriend in tow for a special birthday party for the family friend's daughter, who was her age. The night before the party, she received a call telling her that the catering had been ordered and that there would not be enough food for my friend to bring her boyfriend, even though they both had flown into town specifically for the party. She had RSVP'd for one person, not two. Sorry. We came from a family where my mother delighted in cheerfully setting another place at the table, singing, "The more the merrier!"

Jesus was obviously not a strict adherent to the RSVP policy. Not only that, but he also basically canceled his vacation to Aruba because unexpected guests showed up unannounced at his door. And they ran to get there. He not only welcomed them, but he also decided there would be enough food to invite everyone to dinner. Every single one of them.

This is the only miracle reported by all four of our gospel writers: Matthew, Mark, Luke, and John. We must remind ourselves that the Twelve have just returned from their road trip, healing and casting out demons. Surely, they remember the incredible power and authority God gave them. No? "We better send them away to find food," they tell Jesus.

Jesus asked his disciples to do something they could not do. No one could have done it: "Feed the people." The task was impossible, and the cost was too great. Philip calculated the money needed, which would only buy a taste. Andrew had found a little boy with five barley loaves and two fish—barely an appetizer for a grown man.

In the hands of Jesus, it will be enough.

Blessed. Broken. He teaches them that God is so much bigger than they can imagine. The little they have, five small loaves and two dried fish, are just enough to feed a young boy supper, and when offered to God, they can become a feast for thousands. With leftovers.

And don't you wonder about that boy? He didn't stay quiet in the crowd. He didn't hold back what he had, thinking he had little to offer. He held it out with open palm.

There is green grass, so it is spring. The crowd is divided into smaller groups, perhaps families sitting together as they had when traveling in the wilderness for 40 years. And bread comes from heaven from the hand of Jesus to fill their stomachs. Almost like manna. There were 5,000 men. How many more women and children? They ate their fill. And there were leftovers. Twelve baskets full.

What did these baskets look like? How big were they? And why were they there? Made of twigs or branches, these kophinoi (Greek) were baskets or hampers that could be carried on the back to hold provisions, like a knapsack. It is possible that they were ephah size, about 3/5 bushel. But they could have been larger (Paul was lowered over a city wall in one!).[3] I have also heard that every Jewish man had a small basket to carry "clean" food since they often traveled in Gentile lands. Large or small, the point to hold onto here is everyone ate until they were "satisfied" and there was still more!

This is my favorite part of the story: leftovers. God supplies more than we need. There will be enough. He is adequate. His provision is abundant. There is no need to hold on too tightly to our stuff. When we hand it over to Jesus, it returns to us in abundance—enough to share with others.

I ask myself, what am I holding back? Where do I hunger, thinking there is "not enough"? In my hand, the offering is meager and small. Once it is held in Jesus's hands, offered to the Father with gratitude, it will be broken and multiplied. There will be more than enough. There will be leftovers.

This is the story of two feasts. One took place in a palace; the food and wine flowed, the guests were entertained, and death was ushered in on a golden platter. The other was quite different. It took place in the wilderness, without walls or doors; the invitation list was open to anyone who wanted to attend. The only entertainment was the words that taught the glory of the King. There were no fine delicacies, only the broken bread from the hands of the Son. Everyone ate until they were satisfied. And there were enough leftovers for each disciple to fill a basket for another day.

Which banquet would you like to attend?

57

Trampling the Waves

Read Matthew 14:22-36; Mark 6:45-56; John 6:16-21

It is getting late, and the sun will soon be setting. There is an urgency in the telling of these stories. All the passages telling of the end of the day have the word *immediately* embedded within them. But I am going to go off-script. It is all the unsaid that speaks so quietly here. What these disciples of Jesus have left unwritten are the very human emotions. Emotions. Pause a moment with me, and let's slowly walk the path of these past days with this man named Jesus.

First, underneath all the miracles lay the rawness of rejection. Remember our visit, Jesus, to your hometown? Those who were the closest and had been so influential on you while growing up mocked you and dismissed your message, unwittingly closing the door on seeing God. In person.

And then comes the horror of John's sudden death – as a party favor. You feel the sharp slap of losing the only one who truly understands who you are and why you are here. With heavy heart, you comfort John's disciples, knowing full well that your disciples will soon come to a time when they will feel just as bewildered and abandoned. Numb with grief and sorrow, you withdraw, seeking quiet and time to heal, but the feet run faster than the boat can travel, and thousands wait for you, expectantly, on the shore. As the boat moves closer, you see it on their faces: hope.

For just a moment, Matthew and Mark write it, and we can read it: your emotional state: *He had compassion on them and healed their sick.* Such a small nod to your big and full shepherd heart, aching for your sheep. Binding up their wounds. Running your hands along their heads. Filling up their bellies. As the day had started to wind down, it would have been easier to send the crowds away - but the teacher in you won out. You teach the people; you teach your disciples about the generosity of your Father. And the glory of his Son.

It has been a long day, and exhaustion weighs heavy on your body and your mind. Finally, you send them all away—the crowds down the road, the disciples across the lake—and you climb the mountain alone. Bone-tired, emotionally drained, and spiritually empty, rest is waiting as you settle in with your Father.

Time with him in the stillness gives you what nothing else can. Comfort. Encouragement. Life renewed. It is cool rain in the desert. It is a breeze of fresh air in the heat of the sun. It is quiet in the rabble of the crowd. It is the only thing that can fill you up after you have poured everything out. You pause. You breathe deep. Your spirit receives peace. Your body regains strength. Your thoughts clear. Quiet. Be still and know that I Am God.

Through the darkness of night, down below the heights of the mountain, across the waves of the water, a small boat moves too slowly; your beloved disciples pull against the oars, the wind against them, holding them back. And so you go to them. Walking where no man has ever walked.

For good reason, they are terrified. The winds are high. The land is far away. They are exhausted, rowing continuously against waves that have no end. It is after three in the morning, and the skies are still dark. Something moves in the distance: fog or mist on the water, a blurred apparition, or a ghost on the sea? They cry out in fear.

Here is where we notice that word: immediately. But immediately Jesus spoke to them, saying, *"Take heart; it is I. Do not be afraid" (Matthew 14:27).*

What is the meaning of this *immediately*? As I underline it, I look at the other writers telling of this dark night when the disciples battled the sea alone. Now I notice it is there at the end of the day, the beginning of the evening as the sun lowers. Jesus *immediately* sends the disciples on their way, into the boat and out into the water, while he alone dismisses the crowds and says his goodbyes (Matthew 14:22, Mark 6:45). This seems so odd, doesn't it? Why would he do that?

He has just pointed to the generosity and abundance of God by miraculously feeding 5,000 men (not even counting the women and children). Yet, Jesus immediately removes the disciples and closes the curtain because he realizes the crowd is overwhelmed with his power and potential and plans to force him to play the role of king. Jesus removes the possibility for more ovations and curtain calls and essentially makes the announcement that disperses the crowds: "Elvis has left the building!" It is time for everyone to go home. The crowd realizes that someone like God is in their midst, but they intend to elevate him to the rank of mortal king. God (and Jesus) have a much bigger plan in mind.

And there they are, those disciples alone and terrified in the wind, in the dark, in the boat. Jesus calls out immediately to reassure them. He is nothing to be afraid of. He is there for their protection. He is their salvation. His presence leads to life, not death. He doesn't want them to feel fear – even for one second! Immediately, he speaks words of comfort and encouragement. His words remind us when we feel exhausted and hopeless with no help in sight - Jesus never loses sight of us rowing against the waves. He is there, even in the darkness, walking right beside us.

As John tells the story, they all immediately arrive at their destination once Jesus climbs into their boat. *Then they were glad to take him into the boat, and immediately the boat was at the land to which they were going (John 6:21).* The wind has ceased; they are all on dry land. Mark records that they landed at Gennesaret. *And when they got out of the boat, the people immediately recognized him (Mark 6:54).*

Our story will end very differently from how it started in Jesus's hometown of Nazareth. Gennesaret was a plain on the northwest coast of the Sea of Galilee. The people there recognize Jesus as someone who seems to be more God than man. They spread the good news that he has arrived. The crowds flock to him. To touch the hem of his robes will be enough. It reminds us of the woman in the crowd who knew she would be healed if she could only touch his robe. Jesus stopped everything to remark on her great faith. These people of Gennesaret believe that to touch him is to be healed. And so they are.

But there is one more use of the word immediately that we have skimmed right past. I must look at these passages to make sure I am correct. Is it only Matthew who records what happens after Jesus calls out to his disciples on the water? You would think it would be front-page news across the land. "Peter, the Fisherman, Walks on Water!"

Peter. Lovely, impetuous Peter, who always wants to be wherever Jesus is. And there he is, the only one who asks, "Can I come to you?" And yes, the wind overwhelmed him when he took his eyes off Jesus and looked at the waves crashing around him. Yet, we see that word again: *immediately*. Immediately, Jesus reached out his hand and caught him.

I'm afraid I have to disagree with the scholars who see this private conversation between Jesus and Peter as a reproof. I hear it as a loving parent who catches his toddler in his arms after his first three steps. "Oh, you, of little faith! You were walking! Why did you ever doubt? I have you!"

In fifth grade, I made a new friend, Pam, who invited me to the lake with her family for the weekend. Pam's father sat with me on the shore, positioned me with legs bent, ski-tips high, and arms straight, and talked me through what would happen as the boat pulled me out of the water. As I bobbed unbalanced in the water, my friend Pam, with two skis on (even though, unknown to me, she had learned to slalom at age four!), waited in the water beside me, shouting encouragement. The boat surged forward, I fell over, dropped my rope, and Pam dropped her rope. Second try, the same thing happened. On "our" third try, I suddenly stood on the water, my skis sliding along the surface, Pam shouting hurrahs beside me, her mother cheering me on from the boat. Exhausted, when I finally fell, I was scooped up into the boat, wrapped in a white terry cloth robe, and everyone was jubilant with the excitement of learning to ski. I was on cloud nine. In my mind, I had just done something impossible.

I believe Peter felt the same way. He got out of the boat in high waves and stiff wind, and he walked to Jesus. On water. Can you imagine? I hear no shame in the words of Jesus. I hear encouragement. "You have little faith, Peter. But it will grow. This is not the last time you will fall. Keep getting out of the boat. Keep your eyes on me. I am exactly who you think I am. There is no need for doubt. Trust me. And you will do far greater things than walk on water."

These same men had asked earlier when the waves were high and the storms were raging: "What sort of man is this, that even wind and sea obey him?" Perhaps on this night, they called to mind Job's description of God, *"who alone stretched out the heavens and trampled the waves of the sea" (Job 9:8).* Their declaration justified their actions of worshiping a man named Jesus: *"Truly you are the Son of God" (Matthew 14:33).*

Don't rush by this. We have heard this title for Jesus a million times. We think little of it because we know it down to our very toes – but this was brand new for this odd assortment of very Jewish men who were taught from childhood to have no other gods other than the Great I Am. Could this man who just trampled the waves of the sea be more than a man? Could he indeed be the Son of God? Something had changed. And they did something they had never done before: they worshipped him.

Where do we find ourselves in these stories? Are we so familiar with this hometown boy that we fail to see the glory of God right in front of us? Or are we just there for the party with the influential people, hoping to make meaningful connections that will better our position on this earth… willing to overlook the prophet's head on the platter as long as we are entertained? Did we run to hear the words of life and discover the Father's abundance and the Son's compassion? Are we the hurting ones in the crowd, believing Jesus can cure what ails us if we can get close enough to touch his robe? Or are we his disciples, following him into the wilderness and through the storm, sure that he indeed is the Son of God?

Are we faithful enough to make fools out of ourselves? Are we brave enough to ask him, "Can I come to you, out on the water?"

58

Does This Offend You?

Read John 6:22-71

Walk through this conversation slowly. Our dear John writes it out for us line by line. It is a discussion of division; it is a debate of opposing intentions. The crowd following this miracle worker is in it for the sparkle and flash, thinking they might learn his tricks. Jesus is telling them this is more than a parlor game; in this game, they play for keeps. What happens here determines life or death.

The crowd noticed he almost got away from them. They were looking for him where the bread was easy and plentiful. Word of his wonders has spread. Boatloads of people wanting to see the circus have arrived from Tiberius. They realize the traveling show has moved on to Capernaum across the sea.

Jesus immediately knows their motives: "You did not come seeking the Lord God, whom the signs point to—you came to have your belly filled. You are not seeking the Spirit of God or things eternal; you are only concerned with your physical desires and the temporary here and now. There is food I can give you that leads to eternal life. God the Father has placed his seal of approval on me, his son who looks like a man."

When I was growing up, my mother subscribed to *Good Housekeeping Magazine.* (The name even sounds odd now in this current day and time!) In our house, it was read from cover to cover. It featured economical and easy-to-prepare recipes, the new styles in home decorating, and most importantly, information about products they tested and reviewed. It was quite an endorsement if the magazine put its Good Housekeeping Seal of Approval on a product. That assured every housewife that their institute had thoroughly investigated the product and assessed that it "performed as intended." Since 1909, their seal has been a quality warranty, which they have stood behind. It was the symbol of their promise to protect you, the customer.

When I hear Jesus tell the hungry crowd that God the Father has set his seal on him, the Son of Man, I imagine those white lab-coated scientists standing behind him nodding their approval.

But the crowd doesn't seem to hear what he is telling them. They aren't interested in "food that leads to eternal life." They ask how to do the things he is doing. They want to perform tricks themselves.

Jesus knows their intentions and dives into the deep end of the pool, metaphorically speaking. Let's see who will follow. He shakes his head with a smile, I imagine. "No, no, no. This isn't about 'works' but about 'believing.'" They stand at the edge, not too sure they want to get their feet wet. Mind you, they still want those miraculous works, so they try again. "What sign will you do that we may see? Maybe then we could believe you. Perform for us. You know, like Moses! Make manna rain down from heaven. That would convince us!"

Jesus is so onto them. I imagine he is gently treading water, maybe even floating in the deep blue as he looks up at them looking down on him, their feet firmly planted on concrete-clad solid ground. "Here is the truth, my friends," he says, with a twinkle in his eye. "My Father is the bread maker. He was the One who provided the bread that sustained your fathers in the wilderness – but that was temporary bread. Bread that only lasted for a day. My Father is offering you his true bread from heaven. This bread is everlasting, multiplying, never-ending." They are listening. He has their attention. "I am the bread of life. Whoever comes to me will never go hungry and will never thirst."

Their eyes narrow. This is not what they want. They want action, and they want it now. They want to see this man perform for them. Entertain them. Instead, he is talking about things they cannot see. Things that cannot be.

He is talking about believing. He is talking about God giving him authority and people. Did we hear that right – people? He talks about coming from heaven, doing God's will, not losing those given to him, and eternal life. They shake their heads. He has totally lost them now. It is their turn to scoff and mock. "He is not the Son of God! He is merely the son of the carpenter!"

But this son of the carpenter is not done. He answers their grumbling and discontent. *"No one can come to me unless the Father who sent me draws him. And I will raise him up on the last day" (v. 44).*

This is a truth that humbles me. It should. It should draw all of us who believe up short. I can only see and believe because the Father draws me to Jesus. Unless God opens my eyes, I cannot see! Without that, I would be standing with the scoffers on the edge. Jesus wants to make sure we always know the power of his Father; it is his Father who draws us to him and gives us to him. I read over all these red-letter words again. Three times, Jesus explains that we do not come of our own will but by the will of the Father. I whisper, "Draw them to your Son, my Father, those I love who do not see, who do not know, who do not believe!"

Jesus continues. It seems they are no longer listening, but there will be others from generation to generation who will. And this is the heart of what those who hear will believe. Get ready, here it is: *"Truly, truly, I say to you, whoever believes has eternal life" (v. 47).* That is the bottom line. Belief. Just belief. But what do we believe in? Jesus, the living bread of life. *"I am the living bread that came down from heaven. If anyone eats of this bread, he will live forever. And the bread that I will give for the life of the world is my flesh" (v. 51).* Jesus is the bread of heaven that nourishes us, sustains us, and enables us to live forever in his Father's kingdom. He is very clear – he will give his own living body for ours.

The most incredible, unbelievable thing I have ever experienced was bringing life into this world. I suspected I was pregnant when I lit a cigarette one evening when I was out with my girlfriends and immediately became nauseous. My body refused to accept anything that could harm the tiny little life within my womb. For nine months, my body sheltered my little one as the heart, kidneys, and lungs developed. It all happened unseen within my own body. Everything needed was already there. And then, when that child was born into our world, I marveled at this perfectly formed life I held in my arms. For the first five months of his life, he grew – getting longer and fatter and more developed – sustained on my breast milk alone. His life had everything it needed in my life. It was truly unbelievable to me.

These words of Jesus about eating his flesh and drinking his blood sound so awful until we pause to remember that this is how life begins! All of us – every single one of us – were created, protected, and nourished within our mother's womb. So now, hear the promise of Jesus, *"Whoever feeds on my flesh and drinks my blood abides in me, and I in him" (v. 56).*

Jesus has been teaching so very carefully, so clearly, step by step. Think back over these past hours with Jesus to what John has told us. Jesus had provided for physical needs with abundance; a few fish and loaves fed the multitude with leftovers. Jesus provided emotional comfort when he walked on the waves and through the mighty wind to reassure his disciples and see them safely to shore. Jesus had provided for spiritual needs with his promise that all that was needed to live forever was simple: belief in him, the one who offered eternal life. The one sent by God the Father. "I am the living bread who gives life eternal."

One other little thing we need to remember here is this conversation is with Jews. Jews who were well acquainted with Passover:

Spread the blood of a perfect lamb on the entrance to your house. Eat all the flesh of the sacrificed lamb roasted over the fire. Leave none of it until the morning. (That manna from heaven also needed to be consumed and not saved for the next day.) Those were the necessary components for life in a land of captivity and death. Flesh, blood, bread. This was the story they already knew of God's salvation. God had been teaching them this lesson for a long time. They were to remember it. They were to celebrate it every year with a feast!

But on this day, these miracle seekers could only comprehend the black-and-white facts of the physical world—they could not take the leap into the spiritual world of God, of heavenly truths, of eternity, of things unseen, of bread made of flesh.

They are lost now. They take the wisdom of God through the teaching of his Son and turn it into cannibalism. Isn't this so very human of us? I am reminded of the daily news in our struggling, self-destructive world. I became aware of selective hearing and selective reporting a few years ago. There was a hotly debated political race. The snatches of news I heard on my radio at the top of the hour would astound me. One of the candidates was significantly over the top; honestly, I did not care for him. His personality was overly confident and obnoxious, and everything he said was offensive. He was the proverbial bull in the china shop.

One day, what he was reported to say was so egregious I had to hear it for myself. I looked up the specific speech and listened for the outrageous sentence the reporter quoted. I was astounded. Yes, he said those specific words, but the news reporter had taken them out of context and completely ignored the tone of his voice. It was undeniable he was using sarcasm to say the exact opposite. It was a turning point for me. From that time forward, I began to seek the original source of information. I quickly discovered that the people reporting had a particular agenda: not to report what was being said honestly but to pervert it, twist it, and turn it to make it offensive and insulting.

Jesus said, "You must eat my flesh if you want to follow me." The news reported he was starting a cult of cannibals. Flesh eaters. Blood drinkers. God's Law had long prohibited the drinking of the blood of an animal – and here is Jesus, claiming to be from God, yet demanding people drink his blood! Get out of town!

No wonder they grumbled! No wonder they turned away in disappointment and disgust! That was the only logical response to these words: *"For my flesh is true food, and my blood is true drink. Whoever feeds on my flesh and drinks my blood abides in me, and I in him" (vv. 55-56).* This was indeed hard teaching. Who could accept it?

Jesus agreed. "Does this offend you?" He knows what they do not know yet. It will not be long before they hear things more unbelievable than this. Would they believe their ears when they heard he was crucified and dead and buried in a grave for three days, only to walk again on the road to Emmaus? Would they believe when they heard that Jesus, escorted by angels, had ascended into the heavens as one angel lingered to tell them he would return in the same way?

"The flesh (that has disturbed you so!) counts for nothing," he reassures them. "I am talking to you, teaching you about the heavenly realm – things you have not seen, but I have. God is not flesh and blood; he is Spirit. His Spirit gives life eternal without end. You can only understand the physical: what you see with your eyes, what you hear with your ears, and what you touch with your hands. I am telling you about something much more, something much bigger. My words are of Spirit. My words are life."

Again, it is Peter. Peter, who got out of the boat to walk with Jesus on the water. Peter, who would fall down three times during the trial of the darkest night. But here, at this tenuous, confusing moment when the future hangs in the balance and he must choose between the easily seen physical world and the unseen spiritual world, he keeps his eyes on Jesus.

"Lord, where else will we go? You alone have the true words of eternal life. Somehow, we know. Unbelievably, we believe. The Father has drawn us to you. *You are the Holy One of God.*"

This, my friends, is the question Jesus asks; "Does this offend you?" You will be invited to a dinner party in an upper room. It will be the time of Passover, the night to remember a people caught in captivity, enslaved in a foreign land. They were instructed to slaughter a perfect lamb, smear its blood on the wooden doorframe of their house, and eat its flesh. Jesus would raise a cup of wine to remind his closest disciples of God's great deliverance from death. He would say these words, "This is my blood, shed for you." He would break the bread again, declaring to them, "This is my flesh, broken for you. Eat. This is for you." No one in the room would understand that the *next day,* he would be slaughtered as the sacrificial lamb. His blood would drip from a wooden cross; his body would be broken, his flesh torn. He would submit to all of this – for them. For us. For you. To defeat death.

It is a hard teaching. Does it offend you?

Epilogue

Laying it Down

When many of Jesus' disciples heard him, they said, "What he says is hard to accept. Who wants to listen to him anymore?"
John 6:60 GW

Exactly. Are you starting to think the same thing? This is not the easy Jesus whose words are so soothing and encouraging and easily transcribed into a frame and hung on your wall. Here in the land of the outsiders, those heathen Gentiles, we are seeing a Jesus that isn't exactly the Jesus we love to love. Following him may be more difficult than we originally thought. If we follow this Jesus, we may not be as popular as we would like. We may end up needing to lay some things down that we have become very comfortable with. It may require more than attending church on Sundays and being a good girl or boy.

Has Jesus offended you yet? Looking in your face does he ask *"Do you want to go away as well?" (v. 67).*

It may surprise you that right here, right now, in the middle of these Jesus stories, I am going to lay my Bible down and walk away for a while. I am not abandoning our journey. I will be back, but I am giving us time to pause and catch our breath.

Things changed during the storm. Beyond teaching and knowing, touching and healing, Jesus showed his hand to those terrified disciples in the boat: he could walk on water, he could calm the wind, and he could invite you to do the same. There sat Peter as proof. There was only one possible response: And those in the boat worshiped him, saying, *"Truly you are the Son of God" (Matthew 14:33)*. Look closely at that little declaration. There is no doubt. They are no longer following a miracle-working prophet. They are worshipping the Son of God!

So we will pause here because soon, those religious leaders will be so offended that they will begin devising traps to silence Jesus... or at least discredit him. And soon Jesus will begin talking about suffering in Jerusalem. Yet right around the corner, there is a mountaintop. Once we climb that height and hear God's own voice claiming Jesus as his Chosen One, his own dear Son, there will be no stopping until we reach the hallelujahs of Jerusalem! And then it will be all over but the shouting.

Not really. That is the problem with the Jesus stories—they seem to have no end. We will find that even a scandalous execution and a stone grave will not be able to silence him. He will continue to show up, inviting us to place our hands into his wounds, holding the door open that leads into his Father's kingdom.

So, for now, we will rest and like his mother Mary, cherish these things in our hearts. Soon we will pick up where we left off, but I must warn you, the path will become more difficult, and many will fall away on account of the words of Jesus. It is not a road for the faint of heart. But Jesus has already told you that. Perhaps we share Simon Peter's response to the idea of turning back:

"Lord, to whom shall we go?
You have the words of eternal life.
We have come to believe and to know
that you are the Holy One of God."
John 6:68-69 NIV

Acknowledgments

The Jesus Stories began in January 2020, when I felt the prompting of the Holy Spirit to draw closer to Jesus by reading the Gospels in chronological order. Not knowing how to begin, while staying with my friend Barbara Finch Thompson for a speaking engagement in Birmingham, I found her One Year Chronological Bible in the New International Version on her kitchen counter. It seemed like a good place to start! As the months progressed, I discovered other chronological Bibles differed in sequence, and to make it even more complicated, I often would become side-tracked by how the gospel writers themselves lined up events!

The first year, I was concerned about following an accurate timeline. I finally decided to simply proceed since no one knows exactly the correct order of events! If you disagree with my timeline, please extend grace! Along the way, our troubled years of pestilence, seclusion, and division forced me to listen carefully to *all* the words Jesus spoke. Sometimes, I didn't like what he said. Sometimes, I was confused by his reactions to the people around him. Sometimes, I wanted to gloss over his hard teachings! My constant guide when I hit a wall was Dr. Thomas Constable, Senior Professor of Bible Exposition at Dallas Theological Seminary and Pastor of Plano Bible Chapel. He could be reached whenever I needed him, day or night, when I clicked open *Dr. Thomas L. Constable's Expository Notes.*

I also often referred to my notes from my years as Teaching Director with Community Bible Study. A teaching conference for CBS under Dr. James C. Martin armed me with the spiral-bound resource *The*

Life and World of Jesus the Messiah: The Gospels in Context. A bible study introduced to my teenage daughter by our Youth Pastor's wife, Jeannie Christian, taught me the beautiful Jewish traditions for marriage in ancient times. Thank you to Denise Glenn's *Restore My Heart: God's Passionate Love For His Bride.* Lee Strobel's *The Case For Christ: A Journalist's Personal Investigation of the Evidence for Jesus* opened my eyes to the outlandish fact that Jesus still lives and continues to change people and history. My friend and encourager Janice Scott placed the well-worn and lovely *Sitting at the Feet of Rabbi Jesus: How The Jewishness of Jesus Can Transform Your Faith* by Ann Spangler and Lois Tverberg into my hands one evening, opening my eyes to the traditional relationship between rabbi and disciple.

Larry Carpenter guided me step by step through publishing my first book, *Genesis: Small Stories of a Big God,* through his company Carpenter's Son Publishing, and Shane Crabtree has guided me through *The Jesus Stories.* Thank you to Ann Tatlock's patient editing and Kathi Roberts's beautiful cover design. Thank you also to Christian for keeping up with my inventory at Ingram Distribution – seeing my books go out into the world has been exciting!

My constant companion during this five-year process has been my own personal Bible. It is filled with handwritten notes in the margins from various teachings and sermons, most recently from Dr. Michael Youssef or his son, Jonathan Youssef, at The Church of the Apostles in Atlanta, where my husband and I are members. Yet my greatest teacher and guide has certainly been God's Spirit. I am grateful that Jesus fulfilled his promise, *"But the Helper, the Holy Spirit, whom the Father will send in my name, he will teach you all things and bring to your remembrance all that I have said to you" John 14:26.* This is my continuing desire: that you will open God's wonderful written Word for yourself and see what Jesus has to say!

Notes

Contents

1. Andreas Köstenberger, "April 3, AD 33: Why We Believe We Can Know the Exact Date Jesus Died," April 8, 2020, accessed August 5, 2024, www. cbs.mbts.edu/2020/04/08/april-3-ad-33-why-we-believe-we-can-know-the-exact-date-jesus-died/.

Introduction

1. W. Glyn Evans, *Daily with The King*, (Chicago: The Moody Bible Institute of Chicago, 1979), April 8 devotion.

2 In the Flesh

1. "The Romans Destroy the Temple at Jerusalem, 70 AD," EyeWitness to History, accessed June 8, 2024, www.eyewitnesstohistory.com (2005).

2. Josephus' account appears in Gaayla Cornfield, ed., Josephus, The Jewish War (Grand Rapids MI: Zondervan Publishing Company, 1982).

3 It All Started in the Temple

1. Kevin Smyth, "Elijah: Hebrew Prophet," Britannica, accessed June 27, 2024, www.britannica.com/biography/Elijah-Hebrew-prophet.

2. "The Messiah Would Be Preceded by Elijah the Prophet," Jews for Jesus, January 01, 2018, accessed June 8, 2024, www. jewsforjesus.org/jewish-resources/messianic-prophecy/the-messiah-would-be-preceded-by-elijah-the-prophet/.

6 And He Shall Be Named Jesus

1. "The Powerful Meaning of Swaddling Clothes," Lanier Christian Church, accessed April 15, 2020, www.lanierchristianchurch.com/blog/the-powerful-meaning-of-swaddling-clothes/.

8 Wisemen and Kings, Angels and Dreams

1. Dr. Thomas L. Constable, "Constable's Expository (Bible Study) Notes, Web-based," Plano Bible Chapter, accessed March 14, 2020, www.planobiblechapel.org/tcon/notes/html/nt/matthew/matthew.htm.

10 A Voice in the Wilderness

1. "Bethany Beyond the Jordan," See the Holy Land, accessed April 30, 2020, www.seetheholyland.net/bethany-beyond-the-jordan/.

12 Temptation in the Wilderness

1. "Why did Jesus need to be led into the wilderness by the Spirit to be tempted," Got Questions Ministries, accessed May 1, 2020, www.gotquestions.org/test-God.html.

13 The Seekers

1. John Newton, "Amazing Grace," published 1829, Public Domain.

2. John Piper, "Why Is Jesus Called 'Son of Man'?", Desiring God, accessed May 9, 2020, www.desiringgod.org/interviews/why-is-jesus-called-son-of-man.

16 A Little Late-Night Conversation

1. "Lesson 16: How Jesus is Like a Snake," Bible.org, June 16, 2013, accessed May 16, 2020, www. bible.org/seriespage/lesson-16-how-jesus-snake-john-314-15-numbers-214-9.

17 Mission Accomplished

1. Denise Glynn, Restore My Heart; God's Passionate Love for His Bride, (Houston: Kardo International Ministries, 2002), 45-49.

19 A Long Story About Water

1. Dr. Thomas L. Constable, "Constable's Expository (Bible Study) Notes, Web-based," Plano Bible Chapel, accessed September 9, 2023, www.planobiblechapel.org/tcon/notes/html/nt/john/john.htm.

2. Dr. Thomas L. Constable, "Constable's Expository (Bible Study) Notes, Web-based," Plano Bible Chapel, accessed May 29, 2020, www.planobiblechapel.org/tcon/notes/html/nt/john/john.htm.

3. George Gershwin and Ira Gershwin, "Let's Call the Whole Thing Off," Library of Congress. Copyright Office. (1937). Catalog of Copyright Entries 1937 Musical Compositions New Series Vol 32 Pt 3 For the Year 1937. United States Copyright Office. U.S. Govt. Print. Off.

24 Demons and Declarations

1. This is the Septuagint version, the Greek translation of Hebrew scriptures written for Christian Greeks in the third or fourth century.

27 Guess Who's Coming to Dinner?

1. The Septuagint uses the word mercy instead of steadfast love.

32 The Sabbath Turned Upside Down

1. Dr. Thomas L. Constable, "Constable's Expository (Bible Study) Notes, Web-based," Plano Bible Chapel, accessed May 18, 2021. www.planobiblechapel.org/tcon/notes/html/nt/matthew/matthew.htm#_ftn882.

2. Dr. Thomas L. Constable, "Constable's Expository (Bible Study) Notes, Web-based," Plano Bible Chapel, accessed May 18, 2021, ww.planobiblechapel.org/tcon/notes/pdf/matthew.pdf ftn883 [Carson, "Matthew," p. 239, listed six possible meanings.]

3. Colin Smith, "Restoration," Open the Bible with Pastor Colin Smith, accessed October 4, 2023, www.openthebible.org/article/greatest-need-restoration.
When I looked at the definition of restoration, I found this lovely description: "We had to be redeemed from sin so that we can be restored to fellowship with God. Restoration is the essence of redemption! The limitless reach of God's restoring work is breathtaking.
"It is easy to think of redemption as the ultimate end, but restoration means that there is more to redemption than the promise of eternal life. The lives of the redeemed are restored to good purpose on earth. God's restored people 'bear fruit in every good work and increase in the knowledge of God' (Col. 1:9-12). We are empowered to walk in obedience and live in harmony with others. Jesus is the one who redeems and restores us to fellowship with God and with the saints in light."

33 The Surprising Servant

1. "Faithful." Merriam-Webster.com Dictionary, Merriam-Webster, accessed August 16, 2020, https://www.merriam-webster.com/dictionary/faithful.

34 Jesus Calls His Disciples

1. Dr. Thomas L. Constable, "Constable's Expository (Bible Study) Notes, Web-based," Plano Bible Chapel, accessed September 12, 2020, www.planobiblechapel.org/constable-notes-html/Matthew and Mark, www.planobiblechapel.org/tcon/notes/html/nt/matthew/matthew.htm,
www.planobiblechapel.org/tcon/notes/html/nt/mark/mark.htm.

2. Dr. Thomas L. Constable, "Constable's Expository (Bible Study) Notes, Web-based," Plano Bible Chapel, accessed September 12, 2020. https://www.planobiblechapel.org/tcon/notes/html/nt/matthew/matthew.htm. The Greek

word translated as "disciple" is mathletes, which means simply "learner" or "pupil."

3. "Apostle." Merriam-Webster.com Dictionary, Merriam-Webster, accessed August 15, 2024, https://www.merriam-webster.com/dictionary/apostle.

4. "West African Vodun," Wikipedia, accessed DATE, https://en.wikipedia.org/wiki/West_African_Vod%C3%BAn.

5. Lee Strobel, *The Case For Christ*, (Grand Rapids MI: Zondervan, 1998), 333-334.

6. "Does the Bible record the death of the apostles?" Got Questions Ministries, accessed August 15, 2024, www.gotquestions.org/apostles-die.html.

36 When You Don't Feel Very Blessed

1. Beatitudes research came from these commentaries:
"The Beatitudes in Matthew 5: Meaning and Significance for Today," June 5, 2020, Zondervan Academic, accessed October 6, 2023, www.zondervanacademic.com/blog/beatitudes.
Dr. Thomas L. Constable, "Constable's Expository (Bible Study) Notes, Web-based," Plano Bible Chapel, accessed October 6, 2024, www.planobiblechapel.org/tcon/notes/html/nt/matthew/matthew.htm.

37 Pass the Salt and Turn on the Light

1. Ray Hermann, "Can the Salt of the Earth Lose its Flavor?" The Outlaw Bible Student, June 26, 2019, accessed September 6, 2024, www.outlawbiblestudent.org/can-the-salt-of-the-earth-lose-its-flavor.

40 Talking to The Secret God

1. Dr. Thomas L. Constable, "Constable's Expository (Bible Study) Notes, Web-based," [The Lord's Prayer contains parallels to 1 Chronicles 29:10–18]. Plano Bible Chapel, accessed October 6, 2024, www.planobiblechapel.org/tcon/notes/html/nt/matthew/matthew.htm.

44 Surprising Faith, Generous Mercy

1. "Roman Centurian," Bible History, accessed May 7, 2021, www.bible-history.com/sketches/ancient/roman-centurion.html.

2. Dr. Thomas L. Constable, "Constable's Expository (Bible Study) Notes, Web-based," [The raising of a widow's son 7:11-17]. Plano Bible Chapel, accessed May 11, 2021, www.planobiblechapel.org/tcon/notes/html/nt/luke/luke.html.

46 An Easy Yoke
1. "Denounce." Merriam-Webster.com Dictionary, Merriam-Webster, accessed June 22, 2021, https://www.merriam-webster.com/dictionary/denounce.

2. "Woe." Merriam-Webster.com Dictionary, Merriam-Webster, accessed June 22, 2021, https://www.merriam-webster.com/dictionary/woe.

3. Geography Note: Capernaum was the hometown of Matthew and a stone's throw from Bethsaida, home to the disciples Simon Peter, Andrew, James, and John. This area of Capernaum became the home base for Jesus.

49 The Unforgivable Insult
1. Beatitudes research came from these commentaries:
"Who was Beelzebub?" Got Questions Ministries, accessed August 16, 2021, https://www.gotquestions.org/who-Beelzebub.html.
Ashley Hooker, "Who is Beelzebub in the Bible? Name Meaning and Bible Significance," Christianity.com, April 17, 2024, accessed August 16, 2024, www.christianity.com/wiki/angels-and-demons/who-was-beelzebub-in-the-bible.html.

2. "Blasphemy." Merriam-Webster.com Dictionary, Merriam-Webster, accessed August 15, 2024, https://www.merriam-webster.com/dictionary/blasphemy.

51 How Does Your Garden Grow?
1. "The Land of Milk and Honey – Agriculture in Ancient Israel," MD Harris Institute, February 3, 2013, accessed December 28, 2021, www.mdharrismd.com/2013/02/03/the-land-of-milk-and-honey-agriculture-in-ancient-israel/.

53 Holding onto the Hand of Matthew
1. "Benjamin Franklin on Rev. George Whitefield, 1739," National Humanities Center, accessed August 3, 2024, https://nationalhumanitiescenter.org/pds/becomingamer/ideas/text2/franklinwhitefield.pdf.

2. Matthew insights from Dr. Thomas L. Constable, "Constable's Expository (Bible Study) Notes, Web-based," Plano Bible Chapel, accessed January 5, 2021, https://www.planobiblechapel.org/tcon/notes/html/nt/matthew/matthew.htm.

55 A Sword and A Cross
1. "Authority." Merriam-Webster.com Dictionary, Merriam-Webster, accessed August 15, 2024, https://www.merriam-webster.com/dictionary/authority.

2. Alexander Maclaren, *The Acts of the Apostles,* (New York: A.C. Armstrong, 1907).

56 A Tale of Two Banquets

1. Compassion: sympathetic consciousness of other 's distress and a desire to alleviate it. "Compassion." Merriam-Webster.com Dictionary, Merriam-Webster, accessed November 19, 2023, https://www.merriam-webster.com/dictionary/compassion.

2. The etymology of "compassion" is Latin, meaning "co-suffering." More virtuous than simple empathy, compassion commonly leads to an active desire to alleviate another's suffering. The English noun compassion, meaning to suffer together with, comes from the Latin. "Compassion." Wikipedia.org, accessed November 19, 2023, https://en.wikipedia.org/wiki/compassion.

3. KOPHINOS was "a wicker basket" (made of twigs or branches) originally containing a certain measure of capacity. This was a relatively small basket that could be carried on the back to hold provisions; it is believed that they were Ephah size, about 3/5 bushel (like a knapsack size.) Rev. Jack Barr, "How Big Were the Baskets Used by the Apostles to Gather the Food Fragments?", The Barr Family Website, accessed August 15, 2024, www.barrfamily.com/god-sword/baskets.htm.

About the Author

Georgia Tanner's journey is a testament to the transformative power of God. Born and raised in a loving Christian family in Greenville, South Carolina, she embarked on a path that led her away from her roots. At 17, she set her Bible on a shelf and embraced the world's values. A successful career as an Art Director, a loving family, and a home in Atlanta, Georgia, seemed to fulfill her life. Yet, after 20 years, she found herself deeply unhappy, realizing that much of what she held tightly to was built on lies and shifting sand.

God sat her down (much against her will!) in a welcoming Bible-teaching church where she discovered her identity was not in her own efforts but in the God who loved her and offered abundant forgiveness. As she surrendered every part of her life to him, he nurtured her through rich relationships and his Word.

Her career as a Film Director flourished under his hand, and he also placed her (with much fear and trembling!) in the position of Teaching Director for Community Bible Study, where she taught pretty much every book in the Bible over 17 years. The little class of 30 women grew to 140 women, men, children, and teens.

Stepping out of her comfort zone, in 2019 Georgia wrote and published *Genesis, Small Stories of a Big God,* which brought additional speaking and teaching opportunities. *The Jesus Stories* looks at the Son of God through the eyes of those who saw him, following along with Matthew, Mark, Luke, and John. Take your Bible off the shelf and see Jesus for yourself. You may be surprised at who you see.

smallstoriesofabiggod.com

THE JOURNEYS, AND DEEDS OF JESUS, AND SCRIPTORAL INDEX ON A NEW MAP OF PALESTINE

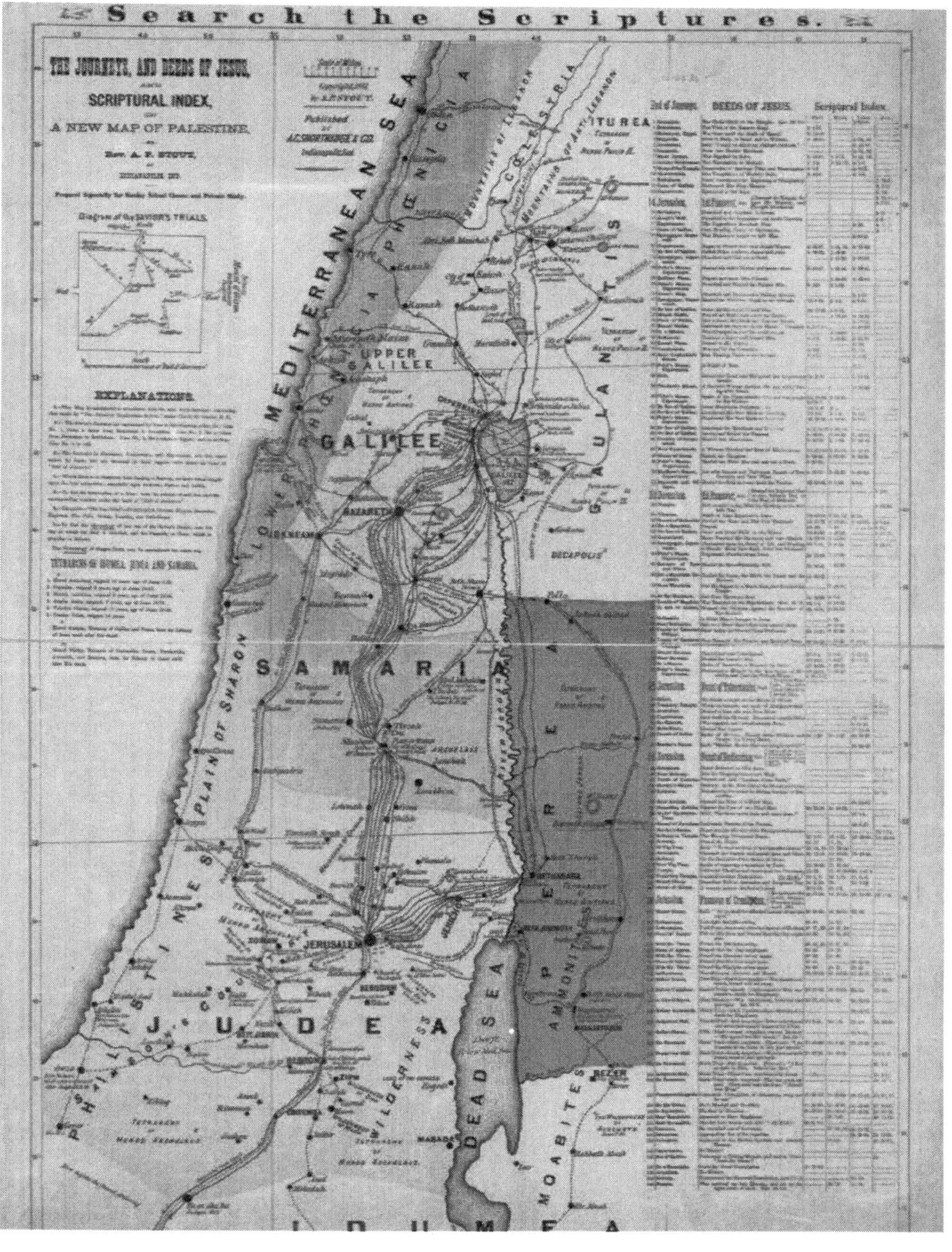